PEOPLE FOR AND AGAINST RESTRICTED OR UNRESTRICTED EXPRESSION

Recent Titles in
The Greenwood Press "People Making a Difference" Series

People For and Against Gun Control: A Biographical Reference
Marjolin Bijlefeld

PEOPLE FOR AND AGAINST RESTRICTED OR UNRESTRICTED EXPRESSION

**John B. Harer
and Jeanne Harrell**

The Greenwood Press "People Making a Difference" Series

GREENWOOD PRESS
Westport, Connecticut • London

Library of Congress Cataloging-in-Publication Data

Harer, John B.
    People for and against restricted or unrestricted expression / John B. Harer and Jeanne
Harrell.
        p. cm.—(The Greenwood Press "People making a difference" series, ISSN 1522–7960)
    Includes bibliographical references and index.
    ISBN 0–313–31758–5 (alk. paper)
    1. Freedom of speech—United States.   2. Censorship—United States.
    3. Anticensorship activists—United States.   I. Harrell, Jeanne E.   II. Title.
    III. Series.
JC591.H37   2002
323.44'3'0973—dc21   2001055617

British Library Cataloguing in Publication Data is available.

Library of Congress Catalog Card Number: 2001055617
ISBN: 0–313–31758–5
ISSN: 1522–7960

First published in 2002

Greenwood Press, 88 Post Road West, Westport, CT 06881
An imprint of Greenwood Publishing Group, Inc.
www.greenwood.com

Printed in the United States of America

The paper used in this book complies with the
Permanent Paper Standard issued by the National
Information Standards Organization (Z39.48–1984).

10 9 8 7 6 5 4 3 2 1

Contents

Series Foreword

Many controversial topics are difficult for student researchers to understand fully without examining key people and their positions in the subjects being debated. This series is designed to meet the research needs of high school and college students by providing them with profiles of those who have been at the center of debates on such controversial topics as gun control, capital punishment, and gay and lesbian rights. The personal stories—the reasons behind their arguments—add a human element to the debates not found in other resources focusing on these topics.

Each volume in the series provides profiles of people, chosen for their effective battles in support of or in opposition to one side of a specific controversial issue. The volumes provide an equal number of profiles of those on both sides of the debates. Students are encouraged to read stories from the two opposite sides to develop their critical thinking skills and to draw their own conclusions concerning the specific issues. They will learn about those people who are not afraid to stand up for their cause, no matter what it may be, and no matter what the consequences may be.

To further help the student researcher, the author of each volume has provided an introduction that outlines the history of the issue and the debates surrounding it, as well as explaining the major arguments and concerns of those involved in the debates. The pro and con arguments are clearly defined as are major developments in the movement. Students can use these introductions as a foundation for analyzing the stories of the people who follow.

Greenwood Press's hope is that each student will realize there are no easy answers to the questions these controversial topics raise, and that those on all sides of these debates have legitimate reasons for thinking, feeling, and arguing the way they do. These topics have become controversial because the people involved have very real, emotional stories to tell, and these stories have helped to shape the debates. Each profile provides information such as where and when the person was born, his or her family background, education, what pushed him or her into action, the contributions he or she has made to the movement, and the obstacles he or she has faced from the opposing factions. All this information is meant to help the student user critique the different viewpoints surrounding the issue and to come to a better understanding of the topic through a more personal venue than a typical essay can provide.

Introduction

Mary Beth Tinker and the black armband

In 1969, during the Vietnam War, thirteen-year-old Mary Beth Tinker and her brother John lived in Des Moines, Iowa. Disturbed about the war, Mary Beth, her brother, and a sixteen-year-old friend, Christopher Eckhardt, decided to wear black armbands, in silent protest. When her school principal told her to remove the armband, Mary Beth refused and said that she had the right to express her dissent. Mary Beth, John, and Christopher Eckhardt were suspended from school for their refusal to retreat from their convictions. With help from the ACLU, her parents sued the school district for violating her First Amendment Rights. Her case went all the way to the Supreme Court. The Supreme Court believed that Mary Beth and students like her were entitled to freedom of speech. They said, "It can hardly be argued that either students or teachers shed their constitutional rights to freedom of speech or expression at the schoolhouse gate."

The moral of this story: Students have rights too, but you may have to stand up for them.

One of our rights as citizens—the right that Mary Beth Tinker defended—is the right to free speech. Freedom of speech is the cornerstone of any free and democratic society. In the United States, the First Amendment to the Constitution guarantees freedom of speech. Because our nation is grounded in the principles of constitutional law, no group in this country has ever advocated eliminating freedom of speech. Thus, free-speech controversies are not about freedom of speech but about what limits, if any, should be placed on free speech. Those who favor limits are sometimes said to advocate censorship.

Identification of those who advocate limits on freedom of speech and those who do not is difficult. Today, free-speech issues cross the lines of political ideology. The defense of freedom of speech has often been seen as very liberal. While it might seem that liberals and liberal groups would be the advocates of freedom of speech and conservatives would be the advocates of censorship, this is not necessarily the case. The American Center for Law and Justice (ACLJ), a legal foundation associated with the Reverend Pat Robertson's Christian Broadcasting Network and the 700 Club, for example, has been in the forefront of several prominent First Amendment cases, advocating freedom of speech for Christians and Christian students, among others, and the Council for Interracial Books for Children has been in the forefront of challenging books that do not use race-neutral language. Indeed, some free-speech advocates have accused the council of outright censorship. G. Gordon Liddy, one of the most famous figures in the Watergate scandal and a conservative radio talk-show host, has received a free speech award from the radio industry for standing up to censorship pressure in his defense of the militia movement shortly after the bombing of the federal building in Oklahoma City, and the National Association for the Advancement of Colored People (NAACP) has actively opposed books with racial epithets, especially Mark Twain's *The Adventures of Huckleberry Finn*. In fact, some conservatives have accused liberals of censoring conservative publications and writings. In his book, *Book Burning*, Cal Thomas, a former Moral Majority associate of Jerry Falwell and now a conservative editorial columnist, has accused libraries and librarians of censoring conservative Christian publications by not including them in library collections. The following story illustrates just how complicated todays issues are.

Bridget Mergens and the Bible Club

Bridget Mergens attended Westside Community District High School in Nebraska. She had a deep, abiding faith in God. She wanted to share her beliefs with friends and to wear her Christian T-shirt in school in the same way that other students wore T-shirts with football slogans or political messages. Bridget formed a Bible Club to hold prayer meetings with other students and to celebrate their Christianity.

School officials believed that Bridget's club violated the principal of separation of church and state and refused to allow the club in the high school. Bridget and her fellow students argued that the club was just like other noncurriculum clubs, such as service clubs or the Chess Club. The Supreme Court agreed with Bridget and said "[I]f the State refused to let religious groups use facilities open to others, then it would demonstrate not neutrality but hostility toward religion."

The moral of this story: Students have rights regardless of the content of their speech activities.

This book highlights the accomplishments of fifty people who are or have been key figures in the debate on the limitations of free speech in the United States. Most of them are active in organizations that either advocate few, if any, limits to freedom of speech or advocate the right to protect primarily children from exposure to pornographic materials and other harmful publications. Organizations such as the People for the American Way, the American Civil Liberties Union (ACLU), the Office of Intellectual Freedom of the American Library Association, and the National Coalition Against Censorship are against most, if not all, forms of censorship. On the other hand, organizations such as the National Coalition to Protect Children and Family, Enough Is Enough, the American Family Association, and Morality in Media exist to combat pornography and to promote family values. These organizations find the growth in sexually explicit language and pictures in publications that are easily accessible to children to be destructive to families and dangerous for the well-being of children. The debate between these two sides, however, is more complex than the description of these organizations implies.

Each of the people included in this book was inspired to join the debate over freedom of speech by something in his or her life. In some cases, it is the individual's profession that has drawn him or her to the problem and to a desire to resolve issues of limits on free speech. For example, because libraries are the repositories of books and materials of all kinds, librarians are particularly disturbed when books of good value are attacked because of objections to words or themes included in the books. As a result, the American Library Association, a professional organization for librarians, has formed the Office for Intellectual Freedom to assist librarians in protecting library materials from such attacks. Other librarians have become strong advocates of intellectual freedom. For this reason, the American Library Association also sponsors the Intellectual Freedom Committee, which develops policy on intellectual freedom. Students who become involved in school newspapers, yearbooks, and literary magazines often find their work coming under the scrutiny of school district personnel as well as others who may object to the topics, articles and words students write. Carl Jensen was a journalism professor at Sonoma State University in California for many years who established Project Censored in an effort to bring censored news stories to the attention of the American public. Mark Goodman, a journalist since his student days, knows at first hand the knife of the censor in student publications. As director of the Student Press Law Center, he has set out on a crusade to ensure that other student journalists have a true learning experience. The student press needs to learn more than the mechanics of writing the news; it also needs to know what rights journalists enjoy as freedom of the press. Jeff Cohen plays a similar role for the national press as director of Fairness and Accuracy in Reporting (FAIR). In recent years, music has also stretched the bounds of acceptability in lyrics and musical expression. Thus, some musicians have joined the debate. Frank Zappa was a pioneer in many ways for the music industry. He constantly challenged the very definition of musical composition. He was the abstract artist of the musical world, and it often brought his music into conflict with the censors. Before his untimely death in 1990, he crusaded against labeling musical recordings. Danny Goldberg, owner of ArtistEnt.com and several recording companies, has also been in the forefront of stemming the tide of record labeling plans. He founded Musical Majority to act as a counterweight to the Parent's Music Resource Center.

In other cases, individuals have joined the debate because they are deeply concerned about the effects of pornography on children and adults. Many individuals in the family values and anti-pornography movements believe there is a direct link between exposure to pornography and sex crimes. The most touted example is the confession of Ted Bundy, a serial rapist and murderer, who confessed to an addiction to pornography. Bundy claimed his addiction to pornography caused him to commit his crimes. Father Morton Hill had the longest record of combating pornography. Hill was the visionary behind Morality in Media, a major anti-pornography organization. His work is being carried out by Robert Peters as the new director of Morality in Media. The Cincinnati area has experienced a long-standing battle with pornography. It is the home of *Hustler* magazine publisher and pornography producer, Larry Flynt. Several anti-pornography organizations have built a national following from their work in Cincinnati. The Rev. Dr. Jerry Kirk, as the founder and CEO of the National Coalition for the Protection of Children and Families, has been very successful in combating pornography. Richard Schatz, as the director of the Coalition, has been fundamentally responsible for its success as a national organization. A more recent entry into the anti-pornography crusade, Enough Is Enough is an organization directed by Monique Nelson as its chief operating officer to assist other organizations and governments in stemming the tide of pornography.

Often people are drawn into the debate over censorship not because their profession is a target of censorship, but because of the very nature of the topic itself. Many individuals believe limits on speech are limits on intellectual freedom. The National Coalition Against Censorship was formed to act on the behalf of several organizations that are combating censorship. Joan Bertin is the current executive director and leads this effective organization in its efforts to educate the American public on the evils of unrestrained censorship. Donna Demac is a counsel for the National Coalition Against Censorship who has written several books on the problems censorship brings to freedom of expression. PEN is an anticensorship organization that was formed to help protect authors and journalists around the world. Many nations do not enjoy freedom of speech or freedom of the press as fully as the United States. In some countries, violations of strict speech laws can lead to a death sentence.

One of the most significant free press organizations began as a project by one of the most well-known newspaper entrepreneurs. Al Neuharth, founder of the national paper *USA Today*, has been the driving force behind the First Amendment Center at Vanderbilt University and has formed the Freedom Forum to promote First Amendment freedoms to a greater audience. Other organizations such as People for the American Way (PFAW) have formed out of fear of the impact of conservative groups promoting a more restricted view of freedom of speech.

No volume of this nature would be complete without the inclusion of the American Civil Liberties Union. The ACLU draws much fire from the conservative elements in the United States because it is the longest running defender of the Bill of Rights. The ACLU does more than defend the First Amendment. Its agenda serves all of the individual rights of the Constitution, but it has been a substantial force in the freedom of speech movement. Well-known names associated with the ACLU over the years include Roger Baldwin and Aryeh Neyer, and Nadine Strossen has been the most recent contributor to the ACLU's success. She has been a prolific writer on First Amendment rights and has been sought as a counsel in many First Amendment cases.

The debate about pornography has also stretched beyond the traditional notions of what is pornography. Advocates of freedom of speech often accuse groups that want to promote family values as blurring the lines between acceptable literature and true pornography. There are twofold issues for free speech advocates. First, the definitive line between true porn and creative works that have sexual themes is pushed to strict limits as censorship wins victories in the courts and in the court of public opinion. Free speech advocates believe that valuable literature and other works of art that push these limits will be unfairly labeled pornography if censorship continues to be unbridled. Second, there is a contention about works that are not sexual in nature at all and could never be misconstrued as pornographic but come under the censors' scrutiny because of objectionable words. On the other hand, some of the individuals included in this book have joined the debate because of their strong Christian values. Their deep abiding faith tells them that violence in the media, abortion on demand, vulgarity, and teachings that tell children that values are relative, as well as pornography, threaten morality in general. They feel that if biblical values are considered relative, then the basic moral foundation of America is threatened.

The Rev. Pat Robertson is a prime example of this movement. Robertson's Christian Broadcasting Network has had an unprecedented national and international impact. Robertson was also instrumental in developing the American Center for Law and Justice (ACLJ), a legal foundation similar to the American Civil Liberties Union, except their work focuses on Christian liberties and values. Jay Sekulow is the main counsel for the ACLJ and has defended many of the court cases that have challenged restrictions on Christian liberties such as forming Bible clubs, saying prayers in school, and defending Christian parents who want to challenge objectionable school materials. The American Family Association (AFA) is another example of a Christian organization that supports the promotion of Christian values. The Rev. Donald Wildmon founded the AFA because of the moral deterioration within society, especially as reflected in the content of TV programming with its excessive emphasis on sex and violence. The Rutherford Institute, founded by John Whitehead, is another example. The Rutherford Institute maintains initiatives for a number of Christian causes and has produced a series of very effective, anti-abortion advertisements. It has also defended students who wish to pray in school. Other organizations and their directors include Citizens for Excellence in Education (CEE), directed by Robert Simonds, which is a grass-roots organization to help local groups and individuals form their own organizations for promoting Christian values, and the Christian Action Network, led by Martin Mawyer and with a similar mission to the CEE. Phyllis Schlafly has been a well-known family-values activist since the 1960s. She was very instrumental in defeating the ratification of the Equal Rights Amendment. Her organization, The Eagle Forum, is a prime force in the family values movement.

The explosive growth of the Internet and its potential for expanding the availability of goods and services has been the latest source of concern for both the advocates of free speech and advocates of censorship. The Electronic Frontier Foundation (EFF) and the Electronic Privacy Information Center (EPIC) are organizations directly involved in promoting a free-access Internet. On the other side, Filtering Facts is an organization founded to combat unlimited access to the Internet because such access can expose children to hard-core pornography. Mike Godwin is the former general counsel most often associated with the EFF and was instrumental in the case before the Supreme Court that struck down the Communications Decency Act. The EFF's executive director is now Shari Steele. Marc Rotenberg has been the driving force behind EPIC and has been active in promoting privacy concerns for Internet users. Both Godwin and Rotenberg are actively involved in the creation and development of the annual Computers, Freedom and Privacy Conference. Filtering Facts, along with Family Friendly Libraries, founded by Karen Gounaud, have been in opposition to the American Library Association's stance on Internet filters. This volume does not include any organization supporting the production or distribution of pornography. Although the pornography industry, which is represented by the Adult Video Association (AVA), has a freedom of speech advocacy program, the AVA exists entirely to promote the free use of pornography rather than freedom of speech or anticensorship activities.

Many individuals who have been active in the anticensorship and family-values movements deserve mention in this chapter and inclusion in this book. Unfortunately, space prevents comments on everyone. The intent of this work is to highlight the most prominent individuals on both sides of the free-speech debate. Anyone wishing to research more individuals would do well to begin with the organizations affiliated with the people featured in this book.

WHAT IS CENSORSHIP?

A ninth grader finds obscenity in a reading assignment

Chris Malpass of York, Virginia, was given Robert Cormier's *The Chocolate War* as a reading assignment in his English class. The novel is about the conflict that occurs in a Catholic boys' school when the main character challenges the school's traditions. Chris had heard about the profanity laced throughout the book and the references to masturbation. Chris's convictions conflicted with his desire to do well in class. He sincerely believed that such topics did not have a place in school. He asked the school to ban Cormier's book. The school formed a committee to review the book to see if it was appropriate. Although Chris was supported by hundreds of people in his hometown, the review committee did not agree with him. They ruled that the novel would remain on the reading list.

The moral of the story: Censorship is a conflict between sincerely held beliefs on two opposing sides.

Censorship is not new. In fact, censorship, sometimes known as "banning speech" and "book burning," has existed in some form or another since at least 4000 B.C.

In ancient Rome, a *censor* was a type of magistrate or local judge who assessed property for taxation purposes, registered people for citizenship and punished people for moral offenses. The punishment for these offenses was usually the removal of the offending person's public rights.

While there are differences of opinion about what constitutes censorship today, Henry Reichman, an attorney and former assistant director for the Office for Intellectual Freedom, American Library Association, has defined it as "the removal, suppression or restricted circulation of literary, artistic, or educational materials of images, ideas, and information on the grounds that these are morally or otherwise objectionable in light of standards applied by the censor" (1988, p. 2). Two aspects of this definition are important. First, action is taken against some form of speech or creative work (a book or printed material, a piece of music, a work of art, a film, a live performance, or a public speech). The action removes, eliminates, or limits access to part or all of the work. Second, action is taken by someone who, after citing a standard or reason for the action, acts as a censor. For instance, recently, the Santa Fe, Texas, school district acted as a censor when it removed the popular series of *Harry Potter* books by J. K. Rowling from all of the school libraries in the district after explaining that several people had claimed the series glorified witchcraft.

There are two opposing views about when censorship exists. The conservative view states that censorship exists only when it is imposed by a governmental authority. In this view, citizens have a right to ask the government to address their concerns about something they find objectionable, but censorship only occurs when a governing body that has the authority to act—a city government that manages public libraries or a school board—takes action to remove the object of complaint. In this view, parents exercise their parental rights by making the complaint, and the government then decides to agree or disagree with the complaint.

The liberal view states that censorship comes into existence with the complaint. According to this view, the complaint and the eventual act of censorship are inextricably linked. In the liberal view, censorship can take many forms and can be imposed by groups other than governing bodies. In the late 1960s, for example, after the Beatles were quoted in the press as saying they were bigger than Jesus Christ, many churches and radio stations, especially in Southern states, organized record-smashing events during which stacks of Beatles' albums and records were publicly smashed. According to the conservative view, the records were privately owned, so the events did not constitute censorship. According to the liberal view these events were a form of censorship that was similar to the public burning of books in Nazi Germany in the 1930s. In the liberal view, groups that threaten to check out books they dislike from public libraries and never return them are acting as censors.

Liberals argue that censorship by any group has what is known as a "chilling effect" on other works. A chilling effect occurs when censorship by any group causes the elimination or postponement of other works out of fear that they will suffer the same fate. When authors write a book about sex education or witchcraft, for example, they know they take a risk that it may be censored. That risk translates into reduced sales and profits if the book is heavily censored, for example, as well as general condemnation in their personal and business affairs. In the past, that risk could also have meant imprisonment for the author. Since these subjects are known to be the subject of censorship cases, authors may hesitate to write about these topics. Death threats made against Salman Rushdie by Iran's Islamic government because of its disapproval of his novel *Satanic Verses* may have caused others to hesitate to write books on Rushdie's subject for fear they, too, would receive death threats. In the liberal view, the chilling effect is a form of censorship.

This discussion has focused on a definition of censorship. It is important to realize, however, that all censorship incidents begin with a complaint. Before censorship can occur, someone or some group has to be offended by a creative work and to express their offense to someone they believe will take action. Several studies of past censorship incidents have found that parents are the most likely to complain about a book held in a library or used in a classroom. According to these studies, coarse language and discussions of sex are usually the focus of their complaints. Parents, for example, may complain about coarse language and an encounter with a prostitute in J. D. Salinger's *Catcher in the Rye* or the frank discussions of sex in Judy Blume's works.

The Nature of Censorship Challenges

Mary Saczawa and the local school board

Mary was a seventh grader in Athens, Alabama, who loved to read. One of her favorite books was Judy Blume's *Blubber. Blubber* is a book about the constant cruel teasing an overweight fifth-grader faces at school. After the school board banned *Blubber* from the school's libraries because of a parent's complaint about the language used in the book, Mary spoke out against the ban at the school board meeting and asked the board to reconsider its decision. The board voted 4 to 3 against Mary's request. In the next school board election, however, three of the four board members who voted to ban the book were voted out of office. One school board member who voted to keep the book said, "You start to throw out the TVs, and then we'll start throwing out the books."

The moral of the story: Censorship challenges do not always end the way you would expect.

There are at least four types of complaints that may lead to some form of censorship:

- benign complaints
- nonconsensus complaints

- consensus complaints
- radical complaints

There is an ascending order of severity in this list. A *benign complaint* is usually a remark or statement that is not accompanied by a request for action. Benign complaints often occur. Patrons frequently ask librarians why a particular book is owned by the library. The answers may satisfy their curiosity, or they may believe a more detailed response is not worth pursuing. Benign complaints can also be formal, such as when a library patron makes a written complaint. A principal, for example, may receive a complaint about a book, review the book, and make a response that satisfies the parent, who does not pursue the matter further.

A *nonconsensus complaint* is more serious. A nonconsensus complaint occurs when the person who complains and the authority to whom he or she complains disagree. This type of complaint is usually formal. A parent, for example, may offer specific objections to a work and ask a school board, principal, librarian, or other person in authority to remove or censor the work in some way. After reviewing the work, the authority may not agree with the complaint, and the work will not be censored. At this point, the complainant may threaten further action. He or she may decide to take the matter to court or may organize a protest. Protests are usually formed to pressure political figures into acting on the behalf of the complainant. In the late 1980s, for example, a group of parents from Long Island, New York, took their complaint about the first book of the popular *Where's Waldo?* picture book series to their local school board. The parents were concerned about a detailed beach scene in the book, which asks readers to locate a character named Waldo, that included a small drawing of a woman that revealed the outline of her breast. A series of authorities reviewed the complaint and decided to keep the book in the school libraries. Several protests were made by concerned parents before and during hearings. Although nonconsensus complaints often become difficult and polarized political events, unless the person or group who has made the complaint is successful in convincing another, usually higher, authority, to censor the work, no act of censorship occurs and the status quo is maintained.

A *consensus complaint* usually leads to the censorship of the work in question. A consensus complaint occurs when the authority to whom the complaint is made agrees with the person or group that complains. The complaint may be formal or informal. For example, a school principal may be approached by a parent who objects to Judy Blume's *Forever*, a controversial novel about teenage relationships, written for high-school readers. If the principal agrees with the parent and removes the book from the school library on his own initiative, the act of censorship is the result of consensus. The censorship resulting from a consensus complaint may be the complete removal of the work or the placement or some form of restriction on the work, such as the need for parental permission to check out the work. No matter what type of censorship occurs, the status quo is not maintained.

A *radical complaint* is an act of censorship that is taken by a group or person who objects to a creative work. Individuals with radical complaints bypass authorities and a review of their objections. For example, a popular movie of the 1980s, *Footloose*, concerns a small town that has banned dancing and music. In one scene, several townspeople have removed a large number of books from the library and are seen burning them in front of the library. This is a good depiction of a radical complaint. The burning of the books in the movie is a very visible and destructive form of censorship and it is being committed by people who are not a government body or authority. The act does not have to be this destructive. In the early 1990s, a feminist student organization at Texas A&M University objected to an eighteenth-century painting in the university library that depicted an Arabic slave trader selling a half-nude slave girl. As a protest, someone taped a picture of a dress over the slave girl. Some groups advocate stealing a book they object to from a library or checking it out and publicly announcing that it will not be returned. In some cases, a radical complaint is the result of the frustration felt by the parents or groups who have lost their case before a governing authority. In other cases, the radical complaint has been the first action chosen by a group or individual. In either situation, the status quo is changed because of direct and illegal action.

What Are the Types of Censorship?

Heidi Webb and the distribution of anti-abortion literature

In 1985, Heidi Webb was a ninth-grade, San Bernadino County High School student in California. Because she believed that abortion was wrong, Heidi began to distribute anti-abortion leaflets at school. When her history teacher told her to stop because what she was doing was illegal, Heidi asked what law she had broken. Her teacher said he would have to get back to her on that. Heidi's principal also asked her to stop handing out the literature and, when she refused to do so, she was suspended from school. Heidi was offered legal assistance by the Rutherford Institute, a religious freedom advocacy group, which led to the revocation of her suspension and an apology from the principal. Heidi could have stopped at this point, but she felt something more was needed. After some discussion, the school district agreed to train its school administrators and teachers in the First Amendment and free speech.

The moral of the story: When basic rights are involved, you may need to do more to promote the principles of free speech.

An act of censorship can take many forms. A book can be burned, but a stone sculpture cannot, for example. Sometimes the type of censorship used is dictated by the type of creative work. There are five types of censorship:

- removal of the entire work from use
- removal of the objectionable part of the work
- restrictions on the use of the work
- re-creating the work to remove the objectionable part
- destruction of the work

The most common form of censorship is removal of the entire work. Libraries and schools may remove a book that is challenged by a parent from the shelves, or bookstores and retailers may decide to remove materials from sales counters or shelves. For example, a library may decide to remove *Wentworth's Dictionary of American Slang* because it contains most of the words that are considered to be vulgar. After the decision to remove the dictionary has been made, the library has the option of throwing the copies in the trash, giving or selling them to another organization, locking them in storage, or burning them. Burning is the most controversial method of disposal. In the late 1970s, after several parents in Bismarck, North Dakota, complained to their local school board about the inclusion of Kurt Vonnegut's *Slaughterhouse Five* on the high-school reading list, the school board removed all of the copies of Vonnegut's book and then burned them. Many nationally known newspapers wrote editorials condemning the school board and suggesting that its actions were like the actions of the Nazi Party in Germany before and during World War II. While individuals may be concerned about the method of disposal, most people who oppose censorship find the act of removing the work to be the greatest wrong. For these individuals, the decision of U.S. military retail shops (known as PX's) to cancel their contracts with *Playboy* magazine and similar periodicals because pictures of nude women in these magazines were considered obscene was just as serious as the action of the North Dakota school board.

Removal of the objectionable part of the work is another type of censorship that may occur when the authorities, after reviewing a complaint, decide the work as a whole is worthwhile but the objectionable parts need to be removed. This type of removal is often called expurgation. The intent of expurgation is to allow access or use to the rest of the work without exposing the user to the objectionable part. The method of removal is usually determined by the type of work. For the printed word, removing just part of the work can be done in many ways. Objectionable words can be blacked out with a pen or marker. Snipping out the words with scissors has been used in the past. Sometimes, whole pages are torn from the book or material. In the film and television, there are electronic means of blurring objectionable pictures. Sometimes, the screen or portion of the screen is blacked out to cover the objectionable visual. If the language is objectionable, the sound track may be turned off or an electronic beep or other sound may be played in place of the language. Music censorship is similar to film censorship. As radio stations are prohibited by the Federal Communications Commission from broadcasting most vulgar language (profanity or obscenity) during daytime programming, a beep is played to block out the words that are to be removed. Late at night, the same song may be heard without the beep. A work of art may have a part of the work covered to block out an objectionable part. In the early 1980s for example, a community college in central New Jersey sponsored an art exhibit that included black and white photos of male nudes. After receiving a complaint from a citizen, the college board ordered triangular pieces of felt to be placed over the male anatomy that troubled some viewers. Attendees could lift the cloth to view the full nude, if they wished.

The third type of censorship—restrictions on the use of the work—may restrict access to a work. A decision to restrict use recognizes that objections to a work may be applicable to only certain categories of users. Many school districts, for example, restrict access to *Go Ask Alice*, an anonymous young adult novel about drug addiction, to high-school students, because they believe younger students may be negatively influenced by the story. If a library deems a book objectionable, librarians may decide to restrict use by placing the book behind the counter. This forces the user to ask the librarian for the book and allows the librarian to deny usage to those for whom the material is thought to be objectionable. In 1991, after many people complained about the nature of the photographs in the pop singer Madonna's book, *Sex*, the Houston Public Library and other libraries across the country placed their copies in a locked cabinet at the reference desk. A note in the catalog instructed patrons to see the reference librarian for access. Patrons who were deemed too young to view the book were turned away. The Motion Picture Association of America's (MPAA) rating codes allow movie theaters to restrict access to films. Movie theater staff may ask people to prove their age before seeing a film that has been found objectionable for certain ages. Within the last five years, the growth of the Internet has spawned a demand for restrictions on web surfing because many web sites are considered pornographic or dangerous. As a result, several companies have developed filtering systems that parents, libraries, and schools can use to restrict access. The most common method of filtering is the creation of a list of keywords that the software then reads as objectionable. When these words are detected in a web site address, the software does not access the web site. Cable TV companies use scramblers to restrict access to specific channels. Adult channels, such as the Playboy Channel, have a scrambler that distorts the picture unless there is a subscription to that channel. Recently, cable companies have allowed parents to place an electronic lock on channels that restricts access through the use of a password.

The fourth type of censorship is the re-creation of a work to remove those parts that have been found to be objectionable. This type of censorship usually occurs in great literature when parts of a particular work are considered vulgar or sexually suggestive. Some people, for example, have found the exploits of the character Sir John Falstaff in Shakespeare's *Henry IV, Part I* to be too suggestive for young readers. Hoping to avoid complaints, many high schools purchase editions of the play that have been edited and rewritten. The works of Thomas Bowdler are the best example of the practice of recreating classics. In the early 1820s, Thomas Bowdler revised Shakespeare's works to remove what Bowdler felt were immoral aspects of the play. This effort was followed by a revision by the Bowdler family of Edward Gibbon's *The Decline and Fall of the Roman Empire*. The Bowdler family's dedication to re-creating works they found offensive led to the word bowdlerism, meaning the practice of revising books and other materials to remove offensive language. Bowdlerism is the classic form of transforming a text for the purposes of censorship. When a publisher sells a work of Shakespeare that has been rewritten to change language that is too sexual or too suggestive into less offensive words, this is an example of a modern form of bowdlerism. In recent years, complaint of racism in Mark Twain's *The Adventures of Huckleberry Finn* caused a middle-school principal in Arlington, Virginia, to attempt to rewrite the novel to eliminate racist language.

The most radical type of censorship occurs when a work is destroyed. The destruction of creative works can occur in mass protests such as the smashing of Beatles records, which was discussed earlier. In Germany before World War II, Adolf Hitler's followers were encouraged to burn books that challenged views of the Nazi Party. Huge public rallies were staged to burn those books the Nazis found objectionable. Because books and other types of creative expression are necessary for a healthy, intelligent society, the destruction of these works by governing authorities often causes outcries, especially in the press. Ray Bradbury, a well-known science-fiction writer, has written a famous novel entitled *Fahrenheit 451*, about censorship and the destruction of books. In Bradbury's novel, a futuristic society believes books corrupt people's minds, so fire departments burn books instead of putting out fires. Today, authorities are reluctant to destroy publicly any creative work for fear of charges of Nazism.

Labeling a creative work to indicate that it contains some form of objectionable expression is a controversial issue in the debate over what constitutes censorship. Take the ratings guide used by the movie industry. Labeling assigns a symbol and/or words to a creative work, usually book, tape, disc, film, or television program. Unlike ratings guides, which assign age limits to products, labeling tells all users that the product contains violent words or action, vulgar language, or sexual content that some people have found objectionable. Another form of labeling is a voluntary rating system guide for the Internet proposed by President Clinton and promoted by several groups concerned with pornography on the Internet. This rating system was never adopted but was similar to the TV ratings or codes for excessive obscene language, sexual themes, or violence, among several codes. In recent years, many individuals have objected to the language used in popular music. Parents have complained of descriptions of drug use in rock and roll songs and violent acts in rap music.

In the conservative view, labeling is not censorship because government bodies do not ban or restrict the work. Proponents of labeling argue that the labeling process provides consumers with information but allows consumers to decide for themselves whether to buy or use a work. Labeling, according to proponents, provides parents with a framework for discussing with their children the issues and problems some music recordings and videos may present. Proponents point out that most labeling schemes are voluntary and thus give the music, or television, or publishing industries the opportunity to police themselves without outright censorship.

In the liberal view, labeling encourages censorship. According to this view, labeling has a chilling effect. Libraries and schools may be reluctant to purchase or provide access to material with a label. Opponents of labeling assert that labels are too generic and cannot provide the information required to evaluate the material in its complete context. A label of "profane language," for example, does not indicate the type of profanity used, which could be anything from a mild expletive to very graphic sexual language. In 1939, Clark Gable spoke the word "damn" in the film *Gone with the Wind* and caused a shock to many people of the day, though today, "damn" would hardly be a concern for censorship. Labeling also does not indicate the preponderance of the profanity, which could be only one sexually graphic word in the entire text or could be the entire text. Opponents also point out that some creative works may need to include objectionable words or material to remain true to their topic. Any biography of General George S. Patton, for example, would have to include and discuss his profane language to be an accurate biography. The liberal view argues that parents and consumers who look only at a label will not know whether the objectionable part is necessary or valuable.

THEORIES OF FREEDOM OF SPEECH AND FREEDOM OF EXPRESSION

The freedom of expression that exists in the United States does so because of a theoretical foundation that influenced the way in which the framers of our government chose to ensure that our freedoms were more than just words on a piece of paper. No other document in the world provides a greater guarantee of freedom of expression than the Constitution of the United States. Indeed, no other nation today or in the past has protected its citizens' rights to free speech and free press more than the United States. In England, for example, it is illegal to criticize the queen. In the United States, public criticism of any elected official, including the president, is acceptable and often expected. British libel laws also are far more strict than those in the United States. Even the most ardent civil libertarian, however, must admit that speech in its many forms has the potential for causing chaos in society. Thus, in any society, there are legitimate limitations to freedom of expression. The dilemma, then, lies in drawing the line between acceptable and unacceptable expression. For more than 300 years, philosophers have attempted to provide at least frameworks for determining what should and should not be allowed. These frameworks are important because they highlight why freedom of expression is important to a free society. Today, six major theories underlie most discussions of the need for freedom of expression in a free society:

- the marketplace of ideas
- social exchange
- social utility
- self-government
- expression versus action
- the communications context

As early as 1644, the English poet John Milton made an impassioned plea in response to publishing restrictions at the time for freedom of speech in a pamphlet entitled *Areopagitica*. Milton is the first and most famous theorist on freedom of speech. Milton argued that people would make wise choices, based on their needs and understanding, if they could freely examine written ideas without restrictions, bias, or undue influence, just as they examined goods in a marketplace. To Milton, in a marketplace of ideas, competition between ideas will provide the regulation necessary to determine what is not acceptable. Milton believed that suppressing any idea before it reaches the marketplace involved the risk that the best idea would not be available to be seen, examined, and chosen.

John Stuart Mill, a well-known and highly regarded nineteenth-century philosopher, argued that speech activities existed in the context of social exchange. Mill's argument is similar to Milton's. Within the marketplace of ideas, Mill said, a social exchange of ideas occurs, which allows people to replace false ideas with true ideas. Mill believed that if the right to express an opinion was denied, both those who agree and those who disagree with an opinion suffered because of the lack of opportunity to trade a false idea for a true one.

The concept of social utility was created by Zechariah Chafee, Harvard law professor and constitutional scholar. Chafee argued that there are two kinds of speech: (1) expression important to the individual and (2) expression important to society. Expression important to society is more important than individual expression because it serves the interests of society as a whole. To maintain public order, whenever individual expression clashes with expression important to society, society needs to favor social interest over individual interest. For example, an author writes a book on how to make a bomb from easily obtained materials. All the information he uses in the book comes from publicly available documents and legally available sources. However, society's interest in protecting citizens from bomb attacks may override this author's free speech and free press rights. Chafee believes that individual free speech is important and should be protected, but he feels individual expression and public order need to be balanced and protected as equally as possible. Chafee has called the point at which individual expression and public order cross paths the point of *social utility*. For Chafee, social utility becomes the overriding concern when individual expression gives rise to acts that threaten social order.

Alexander Meiklejohn, former president of Amherst College and First Amendment scholar, favors the absolute protection of any form of expression that furthers self-government. Like Chafee, Meiklejohn believes there are two forms of speech: public and private. Public forms of speech, in Meiklejohn's view, require greater protection than private speech because they strengthen people's power to govern themselves and to prevent government and government bureaucracies from reducing the power of self-government. A speech or book that either promotes a government policy or disagrees with that policy to offer an alternative is an example of public speech that furthers the good of society. A speech or book that is designed for personal gain by the author or speaker only furthers the good of that author; this is especially true for commercial advertising, a form of private speech. Private expression is not within the scope of the First Amendment protection of freedom of speech as Meiklejohn has argued, and therefore can be regulated.

Thomas Emerson, Yale law professor and constitutional scholar, believes that a distinction needs to be made between expression and action. Sometimes speech leads to actions that may or may not be objectionable. Society needs to condemn actions that destroy public order, but Emerson believes that the First Amendment should protect and maintain the individual's achievement of

- self-fulfillment
- truth
- participation in decision making
- balance between stability and change

When a speech activity contributes in any way to achieving one or more of these values, it must be protected even if there is a link between the speech and the destructive action.

The final theory was developed by Franklyn Haiman, Professor Emeritus of Communication Studies at Northwestern University. Haiman believes that all expression takes place in what he calls a communications context. Expression in one context may have a legitimate interest for society and thus requires full protection, but that same expression in another context may not have the same, legitimate interest. A simple example would be the use of a vulgar or obscene word. If used to harass someone sexually or threaten someone, it may be illegal. If used to make a political statement or as part of a political protest, it may be legal. The most famous such case is *Cohen v. California* (91 S.Ct. 1780, 1971) in which a student wore a jacket with "Fuck the draft" written on the back into a courtroom. This was found to be a part of political protest and therefore legal, but in other contexts, the word "fuck" might not be legal. Haiman argues that the limits of expression should be determined within four specific contexts:

- communication about other people
- communication to other people
- communication and social order for people to make free and informed choices
- government involvement in the communication marketplace

Within each context, limitations vary according to the context of the expression.

HISTORICAL FOUNDATIONS OF FREEDOM OF SPEECH

The roots of the First Amendment rest in the rights provided by English common law and a quiet British revolution, sometimes called the Glorious Revolution or the Bloodless Revolution, that shifted the power to govern from the monarch to representatives in Parliament.

The individual rights of citizens in Great Britain began with the signing of the Magna Carta by King John in 1215. His noblemen demanded that he end the practice of making capricious decisions without their consent. The Magna Carta was the first step leading from the divine right of kings to rule toward the rule of the people through parliamentary government. Although the rights included in the Magna Carta were only enjoyed by noblemen at first, and not the general populace, this set the precedent that began the process for individual rights over the next 450 years.

By 1688, when the Glorious Revolution occurred, Great Britain had endured more than a century of struggle between Catholicism and Protestantism, absolutism and parliamentary government. When James II, a devout Catholic, came to the throne after the death of his brother Charles II in 1685, Protestant leaders in parliament invited William of Orange of the Netherlands, a Protestant, to take the throne. In an almost bloodless coup, (thus the names the Glorious Revolution and the Bloodless Revolution), William conquered James and with his wife Mary, the Protestant daughter of James II, ruled Great Britain. The Glorious Revolution resulted in the Toleration Act and a bill of rights for English citizens. The Toleration Act established in law a form of freedom of religion, and the bill of rights gave the rights to more people than before.

Both the Toleration Act and the British bill of rights were influenced by the philosopher John Locke, whose writings on government and individual rights also influenced Thomas Jefferson, James Madison, and John Adams. Locke argued, among other things, that government was established through the consent of the governed and not by divine right. Both the Declaration of Independence and the Bill of Rights were drawn from Locke's philosophy.

THE FIRST AMENDMENT'S FOUR FREEDOMS

The framers of the Constitution were divided over how much power the federal government should possess. Those who favored a strong federal government were known as Federalists while those who feared that individual rights would suffer under a strong federal government were known as Antifederalists. When the Federalists said that a bill of rights could be added to the Constitution after it was ratified, delegates to the Constitutional Convention signed the documents, and the process of ratification began. Although a presidential election was held after the four largest states had ratified the Constitution, it was clear that some kind of protection for individual rights was needed. James Madison drafted twelve amendments to address this need, and they were submitted to Congress in September 1789. By December 15, 1791, the states had ratified ten of these twelve amendments. The remaining two, which dealt with rules governing Congress, have never been ratified.

Of the ten amendments that we know as the Bill of Rights, the First Amendment is a guarantee of intellectual freedom. It consists of four basic freedoms:

1. Freedom of religion. Two clauses establish this freedom. The first clause states, "Congress shall make no law respecting the establishment of religion." This means that no religion can be established as the official religion of any federal, state, or local government. The second clause is known as the "free exercise" clause, and it prevents government from prohibiting an individual's right to practice a religion in most cases.

2. Freedom of speech. Speech can take many forms, such as a public debate or speech on a government policy or action, a book or other printed matter, and even a symbol such as a sign or piece of artwork. Speech can be categorized in a legal sense as either "protected" or "unprotected" speech.

3. Freedom of the press. The press is the traditional form of broadcasting speech to a larger audience. The press was originally newspapers and magazines, but now includes television, radio, and the Internet when news and other ideas are broadcast.

4. The right to assembly. The First Amendment uses two clauses to define this right: "the right of the people to peaceably assemble" and the right to "petition the government for a redress of grievances." The first clause is the freedom to meet in public as long as the meeting is peaceful. The second clause gives individuals the right to complain about their government and to ask the government to correct problems created by governmental action. These two aspects are purposely tied together to provide citizens with the right to address concerns about their government. Implied in this freedom is the right to associate with individuals or groups.

While people tend to think of censorship and the issues that surround it as matters governed by the guarantees of freedom of speech and freedom of the press, the conduct of our lives is not limited to one freedom at a time. As people interact, their rights often intermingle. Thus, while one person may view an authority's refusal to permit prayer in a schoolyard or the wearing of a T-shirt with a Christian message as a limitation on the right to freedom of religion, another may view it as a limitation on the right to free speech. When these matters reach the courts, the legal proceedings must sort out the differences and distinguish between the rights that apply. Depending on the facts of the case and the arguments made by both sides before a court, the court may decide that an issue is a matter of free speech rather than freedom of religion. Thus, a court may decide to protect the right to wear the T-shirt with a Christian message, for example, on the principle of free speech rather than freedom of religion.

FREE SPEECH: WHAT IS ALLOWED AND WHAT ISN'T

Joellen Stanton and the high school yearbook quote

Joellen Stanton was about to graduate from high school in Brunswick, Maine, in the spring of 1984. At her high school, each senior submitted a quote and a photograph to the school's yearbook. The quotes were usually humorous, celebrating things in life the seniors enjoyed, but Joellen wanted to be different. Because she believed the death penalty was immoral, she submitted an eyewitness account of a prisoner being electrocuted from an article in *Time* magazine. Everyone at the high school was shocked, and the student editors of the yearbook refused to include Joellen's quote. Joellen was taunted at school and received threatening messages from some students. Joellen refused to change her quote and, with the help of the Maine Civil Liberties Union, went to court to win the right to have her quote in the yearbook. Along the way, she lost a lot of friends.

The moral of this story: Sometimes standing up for your convictions can be very unpopular.

As noted earlier, there are legitimate limitations on the freedom of speech and press guaranteed by the First Amendment. There is no easy formula for determining these limitations. They have evolved over time and continue to do so, because the U.S. Constitution allows for change. It would have been impossible to describe in the Constitution every aspect, every nuance, and every contingency that could affect free speech. Therefore, it is up to the courts, particularly the Supreme Court, to interpret the Constitution and determine whether or not a form of speech is protected by the First Amendment. Over the years the courts have decided that the five categories of limitations on free speech are:

- Libel: limitations on individual civil relations in written form
- Slander: a form of libel; slander occurs only in spoken form
- Dissent: limitations on speech that challenges authority
- Obscenity: limitations on vulgar expression
- Limitations on commercial speech: limitations on speech made to sell a product

Speech or some other form of expression that exceeds these limitations is not protected by the First Amendment and may be censored. Joseph Hemmer has described this as a two-tiered approach to free speech. Tier two is speech that is protected by the First Amendment. Tier one is speech that is not protected by the First Amendment. For example, relations between individuals are usually a personal matter; however, they can reach a level where they threaten public order. Libel is a written statement attacking the reputation of a person. Slander is a spoken statement that attacks the reputation of a person. Libel is considered the more serious of the two offenses because it can reach a larger audience. Dissent also has limitations because there is a legitimate interest in maintaining loyalty to the nation and its institutions. Obscenity in its many forms has many limitations because morality is an important factor in the general fiber of our way of life. Finally, information to sell a product is not seen as information needed to promote or maintain self-government, and therefore, commercial speech enjoys less protection than other forms of speech.

Over time, the courts and the government have produced a rough set of guidelines to determine if a form of expression is protected by the First Amendment or exceeds the limitations and is unprotected. These guidelines have developed from cases the courts have tried. The guidelines are not written but are buried in court decisions and subject to interpretation. Using the same guidelines, one court may rule that a particular form of speech exceeded the limitations while another court may decide the form did not exceed the limitations. Although the guidelines are open to interpretation, there are some basic rules that are commonly accepted.

In most libel cases, for example, a false statement is evidence that a libel occurred, and the speech is unprotected. If, however, the person who is charged with libel can show that his or her statement was true, he or she cannot be convicted of libel. Private citizens enjoy greater protection than public citizens because their reputation has not been built by or through the press. Furthermore, a private citizen cannot as easily remedy their reputation by or through the press when damaged by reckless speech since they are relatively unknown. In libel suits, a court considers three aspects of the case in determining what is allowed and what is not. First, the court assesses *intent*. Libel exists if the statement is false and made with the intent to harm someone. If, for example, a local civic lodge decided to honor a person's achievements with a dinner during which satirical jokes and stories were told about the individual, the stories would not have the intent of harming that person. Second, the court makes a distinction between a *private citizen* and a *public citizen* (an elected official, high-level bureaucrat or well-known person, such as a celebrity). Private citizens have more protection than public citizens. Libel involves some form of defamation. Defamation is a printed, written, or spoken word or phrase that tends to injure a person's reputation, especially causing some form of harm, usually harm that can be assigned a monetary value. In the case of a public citizen, *actual malice* must be shown to prove libel. In other words, it must be shown that the false statement was made intentionally with "a reckless disregard for the truth." In the 1960s, for example, several African American clergymen placed an advertisement in the *New York Times* that accused L. B. Sullivan, a city commissioner in Montgomery, Alabama, of brutal police tactics during civil rights demonstrations. Although Sullivan was able to prove that the statements made against him were false, the court ruled that he was a public figure and also had to prove that the clergymen knew before placing the advertisement that the comments were false. Third, the court usually makes a distinction between *individuals* and a *class of individuals*. In most cases, the court decides a class or group of individuals cannot be harmed by a statement. If, for example, someone said all the residents of Smallville were slobs, the statement would not be considered libel. If, however, a specific person is called a slob by another, the statement may be libel.

Dissenting speech is one of the most controversial issues in the United States. Although the Constitution guarantees a person's right to criticize the government, the government needs to protect public order. There are at least six guidelines a court uses to determine whether or not a dissenting expression is protected by the First Amendment.

- clear and present danger
- bad tendency
- advocacy of ideas versus advocacy of action
- balancing
- preferred position
- absolutist principle

When the words expressed in a speech are capable of bringing about an immediate "substantial evil" that the government wishes to prevent, then the speech is said to create a *clear and present danger* to peace and order. During times of declared war, for example, there are often peace activists that protest involvement in the war. During World War I, for example, Charles Schenck made many public speeches urging men to resist the draft. Because his speeches had the potential for immediate harm to the government's attempt to raise an armed forces, Schenck's speeches were considered a "clear and present danger" to peace and order.

In the 1920s, the Supreme Court decided it was not always necessary to prove a clear and present danger to determine that a dissenting speech was illegal and said that a speech could be illegal on the basis of its *bad tendency*. For example, when Benjamin Gitlow published a pamphlet that called for mass strikes of workers in 1925, the courts ruled that the pamphlet was a *bad tendency* and thus was unprotected, illegal speech even though the courts found no immediate harm to public order from the distribution of the pamphlet. Although this test has not been used since the 1940s, it has never been rejected entirely by the courts. During the late 1940s, the courts also made a distinction between *advocacy of ideas* and *advocacy of actions*. When Oleta Yates organized a series of Communist Party activities that included seminars on communism, the courts found that teaching and discussing "abstract ideas" was not advocacy of action and therefore did not present a danger to the government. If Yates had made *statements to take actual steps* to overthrow the government, her speech would have been viewed as advocacy of action.

Two tests, *balancing* and *preferred position*, were created to address the problem of conflicting rights when dissent is expressed. Sometimes rights such as the right to a speedy trial or the right to a fair trial can conflict with the right to freedom of speech. Newspapers, for example, may want to publish the facts of the case as they arise but, in so doing, may jeopardize a person's ability to receive a fair trial. A balance must be maintained between competing rights. Many newspapers, for instance, do not publish the names of a person charged with sexual assault or rape if in doing so it will reveal the names of the victim and violate the victim's right to privacy. This practice has come about because the courts have dealt with balancing the rights of freedom of the press and the privacy rights of victims in past court cases. The *preferred position* test, which is exactly like the balancing test, was developed by Supreme Court Justice William O. Douglas, one of the most liberal justices in the history of the Court, who argued that when there was a conflict between a First Amendment right and another individual right, the First Amendment right should be the preferred position.

The *absolutist* test has never been accepted by the Supreme Court. Its proponent was Supreme Court Justice Hugo Black, who argued that there should be no restrictions on the freedom of speech whatsoever. Black, in *Dennis v. United States*, 71 S. Ct. 857 (1951), believed that "the men who drafted our Bill of Rights did all the 'balancing' that was necessary."

The Supreme Court has also ruled that certain types of words in speech may be legally censored or the person using them may be convicted of a statutory offense, such as disorderly conduct. The Court has made it clear, however, that these words must be taken in context and are not wrong in every instance. There are at least four types of words that, depending on the context, may be illegal:

- fighting words: must be taken in context as words that would cause the ordinary person to be involved in a fight
- provocative words: must be taken in context but seen as words that may cause an immediate danger, such as inciting a riot
- threatening words: similar to provocative words, must pose an immediate threat to a person
- offensive (vulgar) words: considered obscene speech

Fighting words are understood to be those words that ordinary people believe will cause an immediate fight among others who hear or are subjected to them. This restriction comes from *Chaplinsky* v. *New Hampshire* (62 S. Ct. 766, 1942), a well-known case. In this case,

Walter Chaplinsky used vulgar language to describe the local sheriff and called him a Nazi. The Supreme Court found that the words Chaplinsky used could be construed to cause a fight between Chaplinsky and the sheriff and others. In other contexts, however, the word Nazi may not be construed as a fighting word.

Provocative words are those words that a court determines may create a dangerous situation or a clear and present danger if said out loud. The words do not have to be obscene or offensive to be provocative. In 1951, for example, Irving Feiner was giving a speech in front of a hotel, urging students to attend a Socialist rally. When he saw the police approaching, he made derogatory remarks about the police and President Truman and then urged African Americans in the crowd to fight for their rights. Feiner's speech sparked threats from many whites in the crowd. Feiner was arrested and convicted of disorderly conduct. His conviction was upheld when the Supreme Court ruled that his words were provocative words. Threatening words are similar to provocative words. When a statement threatens someone, even a public figure, the police can arrest the speaker for making a threat, unless the statement is what is known as *political hyperbole*. Political hyperbole is a statement made in the heat of a political debate without the actual intent of committing an illegal act. When Robert Watts attended a Vietnam War protest in Washington, D.C., in 1966 and said, "If they ever make me carry a rifle, the first man I'll shoot is L.B.J. [President Lyndon Johnson]," the courts ruled that Watts's remark was made in the context of a political rally and showed no actual intent to shoot President Johnson. *Offensive or vulgar words* within a political context may not be illegal, although they usually are not legal when they are used in public.

The Supreme Court has used three tests to determine whether a publication is obscene:

- Hicklin rule
- Roth test
- Miller test

The *Hicklin rule* is the oldest and rose out of an English court case in 1868 that was adopted by the U.S. Supreme Court in 1879. The Hicklin rule states that if one passage of a book is found to be obscene, the entire work can be declared obscene. This standard kept such books as *Tropic of Cancer* and *Tropic of Capricorn* by Henry Miller from being published and sold in the United States until 1957. In that year, the Supreme Court changed its standards in the case *Roth* v. *United States* (77 S. Ct. 1304, 1957). The *Roth test* requires a work to be judged as a whole, which ended the Hicklin rule, and on the moral standards of citizens of the United States. The Roth test also requires a work to be found to be "utterly without socially redeeming value." The Roth test was superceded in 1973, when the Court ruled in *Miller* v. *California* (93 S. Ct. 2607, 1973) that local community standards, not the standards of all the citizens of the country, were to be used to determine the limits of obscenity. This test recognizes that people in New York, for example, may have a view of obscenity that differs from the view held by people in rural Montana. The *Miller test* requires that a work be declared obscene if it lacks "serious literary, artistic, political or scientific value." This test has permitted more prosecutions of pornography than the Roth test, because its requirements are stricter than the "utterly without socially redeeming value" of the Roth test. The Miller test is the test for obscenity in the courts today.

Obscenity is a difficult issue for advocates of free speech. While they may agree with those who advocate censorship that hard-core pornography has no socially redeeming, literary, artistic, or scientific value, they are concerned about the definition of hard-core pornography. Free-speech advocates point out that legitimate publications may be censored if a definition of hard-core pornography does not take into account the context of the work. In the 1970s, for example, a book entitled *Show Me!* was published as a sex-education book. The book, which discussed sex with simplicity and humor, consisted of photographs of nude children and adults. Some of the pictures showed actual sexual activity. In this context, it is difficult to consider the photograph, and thus the book, pornographic. However, the same photographs used in a book published by a known pornographic publisher would have a different context—one intended to arouse the reader sexually—making the book illegal in most states. Free-speech advocates also worry about where to draw the line between soft-core pornography, which is considered somewhat acceptable, and hard-core pornography. Free speech advocates fear that without some restraint on censorship, depictions of sexual activity could be declared obscene even though the legal standards would not consider them so. For instance, *Playboy* magazine, one of the most popular men's magazines, features pictures of nude women. Many retailers have been picketed by church groups and conservative organizations for carrying *Playboy*, and these demonstrators have called *Playboy* obscene, even though it clearly does not fit the legal definition of obscenity.

On the other hand, the explosive growth of the pornographic industry has raised legitimate concerns about the welfare of children and families. The production of pornography has grown by leaps and bounds, especially since the development of electronic markets, such as the Internet. These markets have allowed both amateur producers of pornography and traditional producers from around the world to sell or disseminate pornography. Especially disturbing is the growth in the availability of child pornography on the Internet. Many organizations, such as Filtering Facts, Enough Is Enough, and the National Coalition to Protect Children and Families, have been created to stem the tide of pornography and eliminate access by children. While many free-speech advocates are sympathetic to the views of these organizations, they are concerned about the legal precedents that may be established by censorship.

Commercial speech is the last major form of speech that is subject to censorship. Commercial speech, primarily advertisements for goods and services, is considered an unprotected form of speech. Governments can regulate advertisements and even censor them. The federal government, for example, banned cigarette and tobacco advertising in the 1970s and convinced the liquor industry to agree to a voluntary ban on television advertising of such hard liquor products as whiskey, gin, and vodka. Commercial speech that is designed to deceive the public is subject to prosecution and cannot be defended as free speech.

CONCLUSION

History has shown that ideas survive and thrive even when authorities try to suppress them. Early debates over censorship were debates over the need to protect ideas, particularly ideas that challenged established authority. If the debate over censorship today was only a debate over the value of ideas, there would be no controversy. However, today's debates are debates over rights. Do parents have the right to challenge government authority when they believe their children will have access to books and other materials contrary to their religious and moral beliefs? Do organizations have the right to challenge publications that they believe destroy the moral fiber of America and may cause irreparable harm to children, even if the marketplace shows that the American public wants access to these materials? Who gets to define what is pornographic and what is obscene—parents, the marketplace, or government?

The fifty people included in this work all believe they can make a difference in the debate on censorship. Some believe that pornography is an immoral national nightmare that can harm children. Others believe that any type of censorship for any reason threatens all forms of expression. All of them hold their views forthrightly, often see each other as adversaries, and play significant roles in today's debates on censorship.

FURTHER READING

Allen, David S., and Robert Jensen, eds. *Freeing the First Amendment: Critical perspectives on freedom of expression.* New York: New York University Press, 1995.

Barron, Jerome A., and C. Thomas Dienes. *First Amendment law in a nutshell.* St. Paul, MN: West Publishing Co., 1993.

Chafee, Zechariah, Jr. *Free speech in the United States.* Cambridge, MA: Harvard University Press, 1967.

Delgado, Richard, and Jean Stefanic. *Must we defend the Nazis? Hate speech, pornography, and the new First Amendment.* New York: New York University Press, 1997.

Emerson, Thomas I. *The system of freedom of expression.* New York: Random House, 1970.

Frohnmayer, John. *Out of tune: listening to the First Amendment.* Golden, CO: North American Press, 1995.

Gabler, Mel and Norma Gabler, with James C. Hefley. *What are they teaching our children?* Wheaton, IL: Victor Books, 1985.

Haiman, Franklyn S. *Speech and law in a free society.* Chicago: University of Chicago Press, 1981.

Harer, John B. *Intellectual freedom: A reference handbook.* Santa Barbara, CA: ABC-Clio, 1992.

Hentoff, Nat. *The first freedom: The tumultuous history of the free speech in America.* New York: Delacorte Press, 1980.

Hull, Mary E. *Censorship in America: A reference handbook.* Santa Barbara, CA: ABC-Clio, 1999.

Meiklejohn, Alexander. *Free speech and its relation to self-government.* New York: Harper & Brothers, 1948.

Mill, John Stuart. *On liberty.* Mineola, NY: Dover Publications, 2002, 1854.

Milton, John. *Areopagitica.* Folcroft, PA: Folcroft Library Editions, 1974.

Reichman, Henry. *Censorship and selection: Issues and answers for schools*. Chicago: American Library Association, 1988.

Sekulow, Jay. *From intimidation to victory: Regaining the Christian right to speak*. Lake Mary, FL: Creation House, 1990.

Thomas, Cal. *Book burning*. Westchester, IL: Crossway Books, 1983.

Gary L. Bauer

Bringing the Importance of Family Values to the National Political Scene

Born: May 4, 1946, Covington, Kentucky
Education: B.A., Georgetown College, 1968; J.D., Georgetown
  University, 1973
Current position: Chairperson, Campaign for Working Families;
  former president, Family Research Council

The political arena often requires outspoken people to champion controversial causes. Gary Bauer has spent more than twenty years in the political arena and has become one of the most passionate and articulate voices in the family values movement, generally espousing traditional marriage and biblical teachings.

Bauer's political life has emphasized conservative values. He has taken strong, principled stands against abortion, homosexuality and same-sex marriages, and assisted suicides, and for prayer and religion in the schools. In 2000, Bauer brought these views to the national political scene when he ran, unsuccessfully, for the presidency.

Bauer was born in Covington, Kentucky, and raised in the nearby, working-class town of Newport, which Bauer has said was overrun by organized crime. Bauer's father, Spike Bauer, was an alcoholic ex-Marine. Despite this background, his father, Bauer says, taught him the value of hard work, education, and family. "I can remember, my father would come home after a bad day at work covered in grime. He would say, 'Look at me. Study, so you don't have to do this,' " Bauer said in the January 20, 1998, edition of the *Washington Post*.

AP Photo/Dennis Cook. Courtesy of AP/Wide World Photos.

He listened to his father's advice and graduated from Georgetown College in Georgetown, Kentucky, in 1968. He went on to receive a doctorate in law from Georgetown University in Washington, D.C., in 1973.

Bauer began his political career in 1980 as the assistant director for policy/communication services for Ronald Reagan's presidential campaign. In October 1982, President Reagan appointed Bauer to the deputy undersecretary of education for planning, budget, and evaluation for the Department of Education. As deputy undersecretary, he was the department's representative on the White House Council for Human Resources and chairperson of the Working Group on

School Discipline. During these years, Bauer often expressed his belief that U.S. academics held the country's political system in contempt. On December 4, 1984, he told the *New York Times*, "Nowhere is one more likely to hear the words 'imperialist, oppressive, militaristic and warmongering' applied to one's own nation and leaders than within the ivy-covered walls of some of the finest schools in America."

In 1985, Bauer was promoted to undersecretary of education and worked to reverse existing school curriculums where courses do not promote one belief or value, especially those beliefs or values grounded in Christian or biblical teachings. Calling them value-free curriculums, Bauer told an audience at the Christian Congress for Excellence in Public Education in that year that such curriculums made it impossible for schools to teach self-discipline, kindness, fidelity, and diligence. Later that year, in a speech to the Denver National Conference on Pornography, he charged that pornographers enjoyed more freedom of speech than conservative religious groups: "When pornography is protected in the name of 'freedom,' our children receive a very disturbing message—since pornography is allowed, it is all right."

Bauer's political agenda expanded as he worked in the Reagan administration. In 1986, he was appointed chairperson of the Special Working Group on the Family. The group conducted and issued a study, written largely by Bauer, that argued that administration policies had led to a decline in crime, drug use, teen pregnancy, and divorce. Bauer's study recommended that families with children receive an increased tax exemption; that in submiting proposals for legislation, all government agencies be required to include a so-called family fairness statement—language to be placed in documents that enumerates how a tax proposal treats families equally and fairly; and that single mothers under the age of twenty-one who refused to live with their parents be denied subsidized housing. Two years later, in 1988, Bauer proclaimed his anti-abortion principles loudly by releasing a draft of an executive order banning the use of fetal tissues in research before an advisory panel had studied the issue and made its recommendations.

In that year, with the Reagan administration in its waning days, Bauer's positions on abortion and other social issues caught the eye of Dr. James Dobson, founder and president of Focus on the Family. Dobson had formed a political advocacy organization in 1982 that was known as the Family Research Council (FRC). Dobson offered Bauer the presidency of the FRC and the position of senior vice president of Focus on the Family. After accepting the offer, Bauer set out to increase the FRC's membership and influence, and by 1998, the organization had a membership of nearly 500,000 and a budget of more than $14 million. The FRC's stated mission is "to reaffirm and promote nationally, and particularly in Washington, D.C., the traditional family and the Judeo-Christian principles upon which it is built" (http://www.FRC.org/). The organization has four goals: (1) to promote and defend traditional family values in the media and in print; (2) to compile statistics and keep a database of research; (3) to develop and promote legislation with traditional family values in the core of the legislation; and (4) to educate citizens on how they can promote biblical principles in our culture.

In 1996 he debated Bob Dole, the eventual 1996 Republican nominee, during the primaries, and then, incensed over the Republican Party's attempt to appeal to moderate, especially pro-choice, Republicans, created a political action committee (PAC) called the Campaign for Working Families (CWF). Bauer explained his reason for doing so in the 1996 edition of the *National Review*: "This is the second failed [Republican] campaign in a row. I'm sick and tired of the political party of death [Democratic Party] being bold and outspoken, while my party appears to be afraid. If we can't find someone . . . to stand up for the sanctity of life, in four more years, I'll do it myself" (Bauer, 1996, p. 51). As the 1996 campaign came to a close he began extensive fund-raising efforts. In 1998, Bauer managed to add an anti-abortion resolution to the Republican National Committee's 1998 election platform and funded an anti-abortion congressional candidate in a special election in California. Bauer's candidate went on to defeat a moderate Republican, who was backed by Newt Gingrich, then Speaker of the House, in the primary. These efforts were a prelude to Bauer's bid for the presidency in 2000. Acknowledging that he was a long shot, Bauer made a valiant effort to gain the Republican nomination but lost the battle for votes and funds. On February 16, he dropped out of the race and stepped away from the moderate Republican, Governor George Bush, the front-runner and eventual winner, to endorse Senator John McCain. Although the move was controversial, Bauer believed he had to uphold his principles.

Bauer stepped down from the presidency of the Family Research Council in the fall of 2000 to devote more time to the Campaign for Working Families (CWF). He is the author of *Our Journey Home* (1992) and, with Dr. James Dobson, co-author of *Children at Risk: The*

Battle for the Hearts and Minds of Our Kids (1994). He continues to write for magazines and other publications and appears on talk shows. He plans to stay politically active to promote traditional family values. He is married to the former Carol Hoke, and they have three children, Elyse, Sara, and Zachary.

SUGGESTED READINGS

Bauer, Gary L. "Family, faith, and freedom." *National Review* 48 (December 9, 1996), pp. 51–52.
———. *Our hopes, our dreams: A vision for America.* Colorado Springs, CO: Focus on the Family Publications, 1996.
———. *Our journey home.* Dallas: Word Publishing, 1992.
Dear, Robert. "Reading, writing, roping liberals." *New York Times*, December 4, 1984, p. 58 (L).
Edsall, Thomas. "GOP victor had the right stuff." *Washington Post*, January 20, 1998, p. A9.

Joan E. Bertin

National Coalition Against Censorship

Born: April 5, 1946
Education: B.A., Smith College, 1968; J.D., New York University School of Law, 1971
Current position: Executive director, National Coalition Against Censorship

---

There are numerous organizations whose missions include an anti-censorship component. The National Council of Teachers of English (NCTE) and the American Library Association (ALA), for example, are professional associations that also work to combat attempts at censorship because their members and their professions are subject to such attempts. Joan Bertin, however, directs the efforts of an organization whose purpose is to act as an umbrella alliance for anti-censorship organizations. As executive director of the National Coalition Against Censorship (NCAC), Bertin and her staff promote freedom of expression whenever censorship occurs or is threatened.

Bertin has enjoyed an illustrious career as an academic and scholar. She graduated from Smith College, *cum laude*, and went straight to New York University's School of Law, where she received her Juris Doctor, also *cum laude*. While at New York University, she earned the school's prestigious Founder's Day Award, which is given for outstanding scholarship, and was awarded a fellowship in the Arthur Garfield Hays Civil Liberties Program. The fellowship, founded in 1958 and named for a well-known American Civil Liberties Union (ACLU) attorney, provides stipends to graduate and law-school students who are interested in civil liberties in recognition of their scholarship. After law school, Bertin spent seven years as a legal services lawyer representing indigent clients and more than a dozen years litigating civil rights and civil liberties cases at the ACLU. During her tenure at the ACLU, Bertin was the associate director of the Women's Rights Project. She has also taught at Columbia University, where, as a member of the faculty, she is a clinical professor of public health. She is also a member of the faculty at Sarah Lawrence College, where she has held the Joanne Woodward Chair in public policy. Her career shows, however, that she prefers activism to academia.

In 1997, Bertin was appointed the executive director of the NCAC. In a press release made on June 1, 1997, Bertin pledged her dedication to combating censorship, which was, she said, an issue that "represents substantial tension in this society, which is dedicated to First Amendment freedoms but still has major disagreements over how those freedoms should be expressed." She directs the programs, special projects, publications, and fundraising functions of the organization and is the NCAC's national spokesperson.

The NCAC, founded in 1974, is "an alliance of fifty national nonprofit organizations, including literary, artistic, religious, educational, professional, labor, and civil liberties groups. United by a conviction that freedom of thought, inquiry, and expression must be defended, we [NCAC] work to educate our own members and the public at large about the dangers of censorship and how to oppose them" (http://www.ncac.org). The coalition's committees deal with various aspects of censorship issues. The Committee on Sex and Censorship, for example, "brings a feminist perspective to censorship debates on issues relating to sexuality, sexual orientation, and gender roles." Other committees deal with countering censorship in schools and libraries; resisting homophobic attacks on education and the arts; and grassroots activism. Bertin has been instrumental in the creation of two new NCAC projects—the Arts Advocacy Project and the Free Expression Policy Project. The Arts Advocacy Project joined several civil liberties groups in a successful defense of rights of the Esperanza Center, an arts center in San Antonio, Texas, when it lost its public funding for art exhibits in 1997. The San Antonio City Council had stripped the center of funds, claiming it supported pro-homosexual, pro-abortion, and antifamily values.

Bertin has made her position on freedom of speech and censorship clear through writings and her speeches in numerous venues, including testimony before government committees. In a statement released at the 1997 Internet Online Summit, Focus on the Children Summit held in Washington, D.C., she gave her views on children and censorship: "Children are not harmed by free expression. The law should target unlawful actions, not protected speech. We [NCAC] support vigorous enforcement of criminal laws against sexual abuse of children but oppose efforts to suppress protected, nonobscene speech. Children, like adults, receive enormous intellectual and other benefits, from living in a free society." Bertin also provided an introductory letter for *Places I've Never Meant to Be*, a collection of essays and short stories by writers, such as the popular young-adult novelist Judy Blume, who have been censored.

In 1998, in what some have seen as a risky move, Bertin appeared as a panelist at the World Pornography Conference, which was held in Universal City, California, on August 6–9, 1998. There, she discussed the impact of current child pornography legislation and the chilling effect of that legislation on other forms of legally protected expression. On October 6, 1999, Bertin testified before the New York State House of Representatives' Task Force on Youth Violence and the Entertainment Industry. In her testimony, she stated that she was opposed to rating video games for violent content because "it is impossible to distinguish rationally between 'acceptable' and 'unacceptable' forms of violent speech, imagery, or entertainment, as the judgment is inherently subjective. The Constitution accordingly allows each of us to make our own decisions about such content, and parents to set their own guidelines for their minor children, and restricts the role of government in controlling these choices" (http://www.ncac.org/issues/internetmenu.html).

Bertin has an extensive resume of public presentations on legal and policy issues and is the author of more than 30 chapters and articles in professional books and journals. At present, she is an effective leader of one of the most significant anticensorship organizations in the United States and today will undoubtedly continue her activism in whatever capacity she may hold in the future. In a press release on September 22, 2001, during the celebration of Freedom to Read week, Bertin explained her commitment to free speech: "Most people say they believe in the First Amendment, but when you get down to specifics, it's clear that many people don't really understand it. They want the First Amendment to protect the material they like but not necessarily what you like. Those of us who oppose censorship believe that reading about something is a safe way to explore and understand it, and that it is the best way to prepare young people to deal with the issues they face, both in school and later in life. It's true that some material is 'offensive,' but to know how to respond to it, we need to understand it."

SUGGESTED READINGS

Web site for the National Coalition Against Censorship: http://www.ncac.org

Judy Blume

Censored Author Crusading for Freedom of Speech

Born: February 12, 1938, Elizabeth, New Jersey
Education: B.A., New York University, 1960
Current position: Writer; founder and trustee, KIDS Fund

Ask any young people who love to read to name their favorite authors and almost all of them will mention Judy Blume. Blume has written at least eighteen novels for young adult readers. In recent years, she has expanded her reading audience with the publication of three adult novels, *Wifey* (1978), *Smart Women* (1983), and *Summer Sisters* (1998).

Her popularity with young readers is both the source of her reputation as a writer and the reason why she is a constant target of those who want to restrict or ban her books. A study of reported censorship incidents during the 1980s found that Blume's young adult novels were the most frequently censored books of the decade, including *Are You There God? It's Me, Margaret* (1970), *Deenie* (1973), and *Forever* (1975) (Harer and Harris, 1994). In response to those

Photo credit: Peter Simon

who would like to censor her books, Blume has said, "The way to instill values in children is to talk about difficult issues and bring them out in the open, not to restrict their access to books that may help them deal with their problems and concerns" (*Washington Post*, p. 131). Blume is active in anticensorship organizations, a member of the board of trustees of the National Coalition Against Censorship (NEAC), and an active supporter of the Author's Guild.

Blume was born on February 12, 1938, in Elizabeth, New Jersey. Her father, Randolph Sussman, was a dentist and her mother, Esther Sussman, was a homemaker. *Newsmakers 98* notes that "Blume and her older brother, David, grew up in a home brimming with books as well as radio tuned to their favorite shows" (p. 56). Blume was an A student in high school, active in the school chorus, and editor of the school newspaper. She attended Boston University for one year before dropping out because of mononucleosis. She later enrolled in New York University and earned a bachelor's degree in early childhood education in 1961. While attending NYU, she met and married John Blume, an attorney.

Blume began writing her first book, *Iggie's House* (1970), during a college writing course. Unable to find a publisher for it, she wrote a children's picture book entitled *The One in the Middle Is the Green Kangaroo* (1969), which became her first published work. In 1969, Blume convinced Bradbury Press to publish *Iggie's House*. The book was a success, although some critics considered it to be a simplified treatment of racial issues. *Are You There God? It's Me, Margaret*, published by Bradbury Press in 1970, firmly established Blume as a significant young adult author. In a review for the *New York Times Book Review* on November 8, 1970, Dorothy Broderick praised this work as "a warm, funny, and loving book, one that captures the essence of adolescence."

The topics of Blume's novels—sexual development, divorce, family breakups, and social ostracism—are usually the source of her censorship troubles. As Alice Phoebe Naylor and Carol Wintercorn note in the *Dictionary of Literary Biography* (vol. 52, p. 31), "Blume's books reflect a general cultural concern with feelings about self and body, interpersonal relationships and family problems." Other critics believe her works have revolutionized young adult fiction with their portrayals of sexuality as normal and not subject to punishment.

Blume says she "knew intuitively what kids wanted to know because I remembered what I wanted to know" (*People*, p. 47) as a child. Blume recalls that her father tried to educate her about sexuality by delivering lectures on how babies were made until she was ten but notes that what she really wanted were answers to questions about how she was feeling about her own sexual development. Blume sees a need for the topics she uses in her books. "When you're twelve, you're on the brink of adulthood, but everything is still in front of you, and you still have the chance to be almost anyone you want. That seemed appealing to me. I wasn't even thirty years old when I started to write, but already I didn't feel I had much chance myself" (*New York Times* Magazine, p. 80). When Blume has found herself in the center of debates over the need for censorship, she has expressed disbelief. "I wrote these books a long time ago when there wasn't anything near the censorship that there is now. I wasn't aware at the time that I was writing anything controversial. I just know what these books would have meant to me when I was a kid" (*Chicago Tribune*, p. 16). Judith Goldberger, in the May 1981 *Newsletter on Intellectual Freedom*, noted that concerned parents and critics read Judy Blume out of context and label the books, while children and young adults "read the whole books to find out what they are about. . . . the grown-ups, it seems, are the ones who read for the 'good parts,' more so than the children" (p. 57).

Blume agrees: "What I worry about is that an awful lot of people, looking at my example, have gotten the idea that what sells is teen-age sex, and they'll exploit it. I don't believe that sex is why kids like my books. The impression I get, from letter to letter, is that a great many kids don't communicate with their parents. They feel alone in the world. Sometimes reading books that deal with other kids who feel the same thing as they do, it makes them feel less alone" (*New York Times* Magazine, p. 80). Blume decries what she calls "dishonest books," books that do not address important issues and even try to hide the issues that, for many, are reality. "They [her young readers] see things and hear things. The worst is when there are secrets, because what they imagine is usually scarier than the truth" (*Christian Science Monitor*, p. 10).

Blume has two children, Randy Lee and Lawrence Andrew. She divorced her husband, John Blume, in 1975, then married a physicist, Thomas Kitchens, and moved from the New York area to Santa Fe, New Mexico. In 1979, Blume divorced Kitchens and continued her prolific writing career. In 1987, she married George Cooper, a law professor and writer. She continues to write and works tirelessly for the rights of authors. She is on the board of directors for the Society of Children's Book Writers and Planned Parenthood Advocates, as well as the Authors Guild and the NCAC. When asked by Brangien Davis of Amazon.com what she considered her most significant contribution to literature, she said, "I'm happy that so many children like to read. And if they like to read in part because of what I gave them to read, that's great. To touch lives, I guess, is the best thing that anybody can ask for."

SUGGESTED READINGS

Blume, Judy. *Letters to Judy: What your kids wish they could tell you.* New York: Putnam, 1986.

Broderick, Dorothy. *New York Times Book Review*, November 8, 1970.
Chicago Tribune, March 15, 1985.
Christian Science Monitor, May 14, 1979, p. 10.
Goldberger, Judith. *Newsletter on Intellectual Freedom*. May 1981.
Harer, John B., and Steven R. Harris. *Censorship of expression in the 1980s: A statistical survey*. Westport, CT: Greenwood Press, 1994.
New York Times Magazine, August 23, 1982, p. 80.
People Magazine, August 16, 1978, p. 47.
Washington Post, November 3, 1991, p. 131.
Weidt, Maryann N. *Presenting Judy Blume*. Boston: Twayne Publishers, 1990.

Jeffrey Mark Cohen

Protecting the Rights of Reporters

Born: November 10, 1951, Detroit, Michigan
Education: University of Michigan; J.D., Peoples College of Law School, 1981
Current position: Founder and executive director, Fairness and Accuracy in Reporting

---

Jeff Cohen is one of the most well known of the media critics in the United States today. He is also the founder of Fairness and Accuracy in Reporting (FAIR), a well-known media watchdog group, and acts as the organization's executive director. Along with his close associate, Norman Soloman, Cohen has written extensively on media bias and censorship of the press.

Jeffrey Mark Cohen was born in Detroit, Michigan, on November 10, 1951. After graduating from high school, he attended the University of Michigan but dropped out and shortly thereafter began his career as a journalist in Los Angeles, California. Cohen's articles have appeared in *Rolling Stone, New Times*, and *Mother Jones*, among many other publications. While working full time as an investigative journalist, he attended the Peoples College of Law School, an evening school in Los Angeles that is dedicated to educating the nontraditional student. In 1981, he earned his Juris Doctor and became a member of the California Bar Association.

His growing concern over the political and corporate pressures that often force journalists to exclude or downplay certain stories led Cohen to found FAIR in 1986. The organization focuses on censorship within the national press. In a statement on the organization's web site members note that they have been "offering well-documented criticism of media bias and censorship since 1986" and go on to say, "We work to invigorate the First Amendment by advocating for greater diversity in the press and by scrutinizing media practices that marginalize public interest, minority and dissenting viewpoints. As an anticensorship organization, we expose important news stories that are neglected and defend working journalists when they are muzzled." FAIR accomplishes this through the publication of *Extra!*, an award-winning magazine of media criticism, and the production of a weekly radio program, *Counter Spin*, which brings the stories behind the headlines to the forefront. FAIR has research and advocacy desks that work on specific issues with journalists and advocates. The Women's Desk, for example, analyzes how sexism and homophobia affect reporting and the Racism Watch Desk monitors the media's handling of racism issues.

In addition to his regular column in *Extra!*, Cohen has coauthored four books with Norman Soloman: *Wizards of Media OZ: Behind the Curtain of Mainstream News* (1997); *Through the Media Looking Glass: Decoding Bias and Blather in the News* (1995); *The Way Things Aren't: Rush Limbaugh's Reign of Error* (1995); and *Adventures in Medialand: Behind the News, Beyond the Pundits* (1993). He is a frequent guest on news programs such as *Fox News Watch, Larry King Live, Crossfire* on CNN and various National Public Radio (NPR) programs. He has also lectured on media bias and journalistic ethics at many colleges, including Harvard, Princeton, Columbia, and several branches of the University of California. His political activism goes beyond FAIR and its publications. He has been a board member of the American Civil Liberties Union of Southern California and the Southern Christian Leadership Conference in Los Angeles, as well as several other public interest groups.

During the 2000 presidential campaign, Cohen was an outspoken critic of the format used for televised debates. Along with many others, including Cal Thomas, a conservative columnist, Cohen objected to the exclusion of third party candidates. In recent articles, Cohen has criticized the press for its coverage of the gun control debate, its use of a double standard in reporting on the private lives of politicians, and its approach to campaign financing issues, especially those involving corporate donations to political campaigns. Cohen feels strongly about media bias and believes that people too often assume the media is biased to a liberal point of view. He states at the FAIR web site, "Independent, aggressive and critical media are essential to an informed democracy." Conservatives often claim that reporters have a liberal bias, but a recent survey of journalists found that they are more conservative than the general public on issues such as corporate power and business influence on government (*Extra!*, July/August 1998).

To be close to the headquarters of FAIR, which is in New York City, Cohen moved to Woodstock, New York. He is married to Stephanie Kristal, and he has one daughter, Sequoia.

SUGGESTED READINGS

Cohen, Jeff, and Norman Soloman. *Through the media looking glass: Decoding bias and blather in the news.* Monroe, ME: Common Courage Press, 1995.

Extra!, a publication of Fairness and Accuracy in Reporting.

Lee, Martin A., and Norman Soloman. *Unreliable sources: A guide to detecting bias in news media.* New York: Carol Publishing Group, 1990.

Gordon M. Conable

Defender of First Amendment Rights

Born: January 5, 1947, Buffalo, New York
Education: B.A., Antioch College, 1969; M.S.L.S., Columbia University, 1975
Current position: Vice president, West Coast Operations, Library Systems and Services, Incorporated

Librarians are often the targets of censors because they provide access to books and other materials that some people believe are dangerous to society, especially to children. Sometimes threats of censorship turn an unassuming librarian into a staunch and tireless defender of the First Amendment. Sometimes the commitment to free speech starts earlier. Gordon Conable, former chairperson of the Intellectual Freedom Committee of the American Library Association (ALA), developed his commitment to free speech at an early age. As he explained to the authors when interviewed, "As a child, I used a branch library of a large system that was reluctant to allow me out of the children's section when I was ready to read books housed elsewhere. This was my first encounter with adults who felt that shielding kids from knowledge was a positive value. My parents' permission was insufficient to open the rest of the collection to me, so I took to riding a bus to the downtown library that willingly offered up its treasures to a sixth grader despite my age."

Conable grew up in Buffalo, New York, in the 1950s, the time of the McCarthy era. He attended Antioch College and graduated with a degree in art in 1969. When he became a librarian in 1975, he told the authors in an interview: "I sought out those whose professional values were rooted fearlessly in defense of the unabridged right to read. Dr. Richard Darling, who was the American Library Association's Intellectual Freedom Roundtable Chair the year I completed library school, introduced me to Judy Krug who became a lifelong friend and mentor, as she has for thousands of others." From this early start, Conable has become one the strongest voices for intellectual freedom within the library profession.

He began his career in the Fort Vancouver regional library system in Vancouver, Washington. By 1988, he had become associate director of the system. In that year, he accepted the position of director of the Monroe County Library System, in Monroe, Michigan. In that capacity, he became known as an ardent defender of the right to read.

Most people are inspired by either their parents or a teacher who reached out to make a difference in their lives. For Conable, inspiration came from a librarian. Conable told the authors, "The most effective First Amendment champions that I have known have all come to cherish freedom through some personal experience. My greatest teacher was a librarian known today only to her friends and family, but whose legacy still informs the public library where she worked. She lived most of her life in view of the mountain she loved, and she was as firm in her commitments as Mt. Hood is in the face of both light breezes and serious squalls."

Conable's early forays into the defense of First Amendment rights included combating the exclusion of *The National Lampoon*, a satirical magazine, by a library administration that, ironically, had defended *Playboy*. He also became involved in opposing an attempt to pass an antipornography ballot initiative. Although the initiative was passed by a wide margin, the legislation was later declared unconstitutional. The most difficult censorship battle of his career was a five-year struggle over a book, entitled *Sex*, by the popular singer Madonna. The book, which was attacked in many communities across the country, featured nude photos of the singer. Conable's considerable skills working within the political system were taxed to their limit during this struggle. The support and inspiration he received from his wife, a school librarian, helped him to continue despite threats against his family and intense political pressure. Given his experiences, it is not surprising that the *Library Journal* asked him to explain how library managers should address a censorship challenge in its popular column "How Do You Manage?" in 1993.

Conable has received many honors and awards over the years. On May 5, 1993, at the Museum of Modern Art in New York, five national foundations for First Amendment defense honored him. In 1996, he was added to the Freedom to Read Foundation Roll of Honor, and in 2000, he received the John Phillip Immroth Memorial Award. He has been an active member of the ALA's Intellectual Freedom Committee since 1987 and a member of the board of trustees for the Freedom to Read Foundation since 1988. In the early 1990s, he chaired the ALA's Intellectual Freedom Committee, and the committee has called upon him on numerous occasions to speak to members of Congress.

Conable is married to a librarian, and they have one son. In 1998, Conable became vice president for the west coast operations of Library Systems and Services, Incorporated (LSSI). LSSI is a private management company that provides management services for public libraries. Its west coast operation is headquartered in Riverside County, California.

SUGGESTED READINGS

Conable, Gordon M. "The public's right to know and electronic government information." In Dennis Reynolds, ed., *Citizen rights and access to electronic information: A collection of background essays prepared for the 1991 LITA President's Program*. Chicago: Library and Information Technology Association, 1991.

Rotenberg, Marc, Robert A. Walton, and Gordon M. Conable. *Privacy and intellectual freedom in the digital library*. (Video production). Topango, CA: Sweet Pea Productions, 1996.

Various issues of *The Newsletter on Intellectual Freedom*, a publication of the Office for Intellectual Freedom of the American Library Association.

Donna Demac

Lawyer and First Amendment Interpreter

Born: December 30, 1952, New York, New York
Education: B.A., St. John's College, 1974; J.D., Boston College, 1979
Current position: Copyright lawyer, adjunct professor, Georgetown University

---

Donna Demac has been delving into studies of censorship and changing interpretations of the First Amendment for more than twenty years. Her research is based on a wealth of experience in copyright law. She is a professor of law and a legal counsel for the National Coalition Against Censorship (NCAC).

Demac was born on December 30, 1952, in New York City to Kenneth L. Demac, a computer company executive, and Denison Demac. After graduating from high school, Demac attended St. John's College in Annapolis, Maryland. St. John's College offers a unique academic environment that is organized around the study of the great books of intellectual tradition. Upon graduation in 1974, Demac accepted a journalism fellowship for the Institute of Southeast Asian Studies and spent the better part of a year in Pasir Panjang, Singapore. This experience helped her to secure a position as an associate fellow at the Overseas Development Council in Washington, D.C.

In 1976, Demac left the Overseas Development Council to pursue legal studies. She attended law school at Boston College and worked as a law clerk for Massachusetts Legal Services, an agency that provides legal services and advice to the poor. After receiving Juris

Doctor in 1979, Demac became legal counsel for the Office of Communications for the United Church of Christ in Boston. As counsel, she received invaluable experience in communication law and First Amendment issues, particularly issues concerning freedom of religion and freedom of speech. Since 1984, she has held positions as staff counsel for the NCAC, legal counsel for PEN American Center, the United States arm of International PEN, an organization that works to protects the rights of authors, and as an adjunct professor at New York University and Georgetown University in Washington, D.C. She is also a member of the board of directors for the NCAC.

Among advocates of intellectual freedom, Demac is known primarily for her work with the NCAC and her book, *Liberty Denied: The Current Rise of Censorship in America* (1988). In her book, Demac noted that freedom of speech in America faces some stark realities:

> Many of us believe that the United States is virtually free of such restrictions [on freedom of speech and the press]. People proudly point to the Bill of Rights as an impenetrable shield and boast that we Americans enjoy a kind of free speech that is almost absolute. Even when it is acknowledged that we are confronted with some limitations on expression, the admission is usually accompanied by the claim that such restrictions are much less severe than they are elsewhere in the world. The reality of individual liberties in the United States is far more ambiguous. Although Walt Whitman described America as "Liberty's Nation," the history of freedom of expression in this country has been a complex mixture of a commitment to personal rights—undeniably greater than in most other countries—and a marked intolerance of dissident and unorthodox views. (*Liberty Denied*, p. 1)

Demac devotes individual chapters to what she believes are egregious attacks on the freedom of expression. Among her examples are harassment of leading newspapers by high-level government officials who threaten criminal prosecution if sensitive information is published; the surveilance of citizens by the FBI; the insistence that government employees sign secrecy agreements; the removal of classic works, such as Chaucer's *Canterbury Tales*, and modern novels, such as those by Kurt Vonnegut, from school and public libraries because of complaints; and the ruling by the United States Supreme Court that gives school principals the right to censor student publications.

While at New York University, Demac was the director of the University's Copyright and the New Technologies Program. Since then, she has become a widely sought speaker on the implications of new technologies and freedom of expression in the electronic age. She was only one of ten featured speakers at the Second Annual Telecommunications and Information Technology Summit, which was sponsored by Pennsylvania State University and held at the University of Texas on May 5, 1998. Demac also was chosen by the American Association of University Professors (AAUP) to prepare a report on the association's copyright policies for distance education initiatives, including classes by closed circuit TV, correspondence, and via the Internet. The Freedom Forum, a freedom of expression institution founded by Al Neuharth, authorized Demac to write an article on the state of the First Amendment in 1997. Her article, "The State of the First Amendment," is frequently quoted and widely distributed.

Demac has written a number of articles and books in addition to *Liberty Denied*. Her first book, prior to her work on censorship, was *Keeping America Uninformed: Government Secrecy in the 1980s* (1984). She is also author of *Is Any Use Fair in a Digitized World? Toward New Fair Use of Digitized News, Text, and Music*, which is available from the Freedom Forum, and she continues to contribute articles and commentary for the NCAC's web site and newsletter.

As a highly regarded scholar and author, Demac is a frequent guest at conferences and academic forums that deal with copyright issues and censorship in the electronic age. At present, Demac is an adjunct professor at Georgetown University in Washington, D.C.

SUGGESTED READINGS

Demac, Donna. *Liberty denied: The current rise of censorship in America.* New York: PEN American Center, 1988.

Web site for the National Coalition Against Censorship: http://www.ncac. org

James C. Dobson

Focus on the Family

Born: 1936, Louisiana
Education: Pasadena College; Ph.D. in child development, University of Southern California, 1967
Current position: Founder and president of Focus on the Family

James C. Dobson is the founder and president of Focus on the Family, a nonprofit organization he began in 1977 after several years as a clinical child psychologist on the staff of the Children's Hospital of Los Angeles. Focus on the Family produces his internationally syndicated radio programs, heard on more than 3,000 radio facilities in North America and in nine languages in approximately 2,300 facilities in over 93 other countries. His voice is heard by more than 200 million people every day, including a program carried on all state-owned radio stations in the Republic of China. He is seen on 100 television stations daily in the United States. Dobson is a licensed psychologist in the state of California and a licensed marriage, family, and child counselor in both California and Colorado.

Dobson was born in Louisiana and grew up in Texas and Oklahoma in a family that insisted upon the strict Nazareen code of morality in family life. His father, grandfather, and great-grandfather all practiced in the Nazareen ministry. Dobson graduated from high school in San Benito, Texas, near the Mexican border, and went on to college at a Nazareen institution in California, Pasadena College. Despite his deeply held religious beliefs, he did not choose to enter the ministry but instead studied psychology. In his book *Straight Talk to Men and Their Wives*, Dobson tells of how the death of his father affected him and gave him the inspiration to begin his calling, which would become Focus on the Family.

Focus on the Family has played a significant role in the promotion of family values in the last three decades. The publishing arm of the organization produces educational materials with a strong family-values orientation to counter the sectarian, and some say, secular humanist, materials of mainstream publishers. Dobson also formed the Family Research Council as a think tank on family values and to counter more liberal think tanks and their research on such issues.

Dobson has written 17 best-selling books, the first of which, *Dare to Discipline* (1970), has sold over three million copies. The book was selected as one of 50 books to be rebound and placed in the White House Library. He has also produced three film series, the first of which was "Focus on the Family," and it has been seen by over 70 million people. His second film series, "Turn Your Heart Toward Home," was released in January 1986 and continues in circulation internationally. A third seven-part series, entitled "Life on the Edge" and released in early 1994, was designed to help late teens bridge the gap between adolescence and young adulthood. In 1989, Dobson interviewed Ted Bundy, a notorious serial killer, just prior to his execution. Bundy told Dr. Dobson that his addiction to reading pornography played a significant role in his life of crime. Dobson's interview was taped and then sold to promote his antipornography views. Dobson has been a strong opponent of the influence of pornography on society, especially since his appointment to the Meese Commission, which studies the harmful effects of pornography.

As an advocate for the family, Dr. Dobson has been heavily involved in governmental activities. He assisted presidents Jimmy Carter, Ronald Reagan, and George Bush in a variety of capacities, from informal consulting to chairmanship of the United States Army's Family Initiative, 1986–1988. In 1985, Dobson was appointed to Attorney General Edwin Meese's Commission on Pornography. In December 1993, Senator Robert Dole appointed Dr. Dobson to the Commission on Child and Family Welfare, and in 1996, Senate Majority Leader Trent Lott appointed him to the National Gambling Impact Study Commission. His influence on the Republican party grew substantially in the 1990s. For example, in 1998, Dobson threatened to withdraw his support for the Republicans because the party did not take a stronger stance on abortion, among other family issues. Then Speaker of the House Newt Gingrich hosted several meetings with Republican figures and Dr. Dobson to address his concerns and keep him within the party.

Dr. Dobson has received numerous awards over the years. In 1987, he received the Marian Pfister Anschutz Award in recognition of his contributions to the American family. In 1999, he received the Christian Counseling in the Media Award from the Board of Directors of the Christian Association for Psychological Studies. In addition, he was awarded fifteen honorary degrees between 1983 and 1999. Dr. Dobson is married and the father of two grown children. He lives in the Colorado Springs area where the headquarters of Focus on the Family is located.

SUGGESTED READINGS

Dobson, James. *Dare to Discipline*. Wheaton, IL: Tyndale House Publishers, 1970.
———. *Straight Talk to Men and Their Wives*. Waco, TX: Word Books, 1980.
Web site for Focus on the Family. http://www.family.org

William A. Donohue

Defending Catholicism Against Blasphemy in the Media

Born: July 18, 1947, Long Island, New York
Education: B.A., New York University, 1971; M.A., New School for Social Research, 1974; Ph.D., New York University, 1980
Current position: Director, Catholic League for Religious and Civil Rights

William Donohue grew up on Long Island, New York, where a Catholic upbringing played a significant part in his personal and professional development. He attended only Catholic schools until he graduated from high school in 1966. Donohue then enrolled at New York University where he earned a bachelor's degree in 1971. After graduation, he took a position at St. Lucy's School in Spanish Harlem, teaching children from a largely Puerto Rican background. While working at St. Lucy's School, he began work on a Master's degree in sociology at the New School for Social Research in New York City, a graduate school for the social sciences, completing his degree in 1974. His education continued at New York University where he began work on a Ph.D. in sociology.

In 1977, he accepted a professorship at La Roche College in Pittsburgh, Pennsylvania, while still completing his doctorate at New York University. His dissertation, "Organizational Change within the American Civil Liberties Union" (1980), was the first in a series of works that researched the influence of the American Civil Liberties Union (ACLU). This dissertation laid the groundwork for his first book, *The Politics of the American Civil Liberties Union* (1985), in which he traces the history of the ACLU and analyzes its role in American civil rights and liberties law and in judicial history. He concluded that the ACLU is a left-liberal organization out of step with American values.

His book attracted the attention of the Heritage Foundation, a conservative think tank that formulates and promotes "conservative public policies based on the principles of free enterprise, limited government, individual freedom, traditional American values, and a strong national defense" (http://www.heritage.org/aboutus/). The foundation then provided him with a scholarship to research and write his second book, *The New Freedom: Individualism and Collectivism in the Social Lives of Americans* (1990). During his association with the Heritage Foundation, Donohue produced a number of works, including pamphlets and position papers, on individual liberty and conservative values. He also began work on his second book about the American Civil Liberties Union, *Twilight of Liberty: The Legacy of the ACLU* (1994).

In 1993, Donohue was appointed director of the Catholic League for Religious and Civil Rights. The Catholic League was founded in 1973 by Father Virgil C. Blum, S.J., to defend the rights of Catholics. The league participates in a number of initiatives to promote and protect the rights of Catholics, including publishing news releases, position papers, and pamphlets, testifying before government hearings and panels, and, on occasion, entering into legal cases to protect individuals or groups where rights as Catholics are in jeopardy. The Catholic League is neither affiliated with nor funded by the Roman Catholic Church, but functions as a lay organization with its own mission. Donohue provides much of the direction for the league's work, and he serves as editor of the league's newsletter, *Catalyst*.

Under Donohue's leadership, the Catholic League has found much that threatens Catholic rights, especially in the media and the entertainment arts. In the last decade, Donohue has used the league's resources to oppose the staging of Christopher Durang's play, *Sister Mary Ignatius Explains It All for You* (1981), whenever it is produced with public funds or through government subsidies, usually by pressuring the government authority to drop its funding and support. The play depicts four former students of a Catholic school nun whose troubled lives are the result of her teachings. Specifically, Donohue has objected to the anti-Catholic humor and negative portrayal of the nun. More recently, Donohue has objected to the play *Corpus Christi* (1998) by Terrence McNally, which depicts Jesus Christ as a homosexual.

Through the Catholic League, Donohue has been able to target other media offensive to Catholics. In 2001, Donohue pressured eBay, the Internet auction site, to remove two items available for sale. One was a CD by the group The Grey Wolves, entitled "Catholic priests f—— children," and another was a statue listed as "weird tattooed Jesus" (http://www.catholicleague.org). In October 2001, Donohue objected to the October 18 episode of the television show *Law and Order* which featured a Catholic priest who admitted to being a homosexual lover of a junkie. Donohue took particular umbrage at a joke made by a detective on the show that belittled the reciting of "Hail Mary's" for penance (http://www.catholicleague.org). The December 17 production of the World Wrestling Federation's RAW episode also came under scrutiny. Donohue argued that the wrestlers Booker T. and Stone Cold Steve Austin ridiculed the Catholic Sacrament of Reconciliation, the requirement for confession of sins and penance (http://www.catholicleague.org).

Donohue continues to direct the activities of the Catholic League for Religious and Civil Rights for the foreseeable future. He also serves on the board of advisors for a number of Catholic charities and legal foundations. His energies are devoted to the success of the League through fundraising as well as promotion of its viewpoints on Catholic religious rights.

SUGGESTED READINGS

Donohue, William A. *The new freedom: Individualism and collectivism in the social lives of Americans.* New Brunswick, NJ: Transaction Publishers, 1990.

———. *The politics of the American Civil Liberties Union.* New Brunswick, NJ: Transaction Publishers, 1985.

———. *Twilight of liberty: The legacy of the ACLU.* New Brunswick, NJ: Transaction Publishers, 1994.

Web site for the Catholic League for Religious and Civil Rights: http://www.catholicleague.org/

Andrea Dworkin

Combating Pornography to Protect Women from Abuse and Oppression

Born: September 26, 1946, Camden, New Jersey
Education: B.A., Bennington College, 1968
Current position: Writer and lecturer

Andrea Dworkin calls herself "a radical feminist . . . against the way American culture treats women" (*New York Times*, October 29, 1989, p. 11). Although she is associated with the fight against pornography, most of her work—from works on the brutality of rape and spouse abuse to works on the exploitation of women in the sex industry—can be characterized as a crusade against the victimization of women. In *Life and Death* (1997), Dworkin writes, "I love life, I love writing, I love reading—and these writings are about injustice, which I hate. They are a rude exploitation of it, especially its impact on women" (from Preface, p. xiv). Dworkin has experienced injustice firsthand, and it has catapulted her into becoming a well-known name in feminist writing.

Dworkin began to wonder about the place of women in society as a child. She knew her mother suffered from heart disease as a result of scarlet fever, which she had contracted as a child. Among poor Jewish immigrant families at the time her mother was young, spending money on a doctor for a sick girl was considered inappropriate, so the disease went untreated and damaged her mother's heart. Dworkin's Jewish background also influenced her views on pornography: "For me, the *Shoah*, the Hebrew word for annihilation, is the root of my resistance to the sadism of rape, the dehumanization of pornography. In my private heart, forever, rape began at Auschwitz, and a species of pornography—sexualized anti-Semitic propaganda—was instrumental in creating hate" (*Ms.*, November/December, 1994, p. 52). For Dworkin, the Holocaust is not just an intellectual topic or recent history lesson. At the age of ten, she discovered the brutality of the concentration camps from the frightening emotional flashbacks of her aunt, a Holocaust survivor of Auschwitz-Birkenau.

After graduating from high school, Dworkin, with the financial help of her father, a school teacher, attended Bennington College. While at Bennington, however, Dworkin, who had been raped as a child, was raped twice. Shortly afterward, she was arrested at a Vietnam War protest and imprisoned at the Women's House of Detention in New York City. Although the brutal and humiliating medical exam by prison doctors shocked Dworkin, she was even more shocked by the lack of concern her male associates showed for the way she had been treated. Her own family was embarrassed and angry with her attempts to report the incident. Eventually, the writer Grace Paley helped Dworkin tell her story, and her charges against the prison staff were investigated but ended with the exoneration of the doctors involved.

Given her background, it may not be surprising that Dworkin is a crusader against pornography. With Catherine MacKinnon, Dworkin has drafted legislation on pornography. The legislation, which was adopted in Indianapolis, Indiana, relies on Dworkin and Mac-Kinnon's argument that pornography is a form of sexual discrimination and, thus, illegal.

Her crusade against pornography has not been limited to these civil statutes. Her book *Pornography: Men Possessing Women* (1989) has had a significant impact on many. In a review of the book for *Punch*, Stanley Reynolds wrote that Dworkin's crusade may be unrealistic at times but that she possesses relentless courage in calling for drastic social reform. Dworkin also coauthored with Catherine MacKinnon *Pornography and Civil Rights: A New Day for Women's Equality* (1988).

Dworkin is also a novelist. Her first novel, *Ice and Fire* (1986), begins with childhood memories of a struggle with disillusionment. The narrator, who descends into a wretched life of drugs, prostitution, and panhandling, becomes increasingly contemptuous of men and the violence that often occurs in their relationships. She is finally rescued by writing and becomes a poet and author. One critic has described Dworkin's third novel, *Mercy* (1991), as the story of "a young woman whose journey through the misogynist world . . . constitutes an almost encyclopaedic survey of male sexual violence" (*Times Literary Supplement*, October 5, 1990, pp. 10–12). Because of her views on women, men, and pornography, Dworkin has experienced difficulty in finding a publisher, but she states that she has been inspired by Elizabeth Barrett Browning's letters exhorting women to not ignore the wrongs perpetrated against them: "My aspirations for dignity and equality do not hinge on perfection in myself or in any other woman; only on the humanity we share, fragile as that appears to be" (Dworkin, 1997, p. 32). Dworkin tells anticensorship advocates who say that her writings promote censorship that she believes there are exceptions to First Amendment protection and that First Amendment rights are not absolute.

Dworkin suffered a great personal loss in 1992 when her brother Mark, a molecular biologist, died of cancer: "I am less alive because I lost my brother. Yet I used what I felt while I watched him dying to write something I considered necessary. I think this is a deep and perhaps terrible truth about writing. Surely, it is a deep and terrible truth about me. As long as I can, I will take what I feel, use it to face what I am able to know, find language, and write what I think must be written for the freedom and dignity of women" (Dworkin, 1997, p. 38). Her latest book is *Heartbreak: The Political Memoirs of a Feminist Militant* (2002).

SUGGESTED READINGS

Cornell, Drucilla. *Feminism and pornography*. New York: Oxford University Press, 2000.

Dworkin, Andrea. "Against the male flood: Censorship, pornography and equality." In Catherine Itzin, ed., *Pornography: Women, violence, and civil liberties*. Oxford, England: Oxford University Press, 1992.

———. *Life and death*. New York: Free Press, 1997.

———. *Pornography: Men possessing women*. New York: Perigree Books, 1981.

———. *Woman hating*. New York: E. P. Dutton, 1974.

Bruce J. Ennis

Attorney for Freedom of Speech

Born: May 22, 1940, Knoxville, Tennessee
Died: July 29, 2000, Boston, Massachusetts
Education: B.A., Dartmouth College, 1962; J.D., University of Chicago, 1965

Former position: Managing partner, Jenner and Block, Attorneys-at-Law

---

Bruce Ennis passed away during the production of this book, but his contributions to the defense of the First Amendment transcend his death. He has been noted as one of the foremost experts on the First Amendment and on Supreme Court and appellate court practice.

Ennis was born in Knoxville, Tennessee, on May 22, 1940. After high school, he attended Dartmouth College and graduated *cum laude* in 1962 with a degree in English. He went on to study law at the University of Chicago. In law school, he was elected to the Order of the Coif, an academic excellence honor, and was a member of the *University of Chicago Law Review*. He received his Juris Doctor in 1965.

Ennis did not begin his legal career as an advocate for the First Amendment. After graduation, he spent three years as a clerk for a federal judge. In 1968, he moved to New York City and joined a Wall Street financial law firm. Within that same year, Ennis became a staff attorney for the American Civil Liberties Union (ACLU), which is dedicated to the protection of the rights guaranteed to citizens by the Constitution, particularly those guaranteed by the Bill of Rights. Ennis's views on the Bill of Rights made him a strong civil liberties advocate. From 1976 to 1981, he was the national legal director of the ACLU and directed a staff of twenty-six attorneys. In his first case for the ACLU, *O'Connor* v. *Donaldson* (422 U.S. 563) (1975), Ennis defended the rights of mental patients. Prior to this case, a mental patient could be confined to an institution without his or her consent. Ennis successfully argued that psychiatric patients had important civil rights. From his extensive study of this topic, Ennis wrote *Prisoners of Psychiatry: Mental Patients, Psychiatrists, and the Law* (1972) in which he stated his belief that mental patients have been denied their basic rights as citizens.

In 1981, he entered private practice. After joining the law firm of Jenner and Block in Washington, D.C., Ennis served as lead counsel for more than 250 cases that had a First Amendment argument as their core. In sixteen cases, he delivered his arguments before the U.S. Supreme Court, an extraordinary feat for an attorney in private practice.

During his career, Ennis was either the lead attorney or filed significant *amicus curiae* (friend of the court) briefs in many free speech cases, including *McDonald* v. *Smith* (the right to petition under the First Amendment), *Peel* v. *Attorney Registration and Disciplinary Commission* (constitutionality of restriction on commercial speech by attorneys), *Barnes* v. *Glen Theatre* (constitutionality of a city ordinance banning public nudity as applied to strip tease or nude performance dance), *Bentsen* v. *Coors* (constitutionality of restrictions on commercial speech), *Turner* v. *FCC* (constitutionality of government regulation of cable television), and *Reno* v. *ACLU, et al.* (constitutionality of the Communications Decency Act (CDA), which made it a crime, with prison sentence and/or fines to use what the law said was indecent or patently offensive speech on a computer network if that speech could be viewed by a minor).

One of Ennis's most famous cases, and one with significant First Amendment implications, was never appealed to the U.S. Supreme Court. In 1979, *The Progressive*, a political analysis and commentary journal, attempted to publish an article about secrecy in the hydrogen bomb program. In the article, Howard Morland, a freelance writer, included declassified government information on nuclear bomb designs. The editors submitted the final draft of the article to the U.S. Department of Energy for a review of its accuracy. After seeing the article, the Department of Energy consulted with the attorney general and then asked a federal judge in Minnesota, where *The Progressive* is published, to stop publication. Prior restraint of the press before publication is considered to be unconstitutional except to protect national security. Arguing that the government had not met certain tests of imminent danger to national security, Ennis successfully defended the author and the *The Progressive*. In his brief before the court, Ennis wrote, "The First Amendment does not permit a court to exercise its judgment as to what the press does or does not 'need' to print in order to advance the author's or the publication's political views, or to balance its assessment of such 'need' against the government's national security claims" (De Volpi, 1981, p. 62).

As his reputation as a tireless defender of the First Amendment grew, Ennis held a number of important roles in organizations dedicated to intellectual freedom. He was the director of the Lawyer's Committee for Human Rights and the director of the American Booksellers Foundation for Free Expression. He was also counsel for the Freedom to Read Foundation. For his service to the foundation and for his support of many First Amendment causes, the successful legal challenge to the CDA, the Freedom to Read Foundation presented him with the Roll of Honor Award in 1997. Several organizations, including the American Library Association (ALA) and various Internet interest groups, found the language of the CDA too vague and felt that many individuals could be subject to a criminal charge for using speech that was constitutionally protected. In his statements before the court, Ennis argued, "The government cannot reduce the adult population to reading or viewing only what is appropriate for children" (http://www.cnn.com/us/9703119/scotus.cda/). He also pointed out that parents have many technological options, as well as normal parental controls, to prevent their children from gaining access to indecent speech.

Before his death from leukemia, Ennis represented the ABC television network in a difficult case about reporters' rights. ABC reporters had used secret cameras to record abuses by grocery store management in the Food Lion grocery chain. In this case, ABC had reporters become employees of Food Lion in order to secretly record abuses of health codes and other sanitary conditions. In their suit against ABC, Food Lion argued that this practice of secretly recording conditions constituted fraud and that the ABC reporters, as employees of Food Lion, were subject to the company rules of employment. The Supreme Court agreed and ruled that because the reporters had been hired by Food Lion, the information they obtained was not legally acquired. Although the case was lost by Ennis and ABC, the Supreme Court drastically reduced the financial award granted by the lower courts. A poll of thousands of attorneys, reported in *Media and the Law* in 1995, voted Ennis as one of the "very best media lawyers in America." He is survived by his wife, Emily Newhall Ennis, and his two sons, Alexander and Bradley.

SUGGESTED READINGS

De Volpi, Alexander. *Born secret: The H-bomb*, The Progressive *case and national security*. New York: Pergamon Press, 1981.

Ennis, Bruce J. "Effective amicus briefs." *Catholic University Law Review* 33 (Spring 1984): 525–632.

———. *The rights of mental patients*. New York: Baron Books, 1973.

Various issues of the *Newsletter on Intellectual Freedom*, a publication of the Office for Intellectual Freedom, American Library Association.

Web site of The Freedom to Read Foundation: http://www.frtf.org

Mel and Norma Gabler

What Are They Teaching Our Children?

Born: Mel, 1915; Norma, 1923
Education: Mel, High school in Houston, attended the University of Houston and Paris Junior College; Norma, Hallsville High School, Hallsville, Texas
Current position: retired; founders of Educational Research Analysts

When Mel and Norma Gabler were married on September 6, 1942, they had no idea that they would become nationally known for taking a stand on the content of textbooks used in public schools. What started as a kitchen-table operation has spread around the world, alerting parents to the curriculum taught daily to their children in school. Since the creation of their Educational Research Analysts, the Gablers have become the leading critics of school textbooks and have greatly influenced textbook publishing.

Mel and Norma Gabler were both born in Texas. Mel graduated from high school in Houston, and Norma graduated from Hallsville High School. They met in 1936 in Talco, where Norma's father and Mel worked for Exxon Pipeline Company. During a leave of absence from Exxon to serve in the Air Force, Mel married Norma in Houston in a church in which the Gabler family members were charter members. After World War II, Mel returned to Exxon, and the Gablers lived in several Texas towns, finally settling on a 68-acre ranch near Hawkins, Texas. Norma stayed home to care for their three sons.

Before they became the textbook critics they are known as today, the Gablers saw themselves as typical middle-class Americans who trusted textbooks almost as much as the Bible. Their work on critically reviewing textbooks began in 1961 when their son Jim (who was 16 years old at the time) asked his father to look at his history book. The book emphasized the role of the federal government and pointedly ignored individual and state rights and responsibilities. Jim also discovered that the phrase "under God" had been omitted from the Gettysburg Address in the class's encyclopedia. Alarmed by these discoveries, the Gablers contacted the Hawkins School District superintendent and learned that local school districts in Texas had to select their textbooks from a list of state-approved list of textbooks. As Norma has said, "We looked at other textbooks and really became alarmed. We saw that textbooks had drastically changed for the worse since we were in school in the 1920s and 30s. Everybody who reviews and compares new and old textbooks recognizes this change" (Gabler, 1985, p. 20).

Although the Gablers were learning more about the process used in selecting textbooks for the public schools, they read reviews written by a group known as Texans for America. In September 1961, the Gablers began to regularly participate in a call-in radio program on radio station KWKH in Shreveport, Louisiana. The radio program, called "Party Line," allowed callers to call once a week, so they each called in weekly, sharing sections from their research and urging other parents to begin reading their children's textbooks more carefully. Since the radio station had a large national audience, many listeners who wanted more information soon contacted the Gablers and they began mailing their newsletter to others who made inquiries. The Gablers' *Educational Research Analysts Newsletter*, born from these first mailings, is currently mailed semiannually and reports the findings on textbook errors and objections to specific textbooks. In the winter of 1961, the Texas State House of Representatives appointed a five-man investigative committee to review textbook selection, and the committee invited the Gablers and other interested citizens to appear before the committee. They have been active in the Texas state textbook review process ever since.

Mel continued to work for Exxon for many years, researching textbooks after work while Norma became the main spokesperson for their crusade. When Exxon moved Mel to Longview in the mid-1960s, the Gablers sold their ranch and built a house that soon became a library, with textbooks everywhere. Even after he retired from Exxon in 1973, Mel continued to run the home operation while Norma was out in the public eye. Her persistence won her the right to voice her concerns with the State Board of Education. The Gablers do not view their efforts as a trifling matter. Rather, they believe that textbook content is central to good educational experiences. "It's foolish to underestimate the power of textbooks on what students study. Seventy-five percent of students' classroom time and 90 percent of homework time is spent with textbook materials" (Gabler, 1985, p. 22).

The Gablers' reputation has made them targets for media criticism. For example, they were interviewed by Mike Wallace, for the CBS-TV program *60 Minutes*, for a segment that featured their work on the show. The program was entitled "What Johnny Can't Read" and featured Wallace attempting to have Norma read some of the objectionable texts the Gablers had criticized. Also on the program were critics of the Gablers such as Edward Jenkinson, head of the anti-censorship committee of the National Council of Teachers of English, and two textbook publishers. Jenkinson argued that the Gablers' work was contrary to freedom of the press and academic freedom. For her part, Norma objected to characterization of their work as censorship. "Now it's strange that if they choose it, it's academic freedom; it's a right of selection. But, if we do it, it's censorship. The highest form of censorship is denying a parent's right to be heard, and who is doing that? The professionals. I call that censorship. And if you (parents) don't fight, nobody else will" (Gabler, 1985, p. 8). As recently as 1998, Prentice Hall published a biology text that Mel and Norma criticized as a textbook purely on evolution, not biology. They have cited Texas law that requires that the teaching of the theory of evolution include the weaknesses of the theory, and they have argued that this textbook fails that test.

Mel and Norma have been featured in many different media outlets. Portraits of them have been produced for magazines such as *Time, People Weekly,* and *Parade.* They have appeared on many television programs as commentators or panelists, including ABC's *20/20* and Ted Koppel's *Nightline,* William F. Buckley's *Firing Line,* several news analysis and commentary shows such as *Crossfire* with Pat Buchanan and Tom Braden, and the *McNeil-Lehrer Report,* as well as Christian broadcasting programs, such as Pat Robertson's *The 700 Club* and *Jerry Falwell Live. The Encyclopedia Britannica,* in its 1983 *Yearbook,* listed the Gablers as two of ninety-five individuals who had a worldwide impact in 1982.

The Gablers have worked to educate other parents concerning their rights and how to protest the adoption of objectionable textbooks. The Gablers' legacy goes beyond their reputation with publishers, state education authorities, and teachers. It also lives on in their extensive list of publications, including their newsletter. They have available for distribution over 1,000 printed forms pertaining to textbook content and thousands of textbook reviews. For now, they plan to continue their crusade together. Educational Research Analysts is firmly established and will continue under Neal Frey. He has been with the Gablers nineteen years. Mel Gabler considers him the best textbook reviewer in the United States.

SUGGESTED READINGS

Educational Research Analysts. *Educational Research Analysts Newsletter.* Longview, TX: Neal Frey, 1961–present.

Gabler, Mel, and Norma Gabler, with James C. Hefley. *What are they teaching our children?* Wheaton, IL: Victor Books, 1985.

Hefley, Jim. *Are textbooks harming your children?* Milford, NJ: Mott Media, 1979.

———. *Textbooks on trial.* Wheaton, IL: Victor Books, 1976.

Rudolph William Giuliani

Crusader Against Pornographic and Offensive Art

Born: May 28, 1944, Brooklyn, New York
Education: B.A., Manhattan College, 1965; J.D., New York University, 1968
Current position: Consultant; Former Mayor, New York City

Rudolph "Rudy" Giuliani has become one of the most vocal and visible opponents of obscene art today. As mayor of the city of New York, he used his position to denounce works of art displayed in art galleries in the New York area that he believes are obscene. Until the 1990s, when a furor arose over art that critics labeled obscene, especially a few works funded by the National Endowment for the Arts (NEA), the press had paid little attention to art censorship. In 1999, however, Giuliani raised objections to a painting at the Brooklyn Museum of Art. Giuliani's objections went beyond the issue of obscenity and raised serious questions about art that is offensive to religion, particularly Catholicism.

AP Photo/Stephen Chernin. Courtesy of AP/Wide World Photos.

Rudolph Giuliani was born on May 28, 1944, in the Flatbush section of Brooklyn, New York, where his father, Harold Giuliani, owned a tavern. Because the Giuliani family, second-generation Italian immigrants, had been forced to close the business owned by Giuliani's grandfather when they refused to pay protection money to local organized crime families, Giuliani grew up with a hatred for the mob. After graduating from a local, parochial high school, Giuliani attended Manhattan College, an all-male, Roman Catholic school. He was president of his fraternity and his sophomore class. Although he had planned to enter the priesthood when he graduated, he changed his plans in his junior year and worked toward a career in law. He graduated from Manhattan College in 1965 and entered New York University Law School, graduating *magna cum laude* in 1968. He began his career as a law clerk for Lloyd MacMahon, a federal district judge, and then became an assistant U.S. attorney for the southern district of New York, which covers most of New York City. In this capacity, he gained a reputation as a tough prosecutor of cases, especially of sensational corruption cases.

In 1975, Giuliani, who had begun his career as a liberal Democrat but had come to disagree with the Democrats' view of global politics, switched political parties and became a deputy attorney general in President Gerald Ford's administration. When Jimmy Carter defeated Ford in the 1976 presidential race, Giuliani returned to New York and worked in private practice for a prestigious law firm. Four years later, Ronald Reagan won the presidency back for the Republicans, and Giuliani returned to Washington as an associate attorney general. Although he had a successful prosecutorial record in this capacity, he was roundly criticized for refusing political asylum to Haitian immigrants. Giuliani argued that the Haitian regime was economically and not politically oppressive; therefore the immigrants did not qualify under U.S. law. During this period, he also strengthened the U.S. Justice Department's narcotics task force.

By 1983, according to Giuliani, he had begun to "feel a tremendous nostalgia" for the U.S. attorney's office in New York, where he had "spent five of the most interesting years of my career" (*New York Times*, April 13, 1983, p. A25). As a result, he returned to New York and began a vigorous prosecution of several organized crime figures, including Carmine "The Snake" Persico, a member of the Colombo crime family. He also broke up a national narcotics operation, known as "The Pizza Connection," which distributed narcotics through a chain of pizza parlors across the eastern states and in many midwestern states as well. He also attacked insider trading scandals on Wall Street. After Giuliani gained an indictment against Dennis Levine, a leading investment banker, the state spared the cost of investigating Ivan Boesky, the Wall Street arbitrageur, because Boesky turned himself in before he could be indicted.

By 1989, Giuliani had left the U.S. Attorney's office for politics. He entered the New York mayoral race against David Dinkins, an African-American, liberal Democrat. According to some observers, Giuliani lost this race because of his conservative views, which did not translate well in an election about racial issues. By 1993, Giuliani was ready to try again. Although he defeated Dinkins, the campaign had some difficult moments.

In 2000, he began to run for the Senate seat vacated by Daniel Patrick Moynihan against Hillary Rodham Clinton. A bout with cancer, among other personal difficulties, ended the campaign before he was ever nominated.

During his tenure as mayor, Giuliani attacked crime and drugs in the city as he had when he was a prosecutor, but he also worked on other issues. He won accolades as the first mayor of New York to rid the Times Square area of the worst of the pornography that flourished there. Until he did so, most people in New York and elsewhere assumed the community standards of the city would allow most of the pornography available there. The Times Square area was also known as a major center of street prostitution, but Giuliani pushed through legislation that created an adult zone for sex-oriented businesses in the more remote areas of the city, away from the Times Square area and its legitimate theatre district.

In a controversial move in 1998, Giuliani pushed through legislation that cracked down on street artists in New York City. In late 1998, he was sued by artist Robert Lederman, who had been arrested for staging a public protest against the regulations requiring permits for all street artists. In their legal brief in defense of the regulations, Giuliani's city attorneys argued, "An exhibition of paintings is not as communicative as speech, literature, or live entertainment, and the artists' constitutional interests are minimal" (http//www.infoshop. org/nyork.grt1.html). Later, in 1999, Giuliani began to publicly criticize certain works of art that he found offensive and objected to their being displayed in publicly funded art museums. One of his most publicized targets was an art show at the Brooklyn Museum of Art, which included a painting of the Virgin Mary covered in elephant dung. The painting, by Chris Ofili, entitled "Sensation," as well as other works in the exhibit, outraged Giuliani: "This issue before us is whether hard-earned taxpayer dollars should go toward actively supporting an exhibit that is patently offensive to many of the taxpayers themselves. That many of the taxpayers feel is really just a display of hatred toward a particular religious group or extremely offensive in the way in which it deals with sexuality and other areas. This is a show that glorifies pedophiles, desecrates the Virgin Mary, and displays the carcasses of dead animals, just to name a few things . . . But, the core question is whether it's fair to force taxpayers to fund, with their own hard-earned dollars, what many of them feel is a direct assault on their deepest held religious and philosophical beliefs" (Mayor's address, Oct. 3, 1999, at http://www.nyc.gov/html/om/html/996/me991003.html). In 2001, before the dust had settled on the "Sensation" exhibit, the Brooklyn Museum displayed the photographic works of Rene Cox. In one work, entitled *Yo Mama's Last Supper*, a nude female was posed in the same manner as Jesus Christ in Leonardo da Vinci's *Last Supper*. Giuliani was again upset. Saying the photo was disgusting, outrageous, and anti-Catholic, he announced that he was forming an art decency panel to advise him and the city on standards for art funded with taxpayer dollars.

After completing his second term as mayor of New York City and now barred by term limits from a third term, he formed a consultancy company. His love affair with New York continues, to be sure. He is a New York Yankees fan who took the subway to the "Subway" series between the New York Yankees and New York Mets in 2000 wearing his Yankee hat and coat to tout the power of New York professional sports. Until recently, he was married to Donna Hanover, and they have two children.

SUGGESTED READINGS

Barrett, Wayne, and Adam Fifield. *Rudy! An investigative biography of Rudolph Giuliani*. New York: Basic Books, 2000.

Giuliani, Rudolph W., and Ron Rubin. *Rudy! Rudy! Rudy!: The real and the rational*. New York: Holmes and Meier, 2000.

Kirtzman, Andrew. *Rudy Giuliani: Emperor of the city*. New York: Harper-Collins World, 2000.

Mike Godwin

Cyber Lawyer Protecting Freedoms on the Internet

Born: 1957, Big Spring, Texas
Education: B.A., University of Texas, 1980; J.D., University of Texas Law School, 1990
Current position: Chief correspondent, *IP Worldwide*

As an advocate for freedom of speech in the electronic information age Mike Godwin has defended a computer game maker and argued against censorship of the Internet. Godwin grew up in Houston, Texas, and graduated from Lamar High School in 1975. He enrolled in the University of Texas and earned a bachelor's degree (with highest honors) in liberal arts in 1980. He entered graduate school, but after three years of studying, first, research psychology and then English, he experienced burn-out and left to work as a journalist and, later, as a computer consultant. It was during this time that a friend introduced him to the burgeoning computer bulletin board, or BBSs, phenomena.

After struggling as a freelance journalist, Godwin turned to selling computers and doing computer consulting but soon found that he wanted something more meaningful. He decided to return to the University of Texas to work on a law degree. During his years in law school, he was editor of *The Daily Texan*, the student newspaper for the university. Godwin notes that the source of his inspiration for a career as a First Amendment advocate was the law school's faculty, especially Charles Alan Wright, constitutional scholar, and professors Mike Tigar and Gerry Goldstein.

Godwin's first foray into defending civil liberties in the electronic media came during his law school days when he discovered that the Secret Service was attempting to prove that Steve Jackson Games, a company that produced computer role-playing games, was involved in a national computer-hacking scheme. Godwin knew Steve Jackson, the owner, and was convinced that Jackson would have nothing to do with computer hacking. As a result, Godwin got on the Internet and began answering legal questions about these efforts and making a case in Jackson's defense. His remarks were noticed by Mitch Kapor, the founder of Lotus Development Corporation, and John Perry Barlow. The two men, along with John Gilmore, were forming the Electronic Frontier Foundation (EFF), an organization dedicated to protecting freedom of speech on electronic networks, at that time. Godwin asked the EFF to support Jackson. The foundation hired an Austin law firm to represent Jackson, and in 1993, Jackson and his company won a $50,000 judgment against the Secret Service for its harassment.

Godwin's advocacy of Steve Jackson was the start of his reputation as an ardent defender of the First Amendment, especially in the electronic world. Since 1990, Godwin has written on legal issues for the computer age for such well-known periodicals as *Wired, Macworld,* and *Internet World*. In 1995, he became involved in a widely reported pornography-on-the-Internet incident. In that year, Marty Rimm, an undergraduate student at Carnegie Mellon University, published a statistical study of the amount and types of pornography on the Internet in the *Georgetown Law Review. Time* magazine then featured the study in a story entitled "Cyberporn." According to the study, there had been a huge growth in pornography on the Internet. To gain civil libertarian support before the study was published, Rimm had solicited Godwin's support, telling him that the data could be used to counter the community standards test for obscenity set by the Supreme Court. The report caused an uproar at Carnegie-Mellon and other universities, in large part because of erroneous reports that Rimm had downloaded millions of pornographic images on university computers. As a result, and contrary to what Godwin had hoped, many institutions became more strict about access to the Internet. Godwin now believes the Rimm affair was a trick by Rimm and his faculty advisor: "In fact, the now-notorious article in the June 1995 *Georgetown Law Review* is so outrageously flawed that anyone with even a smattering of statistics knowledge can spot the flaws on the first reading" (http://hotwired.meos.com/spectal/pornscare/marty. html). In 1998, Godwin wrote *Cyber rights: Defending free speech in the Digital Age.*

In 1991, Governor William Weld of Massachusetts appointed Godwin chairperson of the Massachusetts Computer Crime Commission. This commission was instrumental in drafting that state's computer crime statutes. To date, however, Godwin's most singular accomplishment has been as the chief co-counsel for the plaintiffs in the Supreme Court case *Reno* v. *ACLU et al.* in 1996. In this challenge to the Communications Decency Act (CDA), which was passed in 1996, Godwin was supported by a large number of organizations, including Human Rights Watch, Computer Professionals for Social Responsibility, and the Electronic Privacy Information Center as well as the Electronic Frontier Foundation. A parallel lawsuit, *American Library Association* v. *Department of Justice,* also challenged the law. The CDA made it a crime, with a prison sentence and/or fines, to use what the law said was "indecent or patently offensive" speech on a computer network if that speech could be viewed by a minor. The Supreme Court declared the CDA unconstitutional. Echoing much of what Godwin had argued in his brief, Justice John Paul Stevens said, "As a matter of constitutional tradition, in the absence of evidence to the contrary, we presume that governmental regulation of the content of speech is more likely to interfere with the free exchange of ideas than to encourage it. The interest in encouraging freedom of expression in a democratic society outweighs any theoretical but unproven benefit of censorship" (521 U.S. 884, 1997).

Godwin is now the chief correspondent for *IP Worldwide*, a periodical published by American Lawyers Media for lawyers working on legal issues in the electronic world. He continues his defense of freedom of speech on the Internet through public speaking engagements and articles in a number of publications.

SUGGESTED READINGS

Godwin, Mike. *Cyber rights: Defending free speech in the digital age.* New York: Times Books, 1998.
Sterling, Bruce. *The hacker crackdown: Law and disorder on the electronic frontier.* Champaign, IL: Project Gutenberg, 1994.

Danny Goldberg

Fighting Music Censorship

Born: 1950, New York, New York
Education: High School Diploma, Fieldston School, 1967
Current position: Chairman and CEO of Artemis Records; president and CEO of Sheridan Square Entertainment; president of the southern California branch of the American Civil Liberties Union; publisher of *Tikkun*

Danny Goldberg has worked with more popular musical talent than any other recording executive in the 1990s. He also has worked with every major genre of music, from rap to country to folk to classical to jazz to pop to rock to rhythm and blues. In doing so, he has become one of the most vocal of those who oppose music censorship and labeling.

AP Photo/Dennis Cook. Courtesy of AP/Wide World Photos.

As chairman and CEO of Artemis Records, which was formed in June 1999, Goldberg placed three albums on the charts in the company's first year. Based on sound scan sales, *Billboard Magazine* named Artemis Records the number one independently distributed record label of the year in 2000. Prior to his work with Artemis Records, Goldberg was chairman and CEO of the Mercury Records Group, the largest U.S. division of Polygram Records. The Mercury Records Group included the labels Mercury, Motown, Def Jam, Verve, Deutsche Grammophon, London Classics, and Philips and such artists as Shania Twain, Boyz II Men, Andrea Bocelli, Brian McKnight, Kiss, Jay-Z, LL Cool J, Hanson, 311, The Cardigans, OMC, Cake, Elvis Costello, and Lucinda Williams.

Goldberg began his career as a journalist, writing for *Rolling Stone*, the *Village Voice*, and *Billboard*. In the years since, he has been vice-president of Led Zeppelin's Swan Song Records and supervised the music for numerous movies and TV shows, including the movie *Dirty Dancing* and the soundtrack from the TV series *Miami Vice*. He has spent ten years as principal owner and president of Gold Mountain Entertainment, a personal management firm. He was president of Atlantic Records when it achieved a top ranking among U.S. recording companies and was also chairman and CEO of Warner Bros. Records in 1995 when it became the number one record label in the United States.

Goldberg is also on the national board of the American Civil Liberties Union (ACLU) and the New York Civil Liberties Union, and is currently the president of the southern California branch of the ACLU. In that capacity and as a spokesperson for the music industry, he has appeared on the *Today Show, CBS Morning News, Crossfire on CNN* and the *Charlie Rose Show*. He has written for the *Los Angeles Times* and has been profiled in *New York Magazine, Us*, the *Los Angeles Times*, and the *New York Times*. With his father, Victor Goldberg, he is the publisher of the liberal Jewish bimonthly magazine, entitled *Tikkun*.

In 1985, Goldberg read an article in *Newsweek* by Tipper Gore, wife of then Senator Al Gore of Tennessee, and Susan Baker, wife of James Baker, then secretary of the treasury. In the article, the two women discussed how offended they were by popular music lyrics that had explicit references to sex and violence. Among the artists they criticized were Madonna, Prince, and several hard rock bands such as Guns and Roses and Motley Crue. Gore, Baker, and the wives of several other political figures had formed the Parents Music Resource Center (PMRC) with the stated goal of pressuring major recording companies into adopting a ratings system for song lyrics. They advocated using **X** for sexual content, **V** for violence, **D/A** for references of drugs and alcohol, and **O** for the occult. To win support, Gore, Baker, and other members of the PMRC made appearances on television programs such as *The Phil Donahue Show*, did editorial pieces in numerous newspapers, and galvanized press coverage. On September 16, 1985, the issue became the cover story of

People Magazine, which asked in its headline, "Has Rock Gone Too Far?"

As the manager of musical artists for many years, Goldberg was sensitive to the pressures the volatile music marketplace already exerted on the creativity of these artists. He also remembered how some film and television writers, actors, and directors were barred from work by the activities of Senator Joseph McCarthy and the House Un-American Activities Committee (HUAC) in the 1950s. During this period, Goldberg's parents were close friends with an actor named Howard Da Silva who, after he was blacklisted for refusing to "name names" at a HUAC hearing, was unable to find work in films or television for more than fifteen years.

Goldberg believed that a ratings system for lyrics would be unfair and subjective because there were no criteria for categorizing words except for the so-called seven dirty words that the FCC banned from broadcasting. As the ratings desired by the PMRC went far beyond dirty words and there was no objective way of differentiating offensive lyrics from unoffensive lyrics, it seemed clear to Goldberg that different people of goodwill would have different ratings for vast numbers of songs. During a meeting to discuss the issue, Goldberg and Ira Glasser, executive director of the ACLU, agreed to create an ad-hoc coalition called the Musical Majority, which would be affiliated with the ACLU. Several dozen artists, personal managers, and other music business executives joined Goldberg on the committee.

Goldberg's opposition to a ratings system was strengthened by encounters with various artists. Donnie Osmond, who had never been associated with controversial music, joined the committee, after explaining that he had experienced religious intolerance as a Mormon, which made him nervous of any kind of committee rating. John Denver, another mainstream artist, testified at Senate Commerce Committee hearings on September 19, 1985, that his own lyrics frequently had been misinterpreted. His paean to nature, "Rocky Mountain High," for example, had been banned by numerous radio stations that mistakenly believed it was about drugs. Members of the rock group Styx told Goldberg their anticocaine song "Snow Blind" was kept off the radio by the pressure from groups who thought it was advocating drugs. Rock singer Bob Segar told Goldberg he was intending to omit a brilliant anti-drug song called "American Storm" from his album because he feared an unfair rating.

Goldberg's stance against labeling received further support when Tom Bradley, the mayor of Los Angeles, endorsed the opposition to a ratings system in a press conference. *People Magazine* ran a story about the committee's efforts and confessed that the magazine's earlier piece had received the largest quantity of negative mail of any article in its history. Goldberg debated both Tipper Gore and Susan Baker on various television shows and in the press. By the end of 1985, the PMRC had dropped its demand for a ratings system in return for a parental advisory sticker that each recording label would place on albums as it saw fit. Although the Musical Majority would have preferred no stickering at all, the committee believed this was a vast improvement over the original demands.

Although pressure from the PMRC has died down, politicians and social scientists still frequently blame popular music for antisocial behavior in teenagers. In 1999, after the tragic killings at Columbine High School, President Clinton ordered the Federal Trade Commission (FTC) to investigate the marketing of so-called violent entertainment to children. In the fall of 2000, the Senate Commerce Committee again held hearings, and Goldberg was asked to testify. His testimony clearly expresses what he believes about the censorship of musical works.

SUGGESTED READINGS

Foerstel, Herbert N. *Free expression and censorship in America: An Encyclopedia.* Westport, CT: Greenwood Press, 1997.

Gardels, Nathan. "Does rock wreck families?" *New Perspectives Quarterly* 12 (Spring 1996): 31–36.

Wilkinson, Peter. "Goldberg's greatest hits." *Gentlemen's Quarterly* 60 (October 1990): 282–290.

Mark Goodman

Freedom of the Press for Student Journalists

Born: October 31, 1959, Versailles, Missouri
Education: B.A., University of Missouri, 1982; J.D., Duke University School of Law, 1985
Current position: Executive director, Student Press Law Center

As executive director of the Student Press Law Center, Mark Goodman has sought to champion student voices, protect student journalists in the same manner as professional journalists, and to speak out for freedom of the press. Goodman's inspiration for this work comes from a story he did not write. When he was a nineteen-year-old student journalist for the *Columbia Missourian*, the University of Missouri's student paper, a confidential source supplied him with a wealth of information on illegal prostitution in a small Missouri city. The story could have exposed the involvement of city officials and civic leaders. Before preparing the story, Goodman sought the advice of a journalism professor. The professor warned him, "Be prepared to be subpoenaed, to turn over your confidential source, or to go to jail." Goodman decided it would be better to leave the story alone. "Ultimately," he has said, "I was intimidated by what the professor told me. I let [the story] languish and my source moved away. We may never know what happened. I very much regret it" (*Death by Cheeseburgers*, p. 88). The memory of his unwritten story has helped to drive his desire to protect student journalists. "No person should let the fear of the law dictate for them what the public has a right to know."

Goodman, who was born in Versailles, Missouri, became a writer for the *Columbia Missourian* and graduated with honors in journalism. He then enrolled in the Duke University School of Law.

Upon graduating from law school, Goodman took over the leadership of the Student Press Law Center. The center was created in 1974 as a result of a report entitled *Captive Voices* made by the Commission of Inquiry into High School Journalism, created by the

Robert F. Kennedy Memorial Foundation, a charitable institution promoting open government and constitutional rights, after sponsoring a national high school journalism contest. The center is the only national organization whose purpose is to protect the rights of highschool and college journalists. It was formed and supported by professional journalists and educators. The center publishes a newsletter, *The Student Press Law Center Report*, that chronicles incidents of student press censorship and suppression, promotes the ideals of student press rights through other publications and public-speaking engagements and provides free legal advice and information to students and their advisers. It fields approximately 1,700 calls a year from student journalists or their advisers. "In many cases, they'll call us in extreme frustration, often in times of anger and fear. They are trying to do their jobs as journalists and are facing roadblocks" (http://www.splc.org).

During his career as an advocate for the rights of high school and college journalists, Goodman has received the First Amendment Award from the Society of Professional Journalists, the Louis E. Ingelhart First Amendment Award from College Media Advisers, and the Carl Towley Award, the Journalism Education Association's highest honor. In 1992 and 1999, he was also a judge for the Hugh M. Hefner First Amendment Award. He is a frequent lecturer on college campuses and at high schools around the nation and has taught courses on journalism and media law and ethics at such institutions as the University of Maryland, Virginia Commonwealth University, and Michigan State. He has also authored several publications, most notably *The Law of the Student Press* (1994), a book published by the center as a guide for student journalists. In addition to these writings, Goodman has written extensively on the consequences of the 1987 Supreme Court decision in the *Hazelwood School District* v. *Kuhlmeier* case (1085 CT. 562, 1988) for journals ranging from prestigious law reviews to journals for teachers and school administrators. In this case, a high school principal censored two stories, one on teen pregnancy and another on divorce, that were scheduled for publication in the student newspaper. The Supreme Court ruled that the student paper was a practical exercise in student journalism instruction and therefore the school could regulate the content of the articles and stories.

Goodman continues to direct the operations and services of the Student Press Law Center. Recently he spoke to more than twenty-five groups of students, teachers, school administrators and attorneys, both in the United States and abroad. In the 1980s and 1990s, his legal briefs were entered into the court of record in the most important student press cases, especially the Hazelwood decision. Goodman has noted that he learned when he was a teenager that taking a stand on behalf of the rights of others could be a life's work.

SUGGESTED READINGS

Death by cheeseburgers: High school journalism in the 1990s and beyond. Arlington, VA: Freedom Forum, 1994.
Goodman, Mark. *Law of the student press.* Washington, D.C.: Student Press Law Center, 1994.
Web site of the Student Press Law Center: http://www.splc.org

Karen Jo Gounaud

Family Friendly Libraries

Born: April 22, 1947, Omaha, Nebraska
Education: B.A., University of Nebraska, 1969
Current position: retired; founder and former president of Family Friendly Libraries

Karen Jo Gounaud is the founder and former president of Family
Friendly Libraries (FFL), a national organization that is dedicated to
raising people's awareness of the need to protect children from age
inappropriate materials in public libraries. Gounaud holds a degree
in education from the University of Nebraska, is the mother of two
grown children, and has written children's books. In 1981, she won
the Children's Choice Award for *A Very Mice Joke Book* (1981). She
has also written a "pocket policy" book entitled *Making Your Library
Family Friendly* for the Family Research Council (FRC). The book
is available from the FRC.

It was pure maternal instinct that drove Karen Jo Gounaud to become an activist in the fall of 1992. Gounaud calls it her "she bear"
response to protect the young from harm. When she discovered that
age inappropriate and pornographic materials were freely available to
children in her own local library system, she became angry, and her
anger led to action. She met with local school and library officials,
talked to other groups that showed her concerns, and hit the public-
speaking circuit.

Because she believed the problem was not just local but occurred
coast to coast, she spent the next eight years turning her indignation
into action. Although her activities have been criticized by school
and library officials, as well as some organizations, her sense of being
right has been boosted by the support she has received from her

family, friends, other activists, and political leaders across the country as well as her Christian faith.

After reading verses such as Matthew 18:6, "but whoever causes one of these little ones who believe in Me to stumble, it would be better for him to have a heavy millstone hung around his neck, and to be drowned in the depth of the sea," Gounaud decided to make the protection of children a priority in her life and, in 1995, founded the FFL as a grassroots network of concerned library patrons, professionals, staff members, and trustees. The FFL believes that "more commonsense access policies to protect children from exposure to age inappropriate materials without parental consent" should be adopted by all publicly supported libraries. The organization also believes that libraries need to develop policies that are generated through local control, reflect community standards, and answer directly to taxpayer authority. The FFL takes issue with those that claim these beliefs encourage censorship. The organization states, "FFL does NOT encourage removal of collection material. Does NOT support government censorship or censorship by unauthorized persons. Does NOT support any broadbased attack on librarians and library trustees" (http://www.fflibraries.org/).

The FFL believes that "responsible sponsorship" describes the organization's beliefs more accurately. In the FFL's view, libraries should not take a neutral stance on issues that divide or harm society, such as abortion and teen sexuality, but should take a stand on the side of community standards. FFL objects to the intellectual freedom policies and guidelines of the American Library Association (ALA) and believes that the ALA pressures librarians to ignore the wishes of the local community.

Gounaud has spoken to such groups as the National Coalition for the Protection of Children and Families and the Public Library Association. With Carrie Gardner of the ALA's Intellectual Freedom Committee, she was a featured speaker in a conference call on age inappropriate materials conducted and then published by *American Libraries*, the ALA journal, in November 1999. Gounaud recommended placing books and other media that contained age inappropriate material in restricted areas of the libraries so that children could not encounter them while browsing shelves. Access to the material could occur only with parental permission. Gounaud advocated that libraries should encourage parental involvement when establishing library policies. During her conference call with *American Libraries*, Gounaud noted the difficulty parents experience in obtaining information on their children's borrowing habits. "Most complaints we [FFL] get about librarian interference is when librarians refuse to tell parents what's checked out on their card and will tell them it's because of privacy codes; but the state privacy codes are meant to apply from one adult to another, not between parent and child. And that really annoys and bothers parents" (p. 60).

In 1996, Gounaud received the American Family Association's God and Country Award for the State of Virginia. She has recently turned her attention to the issue of pornography on the Internet and advocates the use of filtering software in public libraries. Gounaud retired from the FFL in 2000 but feels the organization is in good hands under the leadership of Phil Burress, a longtime family values advocate and head of Citizens for Community Values in Cincinnati, Ohio.

SUGGESTED READINGS

Gounaud, Karen Jo. *Making your library family-friendly*. Washington, D.C.: Family Research Council, 2000.
Hull, Mary E. *Censorship in America*. Santa Barbara, CA: ABC-CLIO, 1999.
Web site for Family Research Council: http://www.frc.org

Nat Hentoff

Articulate Defender of the Bill of Rights

Born: June 10, 1925, Boston, Massachusetts
Education: B.A., Northeastern University, 1946
Current position: Author, columnist, *The Village Voice*

Because he was born a Jew in the rough Roxbury section of Boston in 1925, Nat Hentoff faced discrimination early in life. Irish youths often roamed through his neighborhood to taunt and even beat up young Jewish people. Even so, he grew up to become what some literary critics have called "one of the great true-blue jazz loving freedom fighters of our time" (*Current Biography Yearbook*, 1986, p. 221). Nat Hentoff has written both fiction and nonfiction on jazz, freedom of speech and the First Amendment, and education reform. He describes himself as an "advocacy writer" and is considered one of the greatest social critics alive today. He was born on June 10, 1925, in Boston, Massachusetts. His father, Simon, who operated a men's clothing store, and his mother, Lena, were Russian Jewish immigrants. In his autobiography, *Boston Boy* (1986), Hentoff describes himself as a rebel and tells how, when he was twelve, he sat on his front porch "eating a huge salami sandwich very slowly" (p. 8) to taunt Jews on their way to synagogue on Yom Kippur, the holiest day of the Jewish New Year. His politics were formed during the Great Depression from the "ceaseless political debate" among socialists, anarchists, communists and other revolutionaries in his neighborhood.

It was Hentoff's sixth grade teacher who encouraged him to take the entrance exam for Boston Latin School, an elite public school in Boston. Hentoff was admitted and speaks well of his experiences there: "For the six years I was there, my closest friends were a Greek and an Irish lad. It took me a long time to believe that was possible" (Hentoff, 1986, p. 35). His teen years were filled with books and jazz. In fact, his keen interest in jazz led him to sneak into clubs in Boston when he was underage to listen to the jazz greats of the era.

Because he was classified 4-F during World War II, which made him ineligible for military service, Hentoff attended Northeastern University in Boston. As editor of the student paper there, he had his first brush with censorship. Indeed, he has attributed his passion for the First Amendment to his experience of being forced to resign as the editor of the student paper by Dr. Carl Ell, then president of the university: "My obsession with the First Amendment is due to Carl S. Ell. James Madison came later. Ell's way of arranging my self-removal from the *Northeastern News* was not a First Amendment matter. Northeastern was a private university, so no state action was involved in the censoring of my paper. Nonetheless, the spirit of the First Amendment had been rebuked and scorned; and ever since the day of my defenestration, everyone's free speech rights have been my business. Actually, I should be grateful to Carl S. Ell for having given me a life's work" (Hentoff, 1986, p. 107).

While at Northeastern, Hentoff also hosted a jazz program on WMEX, a Boston radio station, and ran live broadcasts from Storeyville, a Boston jazz club. Since then, he has written numerous books, both fiction and nonfiction, on jazz. He is the editor of *The Jazz Makers* (1979) and *Hear Me Talkin' to Ya: The Story of Jazz by the Men*

Who Made It (1966). His first novel, *Jazz Country* (1968), is about a white teen who plays trumpet and hangs around jazz musicians.

His interest in jazz led him to become embroiled in a libel suit early in his career. Although he defended himself when a jazz critic said that he was prostituting himself by writing notes for jazz albums on a commercial basis, Hentoff has since said, "It wasn't until later that I began to read Hugo Black and Madison and understand why Black of all the justices (of the Supreme Court) was ferociously against the whole notion of libel. But I was ignorant of the stuff at the time" (*Publisher's Weekly*, April 11, 1986, p. 29). The world of jazz contributed greatly to his stand on civil rights and racial discrimination. "From jazz, I inevitably became involved in the world that jazz itself reflects, and therefore, I began to write about civil rights . . . that naturally led to the problems of poverty—and ways to end it" (*Newsweek*, p. 48).

Hentoff has also written a number of books on education and social reform. In *Our Children Are Dying* (1967), his most notable book on the difficulties urban schools face, he writes a moving account of one person's attempt to improve school conditions in a Harlem community school. In *Peace Agitator* (1963), Hentoff chronicles the life of A. J. Muste, one of the most ardent promoters of nonviolent means to achieve peace. Muste greatly influenced Martin Luther King, Jr. In *A Doctor Among the Addicts* (1968), Hentoff criticizes the direction of government drug treatment programs by describing a more successful Methadone maintenance program administered by Dr. Marie Nyswander in Harlem. Hentoff also profiled the life of John Lindsay, mayor of New York, in his book, *A Political Life: The Education of John Lindsay* (1969).

Hentoff is known as a tireless defender of the First Amendment and freedom of speech. His numerous works on freedom of speech include a young adult novel and several works of nonfiction. *The Day They Came to Arrest the Book* (1982), a book for young adult readers, is the story of a school that tries to censor Mark Twain's *The Adventures of Huckleberry Finn* and the trauma the censorship battle brings to the school. In *The First Freedom: The Tumultuous History of Free Speech in America* (1980), Hentoff traces the history of free speech in America for high-school and college students. In a more recent work, *Free Speech for Me—but Not for Thee: How the American Right and Left Relentlessly Censor Each Other* (1993), Hentoff describes the struggle for freedom of speech in a world of political correctness.

Hentoff has won numerous awards for his support of free speech and intellectual freedom. In 1981, he received the Hugh M. Hefner First Amendment Award for his book *The First Freedom*. In 1993, the American Library Association (ALA) granted him the Robert B. Downs Intellectual Freedom Award for his lifetime of achievement in defending First Amendment freedoms. In 1996, he won the John Peter Zenger Award for his weekly column "Sweet Land of Liberty," which appears in the *Washington Post*. Each week, the column discusses current issues of freedom of speech and freedom of the press.

Hentoff is somewhat cautious about the future of the First Amendment and free speech. In 1991, he said to a group of journalists, "Consider what would happen if—during the 200th anniversary of the Bill of Rights—the First Amendment were placed on the ballot in every town, city, and state. The choices: affirm, reject, or amend. I would bet there is no place where the First Amendment would survive intact" (Hentoff, 1992, p. 386). Hentoff is also concerned that the schools are not promoting the basic tenets of civil liberties, especially free speech and free press. His book *First Freedom: The Tumultuous History of the Free Speech in America* (1980) chronicles several incidents in which schools violated student rights to speak or to publish in the school paper. He believes that schools have a duty to teach the principles of intellectual freedom and argues, "If freedom of expression becomes merely an empty slogan in the minds of enough children, it will be dead by the time they are adults" (p. 10). Although he believes that free speech organizations, with the help of an independent court system, do succeed in protecting the First Amendment, he feels it will always be necessary to fight to protect free speech.

SUGGESTED READINGS

Current Biography Yearbook, 1986, p. 221.
Hentoff, Nat. *Boston boy*. New York: Knopf, 1986.
———. *Free speech for me—but not for thee: How the American left and right relentlessly censor each other*. New York: Harper Perennial, 1992.
———. *Speaking freely: A memoir*. New York: Knopf, 1997
Newsweek, December 21, 1964, p. 48.

Reverend Morton A. Hill, S.J.

Catholic Antipornography Crusader

Born: July 13, 1917, Brooklyn, New York
Died: November 4, 1985
Education: B.S., Woodstock College, 1929; D.D., Georgetown
   University, 1934
Former position: Cofounder, Operation Yorkville

Father Hill was a gentle man with a deep-seated faith in God and respect for the dignity of each individual who found pornography revolting. When a wave of court rulings liberalized the possession of pornography during the 1960s, Father Hill decided to do something to stem the tide. "Every day a new generation of children becomes hooked on pornography and that's intolerable" (http://www.moralityinmedia.org/hillbiog.html), he is often quoted as having said. In 1962, Father Hill, the Reverend Robert E. Wiltenberg (a Lutheran minister), and Rabbi Julius G. Neumann formed Operation Yorkville (now Morality in Media) to combat the rise of pornography in New York City. In time, their organization grew to a national, interfaith initiative to encourage vigorous enforcement of the laws against pornography and to use constitutional means to fight the criminal traffic in pornographic materials.

Father Hill's work began at his local parish school in 1962, when a parent found several sado-maschistic books and periodicals in the possession of a school student. Father Hill began to research the law on pornography and to speak out about the increase in pornographic material. As Operation Yorkville, expanded, so did Father Hill's reputation as a crusader for morality and family values.

In 1966, the U.S. Supreme Court, on in what is known as the *Fanny Hill* case, declared the publication and distribution of the eighteenth-century pornographic novel by John Cleland about a woman's life as a prostitute to be legal. According to the court's ruling, a work had to be "utterly without socially redeeming value" to be declared legally obscene. The Court's decision led to an outburst of outrage. Father Hill declared that, under this standard, nothing could be declared illegal pornography. The uproar resulting from the decision caused President Lyndon Johnson to create the Commission on Obscenity and Pornography and to appoint Father Hill as one of the eighteen commissioners charged with looking into the growth of pornography and its effects on society. When the commission issued a majority report in 1970 that recommended the repeal of all adult obscenity laws on the premise that pornography is harmless, Father Hill authored a scathing dissenting report, called the Hill-Link Minority Report. The Hill-Link Minority Report, which called the commission's findings "a Magna Carta for the pornographers," was praised by Senator John L. McClellan as "a responsible position on the issues" and read into the *Congressional Record* (Hill, p. 1).

In 1976, Father Hill formed the National Obscenity Law Center (NOLC) as a clearinghouse for information for prosecutors and other members of the bar working to reduce the flow of pornography or fighting pornographers in the courts. Today, the NOLC is considered one of the most authoritative sources on obscenity law.

In that same year, Father Hill embarked on a seven-month national tour to alert the country to the emergence of cable pornography and to the growing traffic in illegal pornography. He visited forty-three cities and towns, often saying, "Pornography is no longer just downtown, it's now downstairs" through cable television (*A Gentle Man*, n.p.). He argued that obscenity should be included in the crimes covered by the federal Racketeering Influenced and Corrupt Organizations (RICO) Act.

By 1983, Father Hill had established a close relationship with President Ronald Reagan, who held similar views on combating pornography. In response to Father Hill's call for greater enforcement of the obscenity laws, President Reagan created the White House Working Group on Pornography, which is charged with devising strategies that could be recommended to the Congress for stronger enforcement of the obscenity laws. In that same year, obscenity was added as a crime in the Comprehensive Crime Control Act. The act stiffened obscenity law violation enforcement by giving judges less discretion in determining the punishment for this crime. The law prescribed a precise range of incarceration, from three to ten years, and did not allow judges to reduce this term.

When President Reagan formed the Attorney General's Commission on Obscenity and Pornography (the Meese commission) in

1985, Father Hill pressed his efforts further. He organized the National Catholic Conference on the Illegal Sex Industry in New York City in June 1984, and the Denver National Conference on Pornography in the spring of 1985. Just as his initiatives were beginning to take hold, however, he died. His work has been carried on by his friends and colleagues at Morality in Media, especially Robert W. Peters (see p. 129).

Father Hill received many accolades for his work in fighting pornography and was well respected within law enforcement circles. Attorney General Richard Thornburgh once honored him for his work with prosecutors by saying, "You let in the light, we will bring in the law" (*A Gentle Man Who Led an Ungentle Life*, n.p.).

SUGGESTED READINGS

A gentle man who led an ungentle life: Remembering Morton A. Hill, S.J. New York: Morality in Media, 1992.

Hill, Morton A., and Link, Winfrey C. *The Hill-Link Minority Report of the Presidential Commission on Obscenity and Pornography.* New York: Morality in Media, 1970.

The Morality in Media Newsletter, a publication of Morality in Media. Web site of Morality in Media: http://www.moralityinmedia.org

Reed John Irvine

Ferreting Out Liberal Bias in the Media

Born: September 29, 1922, Salt Lake City, Utah
Education: B.A., University of Utah, 1942; B.Litt., Oxford University, 1951
Current position: Chairman and cofounder, Accuracy in Media, Accuracy in Academia

---

The media are often criticized for favoring one political viewpoint over others and for unethical journalistic practices. While there are organizations of journalists that police their own ranks, Reed Irvine has been instrumental in bringing the politically conservative view of biased reporting to the attention of the American public.

Irvine was born in Salt Lake City, Utah, on September 29, 1922, to William John and Edna Jessup (May) Irvine. After earning a B.A. in economics from the University of Utah in Salt Lake City in 1942, Irvine joined the U.S. Navy and, later, the U.S. Marines and saw action in Asia during World War II.

After his discharge, he began a career in economics and became an international finance adviser for the Federal Reserve Board in 1951. From then until 1963, he traveled throughout Asia and Latin America, working to develop financial stability for nations in these areas. During this same time period, he wrote articles on development economics and became a lecturer at American University and George Washington University in Washington, D.C. He retired from the Federal Reserve Board in 1977.

As the media's influence grew after the Kennedy years, Irvine became increasingly critical of it. In 1969, with a $200 donation from his friend, Wilson C. Lucom, Irvine formed Accuracy in Media (AIM). "I launched on a career of media criticism in 1969, when disgust with the media—particularly television, for pouring gasoline on the flames of riots in our cities and turmoil on our campuses— propelled me, together with a few friends, into founding Accuracy in Media. . . . My connection with journalism was strictly that of a consumer of its products. Like many others during the late 1960s, I had come face to face with many serious defects in what journalists were churning out" (Irvine, 1984, p. 7). At first, Irvine and his assistants produced news releases for publication in the same media he was criticizing. In time, however, instead of relying on the media itself to publish AIM's commentary and criticism, Irvine created an AIM newsletter. *The AIM Report* was begun in 1972, and four years later, in 1976, Irvine began a weekly syndicated newspaper column, which appeared in more than 100 newspapers in its early years. By 1981, Irvine was producing a daily radio commentary program and had developed a speakers' bureau. Irvine has explained that AIM has moved into so many venues because "it is our view that the news media wield great power and play a valuable role as a check on other institutions, but require checking themselves. This check can best be performed by a private organization acting as a professional critic. This is the function of AIM" (http://www.aim.org/).

In 1984, Irvine wrote *Media Mischief and Misdeeds*, a collection of AIM stories that highlight some of the more egregious media errors.

Among the fifty-two stories in the book, which are accompanied by Irvine's commentary on the issues of media inaccuracy, included are numerous stories from specific reports in print news and in broadcasting. For example, Irvine noted that *The Washington Post* printed editorial columnist Jack Anderson's exposé columns on drug use by government officials in which he named conservatives, such as U.S. Representatives Barry Goldwater, Jr. (R-CA), and Charles Wilson (D-TX), but did not print the columns on drug use by liberal U.S. Representatives Gerry Studds (D-MA) and Parren Mitchell (D-MD). He detailed several complaints about CBS News, including a story on their *60 Minutes* program about insurance fraud. A medical doctor featured in the story, Dr. Carl Galloway, was accused by CBS of signing a fraudulent medical form for collecting insurance claims. Irvine accused CBS of staging the interviews of Dr. Galloway and other experts on the program to bias the story against the doctor. In still another entry, Irvine told of how *Newsweek* magazine failed to check its sources on the supposed discovery of Adolf Hitler's diary, which turned out to be a hoax unveiled by the West German government in 1983.

In 1985, believing that students on many college campuses were struggling to sift fact from the personal bias of their professors, Irvine formed Accuracy in Academia (AIA). The aim of AIA was to report on obvious biased teaching. The organization collected class notes or placed student observers in classrooms where complaints had been lodged by other students. University faculty around the country greeted the formation of AIA with some concern and frequently with outrage. The use of observers to criticize the teachings of professors publicly was seen as an attempt to trample on the freedom of professors to state their own opinions. Many in the academic community believed that AIA was only looking to criticize liberal bias and that conservative bias would go untouched.

Irvine continues to direct the activities of both AIM and AIA. The *AIM Report* is still published twice a week, and Irvine still prepares commentary for his syndicated column. The AIM web site includes such features as a text and audio version of *Media Monitor*, a daily radio broadcast, Irvine's weekly column, an online version of the *AIM Report*, and guest columns. Guest columns are written by well-known commentators such as Paul Weyrich, president of the Free Congress Foundation, John Nowacki of the Free Congress Foundation (a conservative think tank) and Marianne Jennings, Arizona State University law professor and syndicated columnist.

In recent years, Irvine and his staff have dealt with media bias in the coverage of political and foreign affairs. Several AIM reports focused on the pardons issued by President Clinton during his final days in office and on the mischief created by his White House staff. Another AIM report noted that the media in general had failed to cover the case of Sheryl Hall who lost her White House job under President Clinton for protesting the transfer of information to the Democratic National Committee. AIM also detailed the underreporting of Secretary of State Madeleine Albright's visit to North Korea. This report noted that the favorable view of the North Korean regime written by Janet Perlez of the *New York Times* was widely published but that reports on the dire conditions of the North Korean people written by Steve Mufson, a *Washington Post* reporter, were rarely covered.

Irvine has been married to Kay Araki Irvine since 1947. In 1982 Irvine's son, Donald, joined AIM and is currently the operations manager of the organization. Overall, Irvine is pleased with the impact of AIM on the media: "The media's antipathy to hard-hitting, factual criticism of their misdeeds and mischief has not measurably abated since 1969. What I call the Big Media—the television networks, the newspapers with national influence, the news magazines, and the wire services have not been eager to run stories about the criticisms that I have directed against them in the *AIM Report*, my column, and on our radio program. But like the steady dripping of water that wears away granite, our criticism has had an effect" (Irvine, 1984, p. 9).

SUGGESTED READINGS

AIM Report, a publication of Accuracy in Media.
Irvine, Reed J. *Media mischief and misdeeds*. Chicago: Regnery/Gateway, 1984.

Carl Jensen

Project Censored

Born: July 25, 1929, Brooklyn, New York
Education: B.A., University of California, Santa Barbara, 1971;

M.A., University of California, Santa Barbara, 1972; Ph.D.,
University of California, Santa Barbara, 1977
Current position: Professor Emeritus, Sonoma State University;
    founder and director emeritus of Project Censored

Even with the flood of people and events that influence one's life,
it is easy to identify those who have a lasting impact. For Carl Jensen
these influences were his father, an immigrant from Denmark, who
taught him to respect every individual no matter his or her circum-
stances, and his mother, an immigrant from Sweden, who gave him
a typewriter when he was seven years old and filled his toy chest
with books.

As a first-generation American, born in Brooklyn, New York, Carl Jensen was taught early on to love his country and to believe that anything is possible in America. He was raised on Horatio Alger and Tom Swift. Horatio Alger taught him that honesty and hard work were the keys to success and that what you did was far more important than who you were. Tom Swift's extraordinary science fiction adventures taught him how to fantasize about what might be rather than despair over what is.

Perhaps because he grew up during the Great Depression and World War II, Jensen is firmly convinced that it is possible to overcome seemingly insurmountable obstacles and that there are solutions to all of the problems that plague us. These convictions helped him to be successful as an intelligence officer in the U.S. Air Force during the Korean War, as a daily newspaper reporter and a weekly newspaper publisher, as a publicist, and as an award-winning advertising executive. At the age of forty, however, feeling dissatisfied and trapped by the commercial corporate world, Jensen quit his position at Batten, Barton, Durstine & Osborn, one of the nation's largest advertising agencies, and went back to college.

Feeling that he could make a more important contribution to society through education, Jensen completed work for a B.A. in sociology and then went on to receive a master's and Ph.D. in sociology with an emphasis on the media. Armed with his Ph.D. and his years of real-world experience, he started teaching sociology and communication studies classes at Sonoma State University (SSU) in northern California.

In his interview with the authors, Jensen has said the idea for Project Censored came to him one afternoon in July 1976 as he was preparing for the fall semester at SSU and wondering why so many people vote or work against their own best interests. The institution responsible for keeping people informed is the nation's news media, he thought, and the media is not providing people with all the information they need to make the right decisions about their lives. This idea helped him to explain, at least to his own satisfaction, many events. For example, he had never understood how Richard Nixon could be elected president by a landslide five months after the Watergate burglary. When he went back to examine the media coverage of the Watergate burglary before and after the 1972 election, however, he discovered that it had not been a major news story in that year. In fact, as Bob Woodward, reporter for *The Washington Press* who broke the Watergate story, later said, Watergate wasn't even a topic of discussion on election eve. It was only in 1973 that the news media put Watergate on the national agenda. Jensen began to wonder if there were other important stories that were overlooked or ignored by the mainstream media. As he examined the alternative media, he found important issues, such as banned pesticides, East Timor, media monopolies, and acid rain, that had not made the front pages of the newspapers or the evening network news programs.

As a result of his research, Jensen began Project Censored. Since 1976, Project Censored has been locating and publicizing important stories that have been ignored by the news media. Today, under the leadership of Peter Phillips, a sociologist at SSU, Project Censored and its staff of more than 100 faculty, students, and media experts is internationally renowned and the nation's longest-running research project on news media censorship. Project Censored provides people with information on issues that the media often do not cover in depth, encourages journalists, editors, publishers, and student journalists to examine issues they have ignored, and promotes discussions of news media self-censorship in high-school and college journalism classes.

Jensen has been a guest on many radio and television news and talk shows. In 1991, he was interviewed by Bill Moyers for a PBS television documentary about Project Censored. In 1999, he was featured in the television documentary, "Project Censored: Is the Press Really Free?" He is the author of the annual Project Censored yearbook, *CENSORED: The News That Didn't Make the News . . . And Why* (1990–1996), *20 Years of Censored News* (1997), and *Stories That Changed America: Muckrakers of the 20th Century* (2000). This book is the story of people—Ida Mae Tarbell, Paul Brodeur, and Frances Moore Lappe, among others—who have made a difference in the United States because they have believed that societal inequities can be corrected and that one person can make a difference. Jensen was consulting editor for *Ready Reference: Censorship* (1997). Among Jensen's many awards and citations are the Hugh M. Hefner First Amendment Award, presented in 1992; the James Madison Freedom of Information Award for Career Achievement, given by the northern California chapter of the Society of Professional Journalists in 1996; and the Outstanding University Professor of Journalism in California Award, given by the California Newspaper Publishers Association in 1996.

Jensen is currently working on a new book, *Censored America: An Epic Prose Poem*, which will be a collection of more than 200 prose poems that are based on issues raised by investigative journalists in the past twenty-five years.

SUGGESTED READINGS

Jensen, Carl. *CENSORED: The news that didn't make the news . . . and why.* Chapel Hill, NC: Shelburne Press, 1993.
———. *The top 25 censored news stories of 1991: and 1972, 1980, 1984, 1992.* Rohnert Park, CA: Censored Publications, 1992.
———. *20 years of censored news.* New York: Seven Stories Press, 1997.

Karen Kennerly

Author's Rights Advocate

Born: July 17, 1940, New York City, New York
Education: B.A., Pembroke College, 1962
Current position: Individual project fellow, Open Society Institute; immediate past director, PEN American Center

Karen Kennerly has had a distinguished career in publishing and as an advocate for the freedom to read and to publish. She was born in New York City to Albert Kennerly, an architect, and his wife, Helen Wolff Kennerly, on July 17, 1940. Kennerly attended Pembroke College in Cambridge, England, and graduated with distinction in 1962 with a degree in English literature.

Kennerly began her career as a writer. Her first work was a children's book entitled *The Slave Who Bought His Freedom* (1971). The story, which is both uplifting and a graphic description of slavery in our early history, is an adaptation of the autobiography of Olaudah Equiano, an eighteenth-century slave in the United States.

During these early years, Kennerly also earned a reputation as a translator of foreign texts, especially those dealing with folklore and fables, and became a senior editor for Dial Press. In the early 1970s, she was awarded a fellowship to do Japanese translations from International PEN. International PEN and its affiliate centers is an organization of prominent writers and editors that, as its Web site states, "seeks to defend the freedom of expression wherever it may be threatened, and promote and encourage the recognition and reading of contemporary literature." The U.S. branch of International PEN is PEN American Center, which is the largest of PEN's 130 centers. PEN American Center promotes its views and carries out its mission in a number of ways. Its Freedom to Write Program is a primary source of advocacy materials in the defense of freedom of expression throughout the world. PEN offers numerous literary awards in different genres, as well as awards for translators and translations and for literary editors. The organization also sponsors the PEN/Barbara Goldsmith Freedom-to-Write Award and the PEN/ *Newman's Own* First Amendment Award, which was founded by the actor Paul Newman and A.E. Hotchner in 1992. These awards honor people for their willingness to stand for free speech and intellectual freedom. In 2000, for example, Dr. William Holda, President of Kilgore College in Kilgore, Texas, was given the PEN/*Newman's Own* First Amendment Award for resisting pressure to ban the performance of a controversial play on campus. Most of these awards were established under Kennerly's leadership.

In the late 1970s, Kennerly became the executive director of PEN American Center and held that position until 1998, when the center became embroiled in interorganizational strife. To build the financial base of PEN American Center, Kennerly and other leaders had begun to seek wealthy nonmembers for board positions and other roles in the organization, which caused some members to question the direction the organization was taking. Kennerly resigned her position in mid-1998 to pursue her literary career and is now an individual project fellow for the Open Society Institute, an international foundation for Free Societies and Nations. She recently wrote a review for the *New Republic* of Lynne Withey's book, *Grand Tours and Cook's Tours: A History of Leisure Travel, 1750–1915.*

SUGGESTED READINGS

Kennerly, Karen, Ed. *Hesitant wolf & scrupulous fox: Fables selected from world literature.* New York: Random House, 1973.

PEN Newsletter, a publication of the PEN American Center. Web site of PEN American Center: http://www.pen.org

Reverend Jerry Kirk

Antipornography Crusader

Born: May 11, 1931, Seattle, Washington
Education: B.A., University of Washington, 1953; M.Div., Pittsburgh Theological Seminary, 1955; M.Th., Pittsburgh Theological Seminary
Current position: Founder and chairman of the board, National Coalition for the Protection of Children and Families

Dr. Jerry Kirk is a Presbyterian minister in Cincinnati, Ohio, and one of the pioneers in the fight against pornography. Realizing early on that pornography can appear in print, film, and electronic form and is not confined to the inner city but available everywhere, Jerry Kirk has worked to organize coalitions from diverse backgrounds to combat it.

Kirk is a native of Seattle, Washington. While attending the University of Washington, he played on the university's basketball and tennis teams. At the time of his graduation, he was named one of the six outstanding students in his class. After earning his bachelor's degree, Kirk went on to earn two graduate degrees and was named a Purdy Scholar, an academic honor at Pittsburgh Theological Seminary. Because of his prominence in religious activities and his work to combat pornography, he has also been awarded two honorary degrees.

For eighteen years, Kirk has been in the forefront of efforts to combat pornography at either the local or national level. He believes that "pornography is antichildren, antiwomen, antimarriage, antichurch and anti-God. God cares about people, but pornography destroys people" (http://www.worldevangelical.org/noframes/ganews13. htm). He has been instrumental in the creation of a number of organizations that work to stem the tide of pornography and obscenity. In 1983, he formed the National Coalition Against Pornography, which has since evolved into the National Coalition for the Protection of Children and Families (NCPCF). The NCPCF is an alliance of representatives from businesses, foundations, citizen action groups,

religious denominations and faith groups who are committed to protecting children and families from pornography and its effect on society. When a local cable provider in Cincinnati offered the Playboy channel to subscribers, Kirk was instrumental in organizing a group of religious leaders in opposition. Over 300 people marched to city hall to demand that the channel be taken off the air. Within two weeks, the cable company announced that it had stopped airing the Playboy channel due to technical difficulties, and it has not been offered since.

In 1986, Kirk worked with Joseph Cardinal Bernardin of the Catholic church to form the Religious Alliance Against Pornography (RAAP). RAAP began after a series of meetings in New York at the home of Cardinal O'Connor, who was known for his efforts to combat pornography in the New York area. RAAP is an interfaith organization with the same aims and objectives as NCPCF. The leaders of nearly fifty denominations support its efforts. William Cardinal Keeler, archbishop of Baltimore, now shares the chairmanship of RAAP with Kirk. In the same year that RAAP was created, Kirk was invited by the Reagan administration to a White House briefing on combating pornography. After meeting with President Reagan and Attorney General Edwin Meese, RAAP received a commitment to the creation of an office within the U.S. Justice Department dedicated to the issue of child exploitation and obscenity.

Dr. Kirk is the author of two books, *The Mind Polluters* (1985) and *The Homosexual Crisis in the Mainline Church* (1978), as well as numerous articles on religious matters and the antipornography crusade. He has been invited to speak about the harms of pornography on such shows as *The Oprah Winfrey Show*, *NBC Nightline News*, and *Prime Time America*. He is also a regular speaker on Dr. James Dobson's radio show, which is sponsored by Focus on the Family. Dr. Kirk is married to Patty Kirk. They have five children and twenty-three grandchildren.

SUGGESTED READINGS

Kirk, Jerry. *The homosexual crisis in the mainline church: A presbyterian minister speaks out.* Nashville, TN: T. Nelson, 1978.
———. *The mind polluters.* Nashville, TN: T. Nelson, 1985.
Web site of National Coalition to Protect Children and Families: http://www.nationalcoalition.org

Judith Fingeret Krug

Intellectual Freedom Advocate for Libraries and the Freedom to Read

Born: March 15, 1940, Pittsburgh, Pennsylvania
Education: B.A., University of Pittsburgh, 1961; M.A., University of Chicago, 1964; graduate work in political theory
Present position: Director, Office for Intellectual Freedom,

American Library Association, and executive director of the Freedom to Read Foundation

For the past thirty-four years, Judith Krug has been the driving force behind the efforts of the American Library Association (ALA) to protect intellectual freedom and the freedom to read. No other individual has gone before the American public and its representatives in so many venues to defend the freedom to read more than Judy Krug. She has been the director of the Office for Intellectual Freedom of the ALA since 1967 and the executive director of the Freedom to Read Foundation since 1970.

Judith Fingeret Krug was born in Pittsburgh, Pennsylvania, on March 15, 1940. After graduating from high school, she attended the University of Pittsburgh and earned a B.A. in political theory. She then entered graduate school at the University of Chicago and completed her degree in library science in 1964. She began her library career as a reference librarian at the John Crerar Library in Chicago, Illinois, but eventually became a cataloger for the Northwestern University Dental School. Soon thereafter, she became a research analyst for the ALA until her appointment as the director of the Office for Intellectual Freedom.

When once asked how she had become involved with defending

intellectual freedom, Krug replied that she had fallen into it because of her position as an ALA research analyst. She went on to explain that she had been writing proposals and doing fund-raising when a supervisor told her that she was going to be replaced by a male researcher because males were "real researchers." In disgust, Krug immediately began searching for a new job. When word of her predicament reached David Clift, executive director of ALA, he told her, "We need people like you. How would you like to be director of the Office for Intellectual Freedom?" This office had been established only three months earlier. She viewed her job in the first year as one of making the office viable, and as she told one interviewer, "making known its existence. . . . [a year later] the phones started to ring like mad after one success had led to another. We were ready" (Deitch, 1984, p. 655).

Krug's stature in intellectual freedom circles has been recognized in a number of ways. She has won almost every significant intellectual freedom award available, especially those for librarians and legal advocates. In 1978, she was awarded the Robert B. Downs Award for outstanding contributions to the cause of intellectual freedom in libraries. In 1983, she received the Carl Sandburg Freedom to Read Award from the Friends of the Chicago Public Library. In 1990, she was given the Intellectual Freedom Award of the Illinois Library Association, and in 1994, she received the Ohio Educational Library Media Association/SIRS Award for Intellectual Freedom. In 1995, she received the Roll of Honor Award from the Freedom to Read Foundation for her leadership of the foundation. Krug has also been honored by the American Civil Liberties Union (ACLU), which presented her with the prestigious Harry Kalven Freedom of Expression Award in 1976. The American Booksellers Association (ABA) also recognized her significant contributions with its Irita Van Doren Book Award in 1976.

Because of her abilities as an advocate for intellectual freedom, she is often asked to serve on advisory boards and governing bodies. She serves on the First Amendment Advisory Council of the Media Institute as well as on the institute's Cornerstone Project Advisory Council and on the board of directors of the Council of Literary Magazines and Presses. She has previously served on the board of directors of the Fund for Free Expression, the board of directors of the Illinois division of the ACLU, the ABA's Commission on Public Understanding About the Law, and the advisory council of the Illinois State Justice Commission. Her keen intellect has made her a popular guest on political commentary shows, talk shows, and television news shows. Krug once told this author that, after Phyllis Schafly charged that libraries censor the publications of the Christian right, including her own works, during a debate with Krug on a news program, Krug brought to the next public debate a large computer printout of libraries that owned copies of Schafly's books and publications and embarrassed Schafly when she made the charge again.

Krug has supported her views on intellectual freedom with several publications, most notably the ALA's *Intellectual Freedom Manual* (6th ed., 2002), which describes the association's history and its policies on freedom of expression, access to library materials, and opposition to censorship. "For intellectual freedom to flourish, opposition to censorship of materials is not enough. Free access to materials for every member of the community must also be assured. ALA first recognized this in the 1939 'Library's Bill of Rights,' " Krug stated in the manual. She is also the editor of the *Newsletter on Intellectual Freedom*, a serial publication of the Office for Intellectual Freedom, the *Freedom to Read Foundation News*, and the *Intellectual Freedom Action News*.

Krug lives in Evanston, Illinois, with her family. She is a member of Phi Beta Kappa, Beta Phi Mu, the Illinois Library Association, and the American Library Association. She has said when asked if she is personally revolted by book banning and censorship, "There is a basic drive to oppose values, principles, and guidelines different from yours—to protect what you think is right. I am not different from anyone else. The difference is that I wouldn't dream of trying to censor anyone" (Deitch, p. 658).

SUGGESTED READINGS

Deitch, Joseph. "Portrait of Judy Krug." *Wilson Library Bulletin* 58 (May 1984):654–658. *The Newsletter on Intellectual Freedom*, a publication of the Office for Intellectual Freedom, American Library Association.

Krug, Judith F., Anne Levinson Penway and Eve B. Burton. "Sexually explicit content and the First Amendment: Twenty years later." In *Book Publishing and the First Amendment* by R. Bruce Rich and Linda Steinman. New York: Association of American Publishers, 1993.

Web site of the Office for Intellectual Freedom: http://www.ala.org/alaorg/oif/

Beverly LaHaye

Concerned Women for America

Born: April 30, 1929
Education: Attended Bob Jones University
Current position: President and founder, Concerned Women for
   America

Although Beverly Ratcliffe LaHaye is now a nationally recognized
advocate and spokeswoman on issues affecting women and the family, as a young woman she never thought of herself as a leader. She
and her older sister grew up in Missouri and Michigan during the
Great Depression. In 1946, when she entered Bob Jones University
in Greenville, South Carolina, she met Tim LaHaye. The two found
they had much in common, and they were married in July 1947. After
her marriage, LaHaye dropped out of college to become a full-time
wife and homemaker, while her husband went on to become a minister. The couple had four children.

LaHaye attended a workshop led by Henry Brandt, a religious
psychologist known for his self-improvement lectures. He helped
LaHaye realize that she was thinking too much about herself and
not allowing her relationship with God to give her confidence in her
own abilities. After the workshop, LaHaye began to take a more
active role in her husband's ministry. In 1971 the LaHayes developed
the Family Life Seminars, a mix of family-centered, old-time religion
and Christian psychology. In 1976, they wrote *The Act of Marriage*, a
best-seller in the Christian book market. The book encouraged frank
communications about sex between marriage partners and was quite
explicit about specific techniques and styles of lovemaking within a
marriage. During this time, LaHaye began to develop a ministry of
her own, writing, counseling, and speaking to women's groups. In
the late 1970s, she was asked to join the board of directors of the
Coalition for Better TV (now the National Federation for Decency),
which attempts to keep sex and violence off the airwaves.

It was in 1979, while watching Barbara Walters interview Betty Friedan (founder of the National Organization for Women) on the equal rights amendment, that LaHaye decided that neither of the women spoke for the women of the United States and resolved to start a movement that would. After advertising her plan through churches in the San Diego area, she called a meeting. The 1,200 women who attended formed the nucleus of the Concerned Women for America (CWA), which was incorporated in 1979. The CWA has stated positions against the Equal Rights Amendment, abortion, homosexuality, pornography, sexually explicit material on TV, and child abuse (but not parental discipline).

In 1983, with the organization firmly established and growing, Beverly LaHaye decided that an office in Washington, D.C., would be in a better location to support the efforts of the CWA, so the family and the national headquarters moved there, in January 1985, once the Washington office was firmly in place. The first major battle for the CWA was the Equal Rights Amendment. LaHaye asked CWA members to pray about the ERA every Wednesday from January 1 until the amendment was defeated, which occurred on June 30, 1982.

In another battle, which occurred in 1986 in the small town of Church Hill, Tennessee, Vicki Frost, a parent of a child in the school system, and other parents, charged their children's textbooks taught witchcraft, humanism, feminism, and one-worldism, among other things, along with the idea that salvation could be had apart from faith in Jesus Christ. The federal judge ruled that the school could not require children to read textbooks that their parents said violated their religious beliefs.

The organization has an active web site that contains current legislative information and links to many related web sites. In addition, LaHaye has a daily radio talk show, *Beverly LaHaye Today*, that is carried by more than seventy-five stations throughout the country, and a weekend program to recap important events of the week, *This Week with Beverly LaHaye*. Numerous publications—policy papers, brochures, booklets, manuals, and a bimonthly journal, *Family Voice*—provide information for members and interested others.

Under the leadership of LaHaye, CWA also has developed Project 535 (named for the total number of senators and representatives in Congress), a volunteer lobbying group that is composed of women from various walks of life (mothers, teachers, business professionals) who live on the East Coast. The women meet once a month to focus on a particular issue and to lobby on Capitol Hill. The project utilizes fax and e-mail alerts to notify members and other interested parties on a weekly basis of legislative action items.

When she speaks before a group, LaHaye conveys high moral and political standards. Her personal style is reflected in the "quilt wall" that is dedicated "to millions of American women who demonstrated the moral strength and character to overcome obstacles, to create beauty and to guide new generations into an understanding of true godliness" (http://www.cwfa.org/about/quilt.shtml) at the national headquarters in Washington, D.C., and in the prayer chapters that bring together small groups of women on a regular basis but leave the location, time, and frequency of meetings to local chapters. LaHaye firmly believes that it is the duty of the CWA "to protect and promote Biblical values among all citizens—first through prayer, then education, and finally by influencing our society—thereby reversing the decline in moral values in our nation" (http://www.cwfa .org/).

SUGGESTED READINGS

Benowitz, June Melby. *Encyclopedia of American Women and Religion*. Santa Barbara, CA: ABC-CLIO, 1998.
Lippy, Charles H., ed. *Twentieth-century shapers of American popular religion*. Westport, CT: Greenwood Press, 1989.
Paige, Connie. "Watch on the right: The amazing rise of Beverly LaHaye." *MS* 16 (February 1987): 24–28.
Web site of Concerned Women for America: http://www.cwfa.org

Gene D. Lanier

Crusader to Protect Libraries from Censorship

Born: March 13, 1934, Conway, North Carolina
Education: B.S., East Carolina University, 1955; M.S.L.S., University of North Carolina at Chapel Hill, 1957; Ph.D., University of North Carolina at Chapel Hill, 1968
Current position: Distinguished Professor Emeritus, East Carolina University

When the *ECU Accent*, the student paper at East Carolina University, interviewed Gene Lanier, it quickly discovered he would rather talk about the First Amendment than himself: "He will be exceedingly polite, as is his way, the way of an old-school Southern gentleman. He won't really answer you. He gives you just enough information to meet the requirements of your question, then takes the conversation where he wants it—to threats to the First Amendment, and to the importance of libraries in keeping information free and available to the public" (*ECU Accent*, p. 1). Lanier's record as a professor of library science is exemplary, but what stands out more than his degrees or his years of experience is his deep commitment to intellectual freedom. Lanier is the recipient of at least eight intellectual freedom and free speech awards, including the Hugh M. Hefner First Amendment Award, the Robert B. Downs Award, and the John Phillip Immroth Memorial Award. During his tenure as the chairperson of the Intellectual Freedom Committee of the North Carolina Library Association, a post he held for over twenty years, he found that he "faced every conceivable type of infringement on the right to read, view and listen. We had over one hundred attempts each year just in North Carolina libraries to infringe on the right to read. I felt that I made a difference in helping people to see how important it is to examine all points of view."

He traces the inspiration for his career to his parents. As he told the authors in an interview, "My parents were a great influence on my life. I was free to read anything I wanted, and they gave me the freedom to make up my mind on most things in life along with their guidance. Their support helped me to open up many vistas." Lanier carried his parents' tradition into his own family. "As a father, I tried to practice what I preached. Both of my daughters felt free to talk with their mother and me about anything affecting their lives. They would come home from school with unbelievable stories. After getting up off the floor from my amazement, I would suggest we talk about these things. Rather than telling them what to do, I could see them forming their own morals, their own ideas, etc." (interview with the authors).

Because it is not enough to believe in the freedom to read to become a champion of intellectual freedom, Lanier notes that his high-school teachers and world events also influenced him. A favorite high-school English teacher encouraged him to speak out on issues. His experiences in the U.S. Army further strengthened his belief in the importance of the First Amendment. In his interview with the authors, Lanier said, "I heard (firsthand) about the Hitler book-burnings and so forth. And I realized how simple that is to happen anywhere in a country where people take their rights for granted."

Lanier decided the library would be his career while completing his bachelor's degree at East Carolina University in 1955. After receiving his master's degree in library science at the University of North Carolina at Chapel Hill in 1957, he was drafted into the army and trained as an intelligence agent working in Europe to counter Soviet Union espionage. Before he could become a full-time operative, however, his cover was blown.

Lanier is a frequent speaker around the country, and in all his speeches his passion for the First Amendment clearly comes first. For example, in a speech for tech.learning, a Web-based company which sponsored the Well Connected Educator's Forum, an online forum on child safety on the Internet in 1997, Lanier argued: "Yes, kids can be kept safe on the Internet in the same way they are protected from other life choices which might be considered threatening. It's called parenting. Parents/guardians help their children/young people make choices such as what books to read, what movies to see, what field trips to take . . . going out on the 'information highway' is just another field trip."

Lanier has been an active proponent of freedom of speech. "I served a total of eight years (four terms) on the Intellectual Freedom Committee of the American Library Association, which gave me an opportunity to become acquainted with the censorship picture nationwide. After receiving a number of awards, I received many invitations to speak on the subject resulting in talks and presentations to professional and social groups on radio, television, and on stage in over forty states." He has also been active as a member of the North Carolina Library Association's Intellectual Freedom Committee and as a member of the board of advisors of the People for the American Way. Lanier told the authors, "I felt a commitment to spread the word on how to prepare before, during, and after the censors arrive. I, indeed, became a fool for the concept of the First Amendment. The words are absolute and should never be changed. You see, a book is easier to burn than explain."

As he told the authors, "Many of our citizens feel helpless and underrepresented and by examining the First Amendment principles, they can find more stability in life and the democratic process." Threats to freedom of speech or to the freedom to read are intolerable to Lanier. "Freedom of speech belongs to the washed and the unwashed. It is necessary to tolerate and stand extreme ideas and thoughts with which you may have problems in order to get the whole package in democracy including due process" (interview). Faced with diverse opposition, Lanier recognizes the need for diligence in defending freedom of speech: "It is important for us to put aside our apathy and take part in the democratic process and vocalize our feelings to our governments at every level. We must acknowledge we have complex problems, but we must realize that the simplistic solutions offered by some may be misleading and wrong."

When he retired from East Carolina University in 2001, the *ECU Accent* honored him with a front-page article chronicling his life. Lanier now lives in a beach cottage in Atlantic Beach, North Carolina. He has sworn off committee meetings but is still in demand as a speaker on the freedom to read.

SUGGESTED READINGS

Lanier, Gene. *The transformation of school libraries into instructional materials centers*. Dissertation. Chapel Hill: University of North Carolina, 1968.
The Newsletter on Intellectual Freedom, a publication of the Office for Intellectual Freedom, American Library Association.
Rabey, Frank. "Standard bearer." *ECU Accent*, May 22, 1999, p. 1.

Catherine A. MacKinnon

Women's Rights Advocate Against Pornography

Born: October 7, 1946, Minneapolis, Minnesota
Education: B.A., Smith College, 1969; J.D., Yale University, 1977; Ph.D., Yale University, 1987
Current position: Professor of law, University of Michigan School of Law

Feminists are divided on the subject of pornography and obscenity. Some feel pornography exploits women, encourages men to abuse them, and is demeaning. Others believe that pornography is protected by the First Amendment and also argue that women in the sex industry claim that pornography and other sex industries provide employment. This employment, they say, represents empowerment, giving them a sense of control over their lives. The conservative feminists feel that pornography exploits women and should be censored. Catherine MacKinnon supports this point of view and crusades to protect women from the victimization of the pornography industry.

Catherine MacKinnon was born in Minneapolis, Minnesota, on October 7, 1946, to George E. and Elizabeth V. MacKinnon. Her father was a federal appeals court judge and an adviser to Dwight D. Eisenhower and Richard Nixon. Her mother was a congresswoman for Minnesota for one term and a Republican nominee for governor. Like her maternal grandmother and mother, MacKinnon attended Smith College in Massachusetts. She graduated *magna cum laude* (with high honors) in government in 1969. She went on to Yale Law School and earned her Juris Doctor in 1977. Ten years later, she earned a Ph.D. in political science from Yale as well. During her years at Yale, MacKinnon, like other students of the day, protested against the Vietnam War and became involved with the Black radical group known as the Black Panthers. She also cofounded a lawyers' collective, became active in the feminist movement, and created the first course for Yale's women's studies program.

It was while researching and writing about a case at Cornell University that MacKinnon began to redefine sexual harassment. Carmita Wood was an administrative assistant at Cornell University who believed that the only way she could avoid her supervisor's sexual harassment was to resign her position. When she applied for unemployment, the university denied her claims, saying she had quit for personal reasons. Although this case had concluded before MacKinnon began her work, she used its substance in her first book, *Sexual Harrassment of Working Women: A Case of Sex Discrimination* (1978), to argue that sexual harassment is sexual discrimination. "I felt that this is about everything the situation of women is really about, everything that the law of sex discrimination made it so difficult if not impossible to address. So, I decided I would just design something." Prior to 1977, courts had ruled that the behaviors involved in sexual harassment were private matters and not something that could be brought to court through a lawsuit. However, in *Barnes v. Costle*, a case before the United States Court of Appeals for the District of Columbia in that year, the court ruled that sexual harassment was a form of sexual discrimination because it was an action taken solely because of the "womanhood" of the victim. One of the three judges who authored the opinion was MacKinnon's father.

In 1986, the Supreme Court heard its first sexual harassment case, *Meritor Savings Bank* v. *Vinson*. MacKinnon was the cocounsel for Mechelle Vinson, who had sued her employer because her supervisor had constantly harassed her by coercing her into having sex on numerous occasions, fondling her in front of others, and following her into the women's rest room. The Court used MacKinnon's arguments in ruling that the two primary types of sexual harassment—direct acts (*quid pro quo*) and a hostile environment caused by constant harassment—were forms of sexual discrimination.

MacKinnon and other feminists have similar views on sexual harassment. Since the 1980s, however, MacKinnon has become associated with that faction of the feminist movement that finds pornography abhorrent and exploitive of women. MacKinnon firmly believes that pornography is a type of sexual discrimination. In her work, she has become a close associate of Andrea Dworkin. It was Dworkin who encouraged MacKinnon to talk with Linda Marchiano. Marchiano, using the stage name Linda Lovelace, was known as the actress in *Deep Throat*, a famous pornographic movie. In her autobiography *Ordeal*, Marchiano had recounted how she was forced, often at gunpoint, into making pornographic movies by a former husband. MacKinnon attempted to prevent the sale and/or public viewing of *Deep Throat* for Marchiano, but the statute of limitations ran out before a court could rule on the matter.

MacKinnon has also worked with Andrea Dworkin in drafting legislation that defines illegal pornography as the "graphic sexually explicit subordination" of individuals, particularly women and, thus, a form of sexual discrimination. While previous descriptions of illegal pornography have attempted to define obscenity on the basis of what is acceptable morally, the MacKinnon-Dworkin bills emphasize the exploitation of women. Both Massachusetts and Florida have had such laws proposed, and a number of cities have drafted similar legislation. Among these cities are Minneapolis, Minnesota, where MacKinnon was teaching at the time, Los Angeles, and Bellingham, Washington. In Indianapolis, Indiana, the legislature was adopted as law. To date, MacKinnon and Dworkin's efforts either have been struck down in the courts or have been rejected by the jurisdictions considering them as law. Using the argument made by MacKinnon and Dworkin, however, the Canadian Supreme Court has ruled in *R* v. *Butler* (1992) that localities and provinces can suppress materials that harm women. That court also redefined obscenity to include the subordination of women. MacKinnon has said, "This makes Canada the first place in the world that says what is obscene is what harms women, not what offends our values" (*New York Times*, p. A1 [N]).

MacKinnon has been attacked for her views by many, including those feminists who do not view pornography as sexual discrimination. In response, she has said, "Pornography isn't protected by the First Amendment any more than sexual harassment is. It's not a question of free speech or ideas. Pornography is a form of action, requiring the submission of women.... Women's experience and empirical research show the same thing: the more pornography men see, the more they enjoy it and the less sensitive they become to violence against women. A rape stops being a rape, the woman stops being a person. It's a terrifying, escalating dynamic, and the prognostication for women is grim" (*New York Times Book Review*, p. 51). MacKinnon has published two works that explain and defend her position on pornography as a form of sexual discrimination: *Pornography and Civil Rights: A New Day for Women's Equality* (1988), which was cowritten with Andrea Dworkin, and *Feminism Unmodified: Discourses on Life and Law* (1987), which is a collection of speeches given by MacKinnon between 1981 and 1986 on a variety of subjects, including pornography, abortion rights, rape, women's athletics, and the rights of Native American women.

In 1982, responding to criticism of her scholarly work, MacKinnon told an audience at Stanford University, "My work is considered not law by lawyers, not scholarship by academics, too practical by intellectuals, too intellectual by practitioners, and neither politics nor science by political scientists." Much of her scholarly work has been accumulated and addressed in *Toward a Feminist Theory of the State*, which was published in 1989. In this work, MacKinnon analyzes politics and sexuality from a woman's perspective and defines pornography as "the technologically sophisticated traffic in women that expropriates, exploits, uses and abuses women.... pornography sets the public standards for the treatment of women in private and the limits of tolerance for what can be permitted in public" (p. 246). She also discusses her theories on pornography in her 1993 book, *Only Words*. In this work, she calls pornography "the theory and rape the practice" of sexual abuse of women (p. 96).

After many years of temporary teaching assignments, MacKinnon became a tenured professor of law at the University of Michigan

School of Law in 1989. She continues to be in the forefront of feminist issues and a crusader against pornography. She has maintained her association with Andrea Dworkin and has collaborated with Dworkin, as co-editor, in editing *In Harm's Way: The Pornography Civil Rights Hearings* (1997). MacKinnon recently represented Croatian and Serbian women and children, particularly those from the Muslim population, at an international tribunal on the genocidal treatment of women during the Bosian and Kosovo conflicts.

SUGGESTED READINGS

Dworkin, Andrea, and Catherine MacKinnon. *Pornography and civil rights: A new day for women's equality.* Minneapolis, MN: Organizing Against Pornography, 1988.

MacKinnon, Catherine and Dworkin, Andrea, eds. *In harm's way: The pornography civil rights hearings.* Cambridge, MA: Harvard University Press, 1997.

———. *Toward a feminist theory of the state.* Cambridge, MA: Harvard University Press, 1989.

New York Times, February 28, 1992, p. A1 [N].

New York Times Book Review, May 3, 1987, p. 51.

Martin Mawyer

Christian Action Network

Born: 1953
Current position: President, Christian Action Network

Born in 1953, Martin Mawyer believes he has been transformed from "misshapen clay, social misfit, drug abuser and former mental patient," as he told the authors, into a national spokesman, founder and president of a multimillion-dollar organization, author, and leading authority on religious and social issues by his faith in God. His poor childhood and drug use, which landed him in a military mental ward after a serious drug overdose while he was in the army, have helped to mold his views.

For Mawyer, the turning point in his life came in 1972 while he was stationed in Germany. His heavy drug use was beginning to take a toll, and he began searching for meaning in his life. He went to the library in the army base and checked out a Bible. "I became fascinated by God's power, His realness, and His personal relationship with each and every person. That's the kind of God I wanted and needed. Soon I accepted Jesus Christ as my Lord and Savior," he has said.

Some time after leaving the military, Mawyer decided to pursue writing, which was his real love, as a career. He first worked as a reporter for Christian publications and then was hired by Jerry Falwell, who was then head of the Moral Majority, as editor of Falwell's *Liberty Report*. During this time, Mawyer developed a keen interest in politics and public issues and wrote his first book, *Silent Shame: The Alarming Rise of Sexual Abuse* (1987). He also realized that he had a talent for fund-raising. Mawyer worked as editor of the *Liberty Report* for the Moral Majority until Falwell reorganized the Moral Majority in 1989.

Finding himself unemployed, Mawyer decided to purchase computer equipment and, shortly afterward, found a freelance job, which required him to use his own equipment, as a copywriter raising funds for needy causes. Months later, in 1994, with just a $75 investment, Mawyer used the equipment to start the Christian Action Network, a political action organization dedicated to promoting family values.

Mawyer told the authors, "I had a heart to confront the major moral and social issues destroying America, and because of my six years as editor of the *Liberty Report*, I probably knew the issues as well as anyone in America. At the time I realized that my purpose in life was to perform the good works that God created me to do—no matter how difficult the tasks ahead may be. The Bible says that 'you will know them [Christians] by their fruit.' And that was what I intended to be: fruitful."

To start the organization, Mawyer sent letters to 200 people asking them to help. Only five donations came back, but Mawyer used that money to mail to another 260 people. With the funds he received from that mailing, he mailed to 300 more, until eventually he was mailing to 3,000 people. The Christian Action Network now has active supporters numbering more than 250,000 people and a web site that states: "The mission of the Christian Action Network is to defend the American family and to advocate traditional American principles of religious liberty, public virtue, and good government."

In the years since he founded the Christian Action Network, Mawyer has lobbied against grants from federal institutions such as the National Endowment for the Arts (NEA) for art that he considers obscene, anti-Christian, and anti-American. In 1997, in a widely publicized demonstration against public funding of such art, Mawyer attempted to display some of the more questionable projects on the steps of the U.S. Capitol in Washington, D. C. The projects were not allowed to be displayed on the Capitol steps because they were deemed unfit for public viewing by Capitol security. After Mawyer and others had lobbied lawmakers for several years and testified at public hearings, the U.S. Congress decreased the amount of the appropriation for the NEA.

Mawyer has written two other books—*Pathways to Success: First Steps for Becoming a Christian in Action* (1994) and *Defending the American Family: The Pro-Family Contract with America* (1995)—and numerous educational booklets on current issues. Articles by him have appeared in *The Washington Post* and *Chronicles*, among other publications. He has also made guest appearances on a number of radio and television programs.

SUGGESTED READINGS

Web site of the Christian Action Network: http://www.christianaction.org

Michael Medved

Promoting Family Values in Modern Cinema

Born: October 3, 1948, Philadelphia, Pennsylvania
Education: B.A., Yale University, 1969; M.F.A., California State University, San Francisco, 1974.
Current position: Author, film reviewer

Michael Medved is the only nationally known film reviewer willing to challenge Hollywood's assumptions about the content viewers want in films. Medved has said that the entertainment industry has declared war on family values, and he has called for a reduction in the amount of sex, profanity, and violence portrayed in today's films.

Medved was born on October 3, 1948, in Philadelphia, Pennsylvania, to David Bernard and Renate Medved. Medved's father was a physicist, and his mother was a chemist. After graduating from high school in California, Medved attended Yale University in New Haven, Connecticut. After receiving his undergraduate degree, he entered Yale Law School but determined, after a year of study, that the law was not his career of choice. He returned to California, and became a speechwriter for various political campaigns. In 1974, while working in an advertising agency, he earned a Master's in fine art from California State University at San Francisco.

Medved has two careers, one as a writer and one as a film reviewer. After completing his master's degree, he began to write full time and went on the lecture circuit, speaking on the cultural influences of the film industry. In 1976, he coauthored his first book, *What Really Happened to the Class of '65*, with David Wallencinsky, a high school classmate and son of the novelist Irving Wallace. The book traced the lives of the students featured in a 1965 cover story in *Time* magazine on the aspirations of the '60s generation. Medved and Wallenchinsky had interviewed these students ten years later and found that their lives had not always lived up to their aspirations. This promise was based on the belief that altruism, combined with a higher level of education, would produce more successful adults who were socially aware. The show chronicled some of the failures of students in the 1960s who were supposed to embody this success.

In 1981, Medved began his career as a film reviewer. During this time, movie review television shows, especially shows such as *Siskel and Ebert at the Movies*, were popular. Medved began as the movie reviewer for WTBS, a cable television station, and Cable News Network in Los Angeles. In 1985, Medved became the cohost of the Public Broadcasting Network's *Sneak Previews*. The program was aired on most PBS stations and featured Medved and Jeffrey Lyons, a film reviewer for New York City television stations, offering commentary in a fashion similar to Siskel and Ebert. Medved's reviews frequently have criticized Hollywood for its failure to understand that the viewing public possesses traditional family values (a concept generally used to describe a belief in monogamous, heterosexual marriage and strong religious, especially Christian, beliefs). "You know that this is a profoundly religious country. Seventy-eight percent of us pray at least once a week, according to a *Newsweek* survey. And you never see this stuff in movies. The only time you ever see people in films as religious is as crooks or crazies" (*Christianity Today*, p. 40). According to Medved, the movies often present negative stereotypes of religion. "Only characters in the past are allowed to be identified with regular religious practices—like the minister in *A River Runs Through It*, which is set in the 1920s, and so he's allowed to go to church. Anyone in the 1980s—forget it. If a character goes to church, chances are he's a crook or crazy—like Robert DeNiro in Cape Fear. . . . No other group in America could be traduced with such breathtaking impunity" (*Christianity Today*, p. 24).

Because of his film reviews, numerous books, and lectures at colleges and high schools around the country, Medved is known as one of the most powerful voices promoting family values in popular culture today. He has said that there are a number of ways to convince the movie studios to produce films with less violence. He has found guides that list the amount of profanity and number of lewd acts in a given film useful. He has also suggested taking a positive approach by supporting films deemed good rather than simply raging against those deemed bad.

Medved has said that his religion is "traditional Judaism" and noted in the March 8, 1993 issue of *Christianity Today* that his religious commitment provides a balance in his work. He has been married twice. He is currently married to Diane Elvenstar, a clinical psychologist. They have three children, two girls and a boy.

SUGGESTED READINGS

Christianity Today, March 8, 1993, p. 24.

Medved, Michael. *Hollywood vs. America: Popular culture and the war on traditional values*. London: HarperCollins, 1993.

Medved, Michael, and Diane Medved. *Saving childhood: Protecting our children from the national assault on innocence*. New York: HarperCollins, 1998.

Ralph Graham Neas, Jr.

Countering the Forces of Conservatism on Freedom of Speech

Born: May 17, 1946, Brookline, Massachusetts
Education: B.A., University of Notre Dame, 1968; J.D., University of Chicago Law School, 1971
Current position: President, People for the American Way

Ralph Neas has brought a strong background in the political process to his leadership of the People for the American Way (PFAW). PFAW is, its web site states, a nonprofit organization dedicated to "defending the values our country was founded on: pluralism, individuality, and freedom of thought, expression, and religion." The organization was created by Norman Lear, the well-known television producer of such shows as *All in the Family* and *The Jeffersons*, to counter the Christian right's views on censorship.

Neas was born in Brookline, Massachusetts, to Ralph Graham Neas and Elsie Marie Barone Neas. After graduating from high school, he attended the University of Notre Dame and earned his B.A. in 1968. He then chose a career in law and graduated from the University of Chicago Law School in 1971. His first job took him to the Library of Congress where he became a legislative attorney on civil rights for the Congressional Research Office. Neas became known for his abilities, and in 1973 he signed on as a legislative assistant to Senator Edward Brooke, a Republican from Massachusetts. When Brooke was defeated for reelection in 1978, Neas, who had become his chief legislative assistant, joined the staff of Republican Senator David Durenberger of Minnesota. During his career as a member of the Senate staff, he became the senior staffer on civil rights and drafted the first Women's Economic Equity Act. He also worked extensively on legislation involving campaign finance reform, consumer rights, education, and reproductive rights.

In 1979, while on Senator Durenberger's staff, Neas was diagnosed

AP Photo/Wilfredo Lee. Courtesy of AP/Wide World Photos.

with Guillain-Barré syndrome (GBS), a type of acute nerve inflammation that can cause paralysis. As a result, Neas became an advocate for the disabled and helped to found the Guillain-Barré Syndrome Foundation (now the Guillain-Barré Syndrome Foundation International). His work for this organization led to an affiliation with the Leadership Conference on Civil Rights, the nation's oldest and largest coalition promoting civil rights and racial equality. The affiliation began because of the conference's work on behalf of the civil rights of the handicapped. In 1981, however, Neas became the first full-time executive director of the Leadership Conference. During his leadership, he directed various national campaigns that strengthened every major civil rights law. Landmark laws enacted in part as a result of the lobbying done by Neas and the Leadership Conference on Civil Rights include the Civil Rights Act of 1991, the 1990 Americans with Disabilities Act, the 1988 Fair Housing Act amendments, and the 1982 Voting Rights Act extension. In a 1995 statement on the floor of the Senate, Senator Edward Kennedy called Neas the "101st senator for civil rights."

Neas left the organization's demanding and hectic schedule in 1995 to become a law professor at Georgetown University. He also opened his own consulting firm, Neas Group. Although he had belonged to the Republican Party when he was a Senate staffer, in 1998, he made an unsuccessful run for Congress as the Democratic nominee for Maryland's eighth congressional district. He has said of his switch to the Democratic Party, "To understand me, you really have to understand what's happened to the Rockefeller wing of the Republican Party—it's virtually gone. The Republican Party has become the party of Ralph Reed, Tom DeLay, Newt Gingrich, and Dick Armey. That was a party I was no longer comfortable with" (*National Journal Magazine*, p. 564).

When he was offered the presidency of PFAW in 1995, he viewed it as a way to challenge the conservative political tide. Since becoming president of the PFAW, Neas has campaigned for gay and lesbian rights, fought the nomination of former Senator John Ashcroft as the U.S. attorney general, and led campaigns against religious practices considered unconstitutional in public schools. In these efforts, he has had the full support of the organization's founder, Norman Lear.

Neas has received numerous awards in his career, including the Hubert H. Humphrey Civil Rights Award from the Leadership Conference on Civil Rights, the Benjamin Hooks Keeper of the Flame Award from the National Association for the Advancement of Colored People (NAACP), the Flag Bearer Award from the Parents, Families, and Friends of Lesbians and Gays (PFLAG), and the Kennedy Lifetime Achievement Award from the Disability Rights Education and Defense Fund. He lives in Bethesda, Maryland, with his wife Katy Beth Neas. They have an infant daughter, Maria.

SUGGESTED READINGS

National Journal Magazine, February 19, 2000, p. 564.

Pelka, Fred. *The ABC-CLIO Companion to the Disability Rights Movement*. Santa Barbara, CA: ABC-CLIO, 1997.

Web site of People for the American Way: http://www.pfaw.org

Monique Nelson

Protecting Children from Pornography

Born: December 16, 1942, Nice, France
Education: High school diploma
Current position: Chief operating officer, Enough Is Enough

Monique Nelson has been an advocate for children's health and safety for the past twenty years. In the biography she uses for her speaking engagements, she states that she realized when her first grandchild was born that she wanted to do something to make the world a safer place for children.

Nelson was born in Nice, France, during World War II. Her parents emigrated to the United States. In an interview with the authors, Nelson stated that "[I] came to this wonderful country when I was 7 years old. The only degree I have is from the school of hard knocks. When I was in high school, my parents didn't think it was appropriate for girls to go to college. So, I went right from high school, into the working world and soon after married and had children. After my children were in school, I started back to work in corporate America and worked my way up the corporate ladder by a lot of hard work."

In 1990, Nelson, who has spent most of her life in California, parlayed her business acumen into the presidency of Web Wise Kids, a foundation that seeks funds for the distribution of a computer game that is designed to educate children about the dangers of pedophiles on the Internet. The game, which is called Missing and was originally developed by two Canadian computer programmers for the Royal Canadian Mounted Police, provides an interactive real-life example in using computer game operations kids are familiar with to show them how to avoid pedophiles.

Since its creation in 1992, Nelson has played a significant role in Enough Is Enough, an antipornography organization headquartered in Santa Ana, California that states that its mission is "to make the

Internet safe for children and families." To accomplish its mission, Enough Is Enough has worked to awaken Congress, media, schools, and libraries to the issue of pornography on the Internet. The organization also has worked closely with the technology community to promote corporate responsibility, especially where the distribution of pornography and obscenity can reach children, such as encouraging companies not to advertise with appeals that would attract children's interests. The organization's web site states that it stands for three values: (1) freedom of speech as defined by the U.S. Constitution, (2) a culture where people are respected and valued; childhood with a protected period of innocence; healthy sexuality; and a society free from the sexual exploitation of children and women, and (3) an environment where people are free to raise their children and conduct their lives without sexual predators or the relentless intrusion of unwanted sexual material. Nelson became the chief operating officer of the organization in 2000.

In 2000, Nelson testified before Congress on the Communications Decency Act (CDA), which made it a crime, with a prison sentence and/or fines, to use what the law said was indecent or patently offensive speech on a computer network that could be viewed by a minor, and criticized the Supreme Court's decision to strike down the act as unconstitutional. In 1997, after the New York State Attorney General's office conducted a program to catch child pornographers using the Internet, Nelson was quoted in the press as saying, "This really underscores the need for a crackdown on this kind of material on the Internet. Our opponents said that child porn on the Internet was sparse, but 200,000 images is not what I'd call sparse. [Through repeated downloads of pornographic images] those babies are exploited over and over again" (ZDNET News Channel). Nelson has also testified before Congress on legislation authorizing the Commission on Child Online Protection (August 3, 2000) to recommend to Congress technological or other methods to reduce the access of minors to harmful material on the Internet. "Pedophiles call the Internet the 'playground of the millennium.' In the privacy of their homes, they can lure children off the net and into their snare. . . . Enough Is Enough believes it is imperative to educate the parents, teachers, and caregivers how to make the Internet a *safe*, educational and entertaining environment." Nelson told Congress on August 3, 2000, that Enough Is Enough has many educational activities to promote its goals, including PTA presentations, Kids Rule mouse pads that are distributed to schools and community groups, its own web site, print publications distributed through normal channels, a video production, and public speaking engagements by Enough Is Enough board members.

Nelson resides in Santa Ana, California. She is a noted national lecturer and a frequent guest on local and national radio and television shows. She has appeared on the *CBS Evening News*, *The Michael Reagan Show*, Fox News, MSNBC, and the *Warren Duffy Show*. She has three children and eight grandchildren, whom she considers her proudest achievement.

SUGGESTED READINGS

Web site of Enough Is Enough: http://www.enough.org

ZDNET News Channel. "Will CDA return after kiddie porn exposed? September 30, 1997. http://www5.zdnet.com/zdnn/content/zdnn/0930/zdnn0019.html.

Allen H. (Al) Neuharth

Defending Freedom of the Press

Born: March 22, 1924, Eureka, South Dakota
Education: B.A., University of South Dakota, 1950
Current position: Writer; newspaper columnist

"Fate made me an S.O.B. I'd like to take credit for it, but I really can't. Fate—and others—had much more to do with it than I did," Allen Neuharth said in his autobiography *Confessions of an S.O.B.* (p. 1). For Al Neuharth, S.O.B. is a proud badge to wear. "People often call me an S.O.B. Some to my face, with a smile. Others behind my back with a smirk. They meant either that:

• I was a thorn in their side or a pain in the ass
• I had won their admiration, affection, even envy

AP Photo-Peter Cosgrove. Courtesy of AP/Wide World Photos.

The nice thing about being called an S.O.B. in today's world is that it means whatever you want it to mean" (p. 1).

Al Neuharth is the founder of the Freedom Forum, a nonpartisan, international foundation dedicated to free press, free speech, and free spirit for all people. The Freedom Forum operates the Newseum, an interactive news museum, the Newseum's NewsCapade with Al Neuharth, and the First Amendment Center, which has offices at Vanderbilt University in Nashville, Tennessee. The Freedom Forum was founded originally as the Gannett Foundation, a philanthropic foundation to support journalism and journalism education, begun in 1935 by Frank E. Gannett. In 1991, Al Neuharth began the Freedom Forum to support freedom of the press in 1991. The Freedom Forum "conducts national and international initiatives to promote its priorities. It does so primarily through programs rather than grants" (http://www.freedomforum.org). These programs range from forums on news events to the Newseum and its activities.

Neuharth earned a B.A. in journalism from the University of South Dakota in 1950 and then became a reporter for the Associated Press. In 1952, working with a fellow journalist, he produced his own statewide weekly tabloid called the *SoDak Sports*. Despite his best efforts, the tabloid failed, and Neuharth went into debt. Neuharth views this failure as one of the greatest lessons he ever learned. "Everyone should fail (or get fired) once before they're forty. . . . I learned more from that failure than from any of the successes in later life. The most important thing I learned is that the sky doesn't fall when you fail. Chicken Little was wrong. The moon and stars are still there. And the next time you reach for them, you're more likely to get them in your grasp" (Neuharth, *Confessions*, pp. 25, 26).

In 1954, Neuharth moved to Florida to continue his career in journalism. He worked for the *Miami Herald* as a reporter and later spent seven years as the assistant managing editor there. In 1960, he became an assistant executive editor for the Detroit *Free Press*. Eventually, he was noticed by the Gannett Company newspaper conglomerate and was hired as the general manager of its two Rochester, New York, newspapers.

Neuharth's first new newspaper for Gannett was called *Today*, later called *Florida Today*, which he began in 1961. Although breaking into the newspaper market with a new product is difficult, *Today* became one of the biggest selling newspapers in the history of Florida.

In 1982, in the face of declining newspaper readership, Neuharth created *USA Today*, a nationally distributed newspaper. Before starting the paper, he asked Lou Harris, a well-known opinion pollster, to find out why the decline was occurring. Harris found that the television generation was not going to read dull, gray newspapers and that it wanted a maximum of information with a minimum of time and hassle. "That more than any other factor caused us to start *USA Today* in 1982. We made it look like TV in print."

Of all his accomplishments, Neuharth may be proudest of the Freedom Forum and his support for freedom of the press. "Free spirit is what makes all of our First Amendment freedoms work. . . . Free spirit has created everything from better moustraps to new nations. . . . When we founded the Freedom Forum in 1991, we wanted a slogan or credo for that international foundation, which is dedicated to fostering freedoms for all people. A study committee suggested: Free Press, Free Speech, Free Spirit. I loved it . . . In my book, free spirit is individualism. Original thinking. Saying no to the status quo. Looking for better ways to learn and live. To succeed and to share" (Neuharth, *Free Spirit*, Prologue). The Freedom Forum has honored many people since 1992. Its first award was given to Terry Anderson, a journalist who endured 2,455 days of captivity at the hands of Islamic terrorists in Lebanon. Originally called the Free Spirit Award, the award is now named after Neuharth himself.

Neuharth retired from the Gannett Corporation in 1989. However, he still writes a weekly column, entitled "Plain Talk," for *USA Today*. "Many have asked me why I keep writing my weekly 'Plain Talk' column . . . since my retirement. Several reasons. It's a part-time, not full-time, job. It's fun. It keeps me in touch with people and them in touch with me" (Neuharth, *Free Spirit*, p. 42).

SUGGESTED READINGS

Neuharth, Al. *Confessions of an s.o.b.* New York: Doubleday/Currency, 1989.
———. *Free spirit: How you can get the most out of life at any age.* Arlington, VA: Newseum Books, 2000.
Web site of the Freedom Forum: http://www.freedomforum.com

Marcia Pally

Sense and Censorship

Education: B.S., Cornell, 1971; M.A., University of California and Los Angeles, 1974; Ed.D., New York University, 1995
Current position: Professor at New York University and Fordham University; author, film critic, and columnist

The feminist movement, born out of centuries of discrimination against women, has united many women in their struggle for fair treatment. In recent years, however, the feminist movement has been divided over the issue of pornography. Although most feminists view the sex industry—from the making of pornographic films to prostitution—as an exploitation of women, some feminists, such as Catherine MacKinnon, believe pornography should be censored because

it is a form of sexual discrimination. Other feminists, such as Dr. Marcia Pally, agree with Betty Friedan, who said, "To suppress free speech in the name of protecting women is dangerous and wrong" (http://www.well.com/user/freedom).

Pally received a B.A. from Cornell University in 1971 and went on to UCLA for her master's degree. She then returned to New York to complete her doctorate in education at New York University. She now teaches at New York University and Fordham University.

Pally told the authors in an interview that "the greatest influence guiding me to become involved with social issues is the Jewish day school that I attended from the first through the eighth grades, The Solomon Schechter School, and the tradition of Jewish social justice that my parents also believe in and work towards." She is the past vice president of The Freedom to Read Foundation, has served on The Media and Communications Committee of the American Civil Liberties Union (ACLU), and is the founder and past president of Feminists for Free Expression (FFE).

"The Feminists for Free Expression," FFE's, web site states, "is a group of diverse feminists working to preserve the individual's right to read, listen, view, and produce materials of her choice without the intervention of the state 'for her own good.'" The organization, which was founded in 1992, opposes censorship because it believes that censorship is a superficial way to solve complex problems. In a position statement on its web page, FFE states, "Feminists for Free Expression is deeply concerned about this trend [censorship of books, art, and so forth], for censoring disagreeable ideas will not make the disagreeable realities go away and only distracts people's attention from addressing the real causes of social ills. Censorship harms all groups working for social change—especially women." FFE has also taken strong stands on abortion, sexual harassment, and pornography.

The organization does not defend the production of pornography but argues that censorship does not end the exploitation of women. "Sexism, not sex, degrades women. Though sexism pervades our culture in many forms, we will not eliminate it by banning sex. Sexism and violence stem from long-standing economic, political and emotional factors. It is these that need addressing" (http://www.well.com/user/pornography.html).

Pally has been a film critic and columnist in the United States and Europe for the past nineteen years. She is the author of two books on censorship and freedom of expression, *Sex & Sensibility: Reflections on Forbidden Mirrors and the Will to Censor* (1994) and *Sense & Censorship: The Vanity of Bonfires* (1991). She has also written for the *New York Times*, the *Village Voice*, *The Nation*, *Film Comment*, *Cineaste*, *Index on Censorship*, *Z Papers*, and *die Zeit*, and lectured at Harvard, Columbia, University of Chicago, Cornell, New York University, and the Cato Institute. (The Cato Institute is a nonprofit, public policy research foundation promoting the principles of limited government and free markets.)

In 1997, along with Mike Godwin (see p. 70) and Stephen Bates, a senior fellow at the Annenberg Washington Program, she was a featured speaker at the Cato Institute's policy forum "Do Movies and Music Cause Violence? Sex, Cyberspace, and the First Amendment." Her remarks addressed the charge that censorship would protect women:

Will life improve if we ban some image, rock music, or movie? . . . Violence and sexism flourished for thousands of years before the printing press and the camera. Today countries where no sexual imagery or Western music is permitted—countries such as Saudi Arabia, Iran, and China—do not boast strong records of social harmony or strong women's rights records. For millennia, teenagers have managed to become pregnant without the aid of sexual imagery, rock n'roll, or matrimony. . . . In light of the historical record of violence and sexual abuse, it is unlikely that their cause lies in a Johnny-come-lately industry such as mass-market pornography or rock n'roll, or rap. Banning sexually explicit material is not likely to reduce those abuses or assist women and children. The social science data come to the same conclusion. (http://gos.sbc.edu/p/pally.html)

Pally has appeared on the *Phil Donahue Show, Pozner & Donahue, Crier & Co.*, and programs on the British Broadcasting Company and the Canadian Broadcasting Company. Her career, however, is not focused entirely on combating censorship. She is the author of *Screening English: Studying Movies for Reading, Writing, and Critical Thinking* (1997), a textbook that uses film studies to develop critical thinking and writing in the English as a second language classroom, and her work has appeared in numerous professional journals, including the *Journal of Adolescent and Adult Literacy, Journal of Second Language Writing, Language and Education, TESL-EJ*, and others.

SUGGESTED READINGS

Pally, Marcia. *The flight from critical thinking*. Berlin, Germany: Verlag/Ber Teslman, 2002.
———. *Screening English: Studying movies for reading, writing, and critical thinking*. White Plains, NY: Pearson Press, 1997.
———. *Sense and censorship: The vanity of bonfires*. New York: The Freedom to Read Foundation, 1991.
———. *Sex & sensibility: Reflections on forbidden mirrors and the will to censor*. Hillsdale, NJ: Ecco Press, 1994.
Web site for Feminists for Free Expression: http://www.well.com/user/

Robert W. Peters

Combating Pornography Through the Law

Born: January 13, 1949, LaSalle, Illinois
Education: B.S., Dartmouth College, 1971; J.D., New York School of Law, 1975
Current position: President, Morality in Media

Robert Peters is the current president of Morality in Media, an organization dedicated to fighting hard-core pornography. The organization was founded by the Reverend Morton A. Hill, S.J. (see p. 87), Robert E. Wiltenberg, a Lutheran minister, and Julius G. Neumann, a rabbi, in 1962. Peters' life was not always so dedicated to Christian beliefs. In fact, the path he has followed to become an antipornography crusader has been a rocky one.

Born in LaSalle, Illinois, Peters graduated from the LaSalle-Peru Township High School in 1967 and entered Dartmouth College. He was the co-captain of the school's 1970 undefeated football team and won the team's award as the team member with the foulest mouth. Peters recalls that life at Dartmouth was unlike anything he had experienced before. The moral consensus he had known in his youth was gone. During his years in college he saw the college's rules change from strict discipline to the point where drugs were sold openly. The collapse of authority extended to the clergy as well. He once witnessed an Episcopal minister struggling to defend the existence of God.

After graduating from Dartmouth in 1971, Peters entered the New York School of Law. However, he entered the school with a drinking problem and, as a result, suffered two nervous breakdowns while there. The first came in September 1972 when, after a heavy drinking party, Peters says, "I spent the better part of two days wandering the streets of New York City." While on a leave of absence after this drinking bout, he met an old high-school classmate who, he explains, touched him profoundly. "From my experience, something happened at that moment before God and man was for me a real experience. . . . My faith is not based on that experience, but I was open once again to claims of the Christian faith. I was now willing to take a chance" (*Daily News Tribune*, p. A1).

After graduating from law school in 1975, Peters became a VISTA attorney in New York City. VISTA, the stateside equivalent of the Peace Corps, works to improve the lives of the poor and disenfranchised in urban and rural America. Peters spent a year representing tenants in Manhattan's landlord-tenants court and then left the practice of law to become an assistant pastor in a small church. The pastor of the church took a stand against gay rights and asked Peters to conduct a campaign against the gay rights bill then before the New York City Council. "It was not long before I was working on the morality issues full-time—sex education, gay rights, you name it. . . . I didn't want to do it at first, but I saw there was something to this morality stuff. There are a lot of things they don't teach in college and I soon saw this was serious stuff" (*Daily News Tribune*, p. A2).

When Peters began as a staff attorney at Morality in Media in 1985, he planned to leave after only a few years. He explains, however, when he told the authors that "I learned about constitutional obscenity and indecency laws. I learned how pornography harms children and adults." In 1987, he was named the assistant director of the National Obscenity Law Center (NOLC). He has been president of Morality in Media since 1992. In his interviews he said, "Part of the challenge of working at Morality in Media is that there will always be people willing to purchase porn and others ready to supply it for a price. At best, law enforcement can drastically reduce the flow of pornography—but not eliminate it."

Although Peters has had numerous successes in combating pornography over the years, he views the provision in the recent telecommunications law that granted cable operators the option of keeping pornography off leased access channels as his greatest success. He was also helped to prepare the language for the Minnesota State obscenity law.

Peters is a frequent guest speaker on television. He has been interviewed on several occasions by Larry King on *Larry King Live!* and was featured on an episode of CBS's *48 Hours*. In 1993, Phil Donohue devoted an entire show to obscenity issues and invited Peters and Monsignor Jim Lisante as his guests. "I can do my best to expose the evils of porn and media sleaze" Peters stated, "and to show people what they can do to fight back; but as I see it, it is not my responsibility to force people to choose good. It is up to the American people and their leaders to make that decision."

Peters authored the article "Information Superhighway or Technological Sewer: What Will It Be?" which appeared in the December 1994 issue of the *Federal Communications Law Journal*. In October, 2000, he described what he sees as the problems with violence and sex in current TV programs before a full hearing of the Federal Communications Commission.

Peters looks for success anywhere pornography can be attacked. As he told the authors in an interview, "It is, of course, my hope and prayer that one day the American people will insist that obscenity and indecency laws be enforced; and that they will also stand up and tell mainstream media outlets, large and small: 'If you continue to pollute our culture and our children's minds, we will no longer do business with you.' If that day does come, the United States will still be an imperfect country; but it will be a much better place to live and raise children. My goal is not a perfect nation, but a better one."

SUGGESTED READINGS

Daily News Tribune, Princeton, IL, June 29, 1998, p. A1.
Morality in Media Newsletter, a publication of Morality in Media.
Web site of Morality in Media: http://www.moralityinmedia.org

Michael Powell

Synergy in the Bookstore Business

Born: July 29, 1941, Portland, Oregon
Education: University of Chicago
Current position: President, Powell's Books

Because most censorship controversies begin in the community, one might think that booksellers would go out of their way to avoid such controversies. After all, these controversies have the potential to polarize the buying public, and in the competitive environment of the book business, it is difficult to overcome the loss of a significant portion of clientele the bookseller serves. Michael Powell, however, believes that nothing is gained by avoiding controversy.

Powell's bookstore business began in 1970 in Chicago, Illinois, when he was in graduate school at the University of Chicago. A group of friends and professors at the University of Chicago encouraged Powell to assume a lease on a bookstore. Powell borrowed $3,000 and opened his store. His used books store was so successful that he was able to pay back the loan within two months. Powell's father, Walter, a retired painting contractor from Portland, Oregon, spent one summer in Chicago working with his son and returned to Portland so excited about the used book business that he opened his own store in 1971.

In 1979, Michael Powell sold his Chicago store and joined his father in Portland, Oregon, in a joint bookstore business. In 1981, he

purchased his father's share in the store. By that time, Powell and his father had so expanded the business that it occupied the space formerly held by a car dealership and repair shop. Powell's City of Books, as they called the store, employs a rather unorthodox concept in its business: Used and new copies of a title are shelved together. The store is open 365 days a year and staffed by knowledgeable and dedicated book lovers. There are now four full-service Powell bookstores (City of Books, Powell's at Cascade Plaza, Powell's on Hawthorne, and Powell's at PDX), three specialty stores (Powell's Technical Books, Powell's Travel Store, and Powell's Books for Cooks & Gardeners), and powells.com, which went online in 1996. The business remains focused on used and hard-to-find titles. Seventy percent of the stock is comprised of used, out-of-print, and rare books.

Michael Powell has been at the center of Portland's social, political, and artistic growth since 1979. As he told the authors in an interview, "When we started bringing authors to town, you couldn't get a decent author to visit Portland. Portland's access to ideas, authors, and books has grown because Powell's has grown. It's not cause and effect, but it's synergy." Powell's store was the first business to sponsor the city's author lecture series, which began in the early 1980s. Carrie Hoops, director of the series, has said, "We get people to come here because Powell's is here. If there's a new edition of the Bible, people expect God to be at Powell's to sign books."

Powell is adamant about the importance of free expression and civil rights. David Fidanque, head of the Oregon American Civil Liberties Union, has said, "When you call Michael on a free-expression issue, if he's not on it already, he'll be there soon" (Press Release for Powell's Books). When *Satanic Verses* by Salman Rushdie was published in 1989 and the Iranian Islamic government issued a death warrant for Rushdie, many large bookstore chains took the book off their shelves, hoping to avoid the controversy, but Powell's continued to carry it. In 1994 and 1996, in response to antipornography initiatives in Oregon, Powell turned his store into an advertisement for free speech and free thought by placing orange tags below all the titles the store carried that had been censored in the past, including *Huckleberry Finn*. In both cases, the legislation was defeated. Powell has been recognized for his support of freedom of expression by a number of organizations, including the American Library Association (ALA).

Over the years, Powell's committed community interests have led him to become involved with numerous civic organizations, including the World Affairs Council, Port of Portland, Association for Portland Progress, Metropolitan Arts Commission, Multnomah County Library Board, Pacific Northwest Booksellers Association, American Booksellers Association, Portland Public Schools Foundation, Portland State University Library Advisory Committee, and the SMART (Start Making a Reader Today) Program Advisory Committee.

The mission statement for Powell's states Michael Powell's stance clearly. It reads, in part, "We have a social responsibility to the community and to our industry to fight censorship, promote literary awareness, and encourage authors and their works."

SUGGESTED READINGS

Hull, Mary E. *Censorship in America*. Santa Barbara, CA: ABC-CLIO, 1999.
    Web site for Powell's Books: http://www.powells.com

Michael W. Roberts

Protecting the Rights of Authors

Born: October 14, 1949, Houston, Texas
Education: B.A., Dartmouth College, 1971; J.D., Harvard University, 1979; Ph.D., Harvard University, 1980
Current position: Executive director, PEN American Center

Michael Roberts has recently taken over the leadership of PEN American Center, one of the most important free speech organizations in the United States. Roberts was born in Houston, Texas, in 1949 to Paul Wakely Roberts and Audrey Roberts. After graduating from high school, Roberts attended Dartmouth College, graduating *summa cum laude* (with highest honors) in 1971. He then entered law school at Harvard University and reached his Juris Doctor in 1979. During his legal studies at Harvard, Roberts found himself torn between the law and literature. Influenced by the poet Robert Lowell who was at Harvard when he was, he decided to keep pursuing literature. Roberts also worked on a Ph.D. in English and American Literature. He completed that degree in 1980.

After receiving his Ph.D., Roberts went into private practice with the law firm of Sullivan and Worchester in Boston, but stayed only long enough to get some experience in the legal profession. He then returned to Harvard to teach literature and enjoy an intellectual lifestyle. In 1991, Roberts began to work for Neil Rudenstein, the new president of the university. By 1992, he had become the secretary of the university, and served as a member of the senior administrative team managing the affairs of the university's two boards, the Harvard Corporation and the Board of Overseers.

By 1998, Roberts was ready to seek a new direction in his career. He joined PEN American Center. PEN American Center, which is an affiliate of International PEN, is an association of 2,600 American writers dedicated to advancing literature and the reading of literature. PEN believes that freedom of expression must be vigorously defended. PEN American Center accomplishes its goals through its Freedom-to-Write Program, which is the prime advocacy arm on behalf of free expression, readers and writers book groups to promote literacy and reading, PEN forums (which are public literary programs), and seventeen literary awards. Roberts sees the mission of PEN American Center as one of promoting, through the prestige of writers, freedom of expression as both an ideal and a reality. "We have to recognize and exploit our character as an organization of *writers* and people who recognize and support distinctive writing. Our great strengths are the lingering, almost magical prestige of writers, the extraordinary distinction of the membership, and our ability to convene the voices that 'forge the uncreated conscience of the race,' to paraphrase Joyce on the role of writers. These give us the wherewithal to do a great deal if we can mobilize effectively" (*PEN Newsletter*, p. 3). Roberts now resides in New York City where PEN American Center is headquartered. He has taken over the reigns of the organization from Karen Kennerly who headed PEN American Center until 1998.

SUGGESTED READINGS

Chute, Marchette G. *P.E.N. American center: A history of the first fifty years.* New York: PEN American Center, 1987.
PEN Newsletter. Issue 101, September–October 1998, p. 3.
Web site for PEN American Center: http://www.pen.org.

Pat Robertson

Christian Service

Born: March 22, 1930, Lexington, Virginia
Education: B.A., Washington and Lee University, 1950; Juris Doctor, Yale University Law School, 1955; M. Div., New York Theological Seminary, 1959
Current Positions: Founder and chairman of the Christian Broadcasting Network; Founder and chancellor of Regent University

---

Televangelism has become a significant media phenomena and a potent force for social and moral change. Marion Gordon Robertson, or Pat Robertson, as he prefers to be called, has been a pioneer in both televangelism and the promotion of conservative Christian ideals. He has spoken out against pornography, abortion, the teaching of evolution, and secular humanism for a longer time and more effectively than many other well-known televangelists, including Jerry Falwell. Robertson has achieved national and international recognition as a radio and television broadcaster, religious leader, philanthropist, educator, businessman, author, and leader in public affairs.

Robertson was born on March 22, 1930, in Lexington, Virginia. He was the younger of two sons of Absalom Willis Robertson and Gladys Churchill Robertson. Robertson's father, A. Willis Robertson, served in Congress for thirty-four years as a congressman and senator from Virginia. Robertson's other distinguished ancestors include two former U.S. presidents, Benjamin Harrison and William Henry Harrison, and a signer of the Declaration of Independence, Benjamin Harrison. Robertson has said that, as a child, he was greatly influenced by his father's love of politics. His mother's born-again Christian faith also made a strong impression on him.

Robertson attended Washington and Lee University in his hometown of Lexington, Virginia, and was a member of the Sigma Alpha Epsilon fraternity. He spent a year studying economics at the University of London in England but dropped out in 1950 to join the Marine Corps. After two years of service in the Marines, Robertson entered Yale Law School. By the time he had received his Juris Doctor in 1955, however, he had become disillusioned with the legal profession for what he considered its lack of moral absolutes and went to work as a financial analyst in New York. While doing so, Robertson told the authors, "I became deeply concerned about my own personal life, and as a consequence, after a time of spiritual searching, I had an encounter with Jesus Christ, accepted His death on the cross as being personal for me, and from that moment on made Him the Lord of my life. To use the phrase of the Apostle Paul, I became a 'new creature in Christ' and embraced a central motivating theme for my life to serve God and to help my fellow man."

As a result, Robertson entered the New York Theological Seminary. After graduating, he and his family moved to Bedford-Stuyvesant, one of the worst slum areas in Brooklyn, New York. At first, he planned to open a mission there, but he came to feel that God had a different path for him. He moved back to Virginia and borrowed money to buy a run-down UHF station in the Tidewater area. In doing so, he acquired both a television and radio station. In 1960, he applied for a Federal Communications Commission license. Robertson's popular *700 Club* came about during this time and gets its name from his appeal to 700 people to pledge $10 per month to keep the station running. Robertson is now the founder and chairman of the Christian Broadcasting Network. Programs that his companies produce are seen in 155 countries and heard in sixty-four different languages, including Russian, Arabic, Romanian, Spanish, French, and Chinese.

Robertson is also the founder of Operation Blessing International Relief and Development Corporation, which he started in 1978. Since then, Operation Blessing has distributed more than $500 million worth of food, medicine, clothing, and services to the poor and needy around the world. In 1996, Operation Blessing completed the conversion of a Lockheed L-1011-50 wide-body jet airliner into a flying hospital. The plane brings state-of-the-art medical assistance to people in developing countries who have little access to basic health care. Robertson has also founded the American Center for Law and Justice (ACLJ), International Family Entertainment, PorchLight Entertainment, CENCO Refining, and Zhaodaola China Internet. In 1977, Robertson founded CBN University, now Regent University, a higher education institution that awards masters and doctoral degrees in law, business administration, communications, education, theology, and government. Robertson is chancellor of the university, which was built at the same time as the CBN Center, a $20 million complex in Virginia Beach. In 1981, Robertson formed the Freedom Council, a tax-exempt grassroots foundation aligned with the National Perspectives Institute, a conservative think tank. Until recently, both the council and the institute were subsidized by the Christian Broadcasting Network.

During the presidential primaries in 1988, Robertson was a candidate for the nomination of the Republican Party. He ran first in five states, second in seven states, and finished third behind George Bush and Bob Dole. Robertson espouses the values that were embodied in Ronald Reagan's presidency. He does not see his constituency as "right-wing," but rather as "the new center" of the Republican Party. In 1990, using the political base he had developed during his campaign, Robertson founded the Christian Coalition, which now has over 1,200,000 active members in fifty states. In 1996, the Christian Coalition distributed 45,000,000 voter guides and has been credited as a major force behind Republican Party victories. The Christian Coalition is a political organization devoted to promoting candidates who support Christian, especially conservative Christian, positions on such issues as abortion, prayer in the schools, and obscenity.

Robertson's values determine the programming on his network, which features news and commentary on such topics as abortion, pornography, and the occult. Robertson's National Legal Foundation, a Christian Public Interest Law Firm, has supported numerous challenges to school textbooks and library materials. In 1989, the National Legal Foundation initiated the legal controversy surrounding the *Impressions* textbook series, which was banned in many schools because of charges that it promoted secular humanism. The series contained over 800 stories for students to read and use for language and literature classes on such topics as abortion, teenage sex, and witchcraft that many conservatives found objectionable. Robertson believes that schools and government sometimes violate the rights of Christians, especially born-again Christians, to practice their faith. Jay Sekulow has worked closely with Robertson to develop the ACLJ into an effective advocacy organization.

Robertson has received many honors over the years, including the Humanitarian of the Year award from Food for the Hungry in 1982 and the Christian Broadcaster of the Year award from the National Religious Broadcasters Association in 1989. In 1992, *Newsweek* listed him among America's 100 cultural elite. He has written ten books, including *The Secret Kingdom* (1992), *Answers to 200 of Life's Most Probing Questions* (1984), and *The New World Order* (1991). He donates his CBN salary to the ministry, using the revenue from the sale of his books and other ventures for his personal income.

Robertson and his wife, Adelia Elmer Robertson, were married in 1954, and have four grown children (Timothy, Elizabeth, Gordon, and Ann) and fourteen grandchildren. Adelia Robertson, better known as Dede, is a nursing instructor. In his spare time, Robertson enjoys horseback riding. It is not known if Robertson will attempt to run for the presidency again. However, he will remain a visible force in the broadcasting world and a significant voice for conservative Christian values.

SUGGESTED READINGS

Donovan, John B. *Pat Robertson: The authorized biography*. New York: Macmillan, 1998.
Foerstel, Herbert N. *Free expression and censorship in America*. Westport, CT: Greenwood Press, 1997.
Robertson, Pat. *The autobiography of Pat Robertson: Shout it from the house tops*. South Plainfield, NJ: Bridge Publications, 1995.
Web site for the Christian Broadcasting Network: http://www.cbn.com/

Marc Rotenberg

Protecting Privacy on the Internet

Born: April 20, 1960, Boston, Massachusetts
Education: B.A., Harvard University, 1982; J.D., Stanford University, 1987

Current position: Executive director, Electronic Privacy Information Center

---

Personal privacy has long been considered integral to a free society and intellectual freedom. With the advent of the electronic age, government and private industry have a greater ability to invade personal privacy than ever before. For that reason, Marc Rotenberg has set out to champion the personal privacy cause.

Rotenberg was born in Boston, Massachusetts, on April 20, 1960, to Michael, a realtor in the Boston area, and Karen Rotenberg. His activism began, he told *Business Week Online*, at the age of seven, when he marched with a sandwich board to protest the Vietnam War with his parents. Rotenberg's interest in electronics and computers began at a young age as well. In the same interview, he recalled burning gouges in his mother's kitchen table with soldering guns while making calculators from kits with his brother Jonathan (*Business Week Online*). Rotenberg earned a B.A. from Harvard University in 1982. While there, he taught a computer science class to freshmen. "I'm probably the only person who has been into computers for 20 years who isn't making any money" (*Business Week Online*). He went on to study law at Stanford University and received his Juris Doctor in 1987.

Privacy of electronic information, especially privacy on the Internet, is Rotenberg's primary concern today. "Privacy is the No. 1 civil liberties issue of the new century and a way to make a difference," he has argued (*Business Week Online*). In 1994, to fulfill his passion for protecting electronic information from government and corporate scrutiny, he founded the Electronic Privacy Information Center (EPIC). Rotenberg has said, "There's this self-interested industry view that says, 'Give up your privacy and we can give you all sorts of benefits for doing so.' I say, lose your right to privacy and you lose your democratic freedoms" (*Business Week Online*). Rotenberg's center is funded by a wide range of nonprofit organizations, from the conservative Fund for Constitutional Government to the philanthropic Ford Foundation.

Rotenberg has realized a number of successes in his efforts to stem the invasion of privacy by corporations and the government, especially online. In 1999, he mounted a campaign to prevent Double Click, an Internet company, from using data on web surfers' behavior (without their knowledge) cross referenced with offline databases as a commodity for sale to anyone. After Rotenberg made consumer complaints to the Consumer Protection Agency, Double Click backed down. Rotenberg also threatened a boycott of Intel for using technology in its Pentium III chips that would make it easy for any organization, including the government, to track Net surfing. AOL Chairman Steve Case has said of Rotenberg, "The guy can cause a privacy uproar at the click of a mouse." Rotenberg believes consumers have become increasingly concerned about privacy. "I think people need to be aware that consumers are very concerned about how their personal information is going to be used. They go to a website and they're asked a lot of questions. It's not just 'What's the address this CD or sweater is going to?' They get asked questions like 'Do you have kids?' and 'How many vacations do you take a year?' People are uneasy about this. I think businesses at the front end really need to make privacy a priority. It's not just about a policy. It's about taking very seriously the fact that a lot of consumers are going to be concerned about how you're going to use the information about them that you collect" (*Business Week Online*).

Rotenberg teaches information privacy law part-time at Georgetown University Law Center. He is a frequent speaker at conferences and in the media. He has also testified before the U.S. Congress on privacy law issues. In June 2000, he and Whitfield Diffie, inventor of the "public key" in cryptography, Phil Karn, another cryptography pioneer, and Phil Zimmerman, inventor of a program called PGP (Pretty Good Privacy), testified before the U.S. Senate at a hearing on Internet privacy. Zimmerman had been under attack by the government and others for his program, which protects the privacy of information that the government considers dangerous to the national defense. Rotenberg told *TechTV* (a cable TV Network and integrated Web Site), "I think privacy legislation would be good for the Internet. There are a lot of people against this. My organization is a big believer in keeping the Internet open. But when it comes to privacy protection, an issue people feel so strongly about and which is so uncertain, some simple, predictable rules would be good. But the question is, if we go into the legislative process, will we be able to get some simple predictable rules out of it? I don't know that we would. But it's worth trying because one of the big problems is a lot of uncertainty both on the business side and the consumer side" (http://www.TechTv.com/story/).

Rotenberg's privacy advocacy has led him to become involved in a number of other activities. He serves on the cryptography policy and computer security panel for the Organization of Economic Cooperation and Development (OECD) and the cyberspace law panel for UNESCO, a United Nations agency, as well as other national and international advisory panels. He is also the editor of *The Privacy Law Sourcebook 2000* (2000) and, with Phil Agre, coeditor of *Technology and Privacy: The New Landscape* (1998). In 2000, he won the prestigious Norbert Wiener Award for professional and social responsibility, which is sponsored by Computer Professionals for Social Responsibility (CPSR). He has also won the Berkeley Center for Law and Technology Distinguished Service Award.

Rotenberg is married to Anna Markopoulos and has one son. In his spare time, he is an avid chess player and plays online. He also enjoy studies on German Expressionists because he believes that German Expressionists, particularly Franz Marc, George Grosz, and Kathe Kollwitz, embody the spirit of free speech. In 1995, in a speech before the American Library Association (ALA), he spoke of coming privacy issues: "One issue, in particular, is the question of anonymity. This is the next frontier of the privacy battle in the United States. Many of you, I am sure, have heard a lot about the battle of encryption. . . . But, anonymity, which is the right to control the disclosure of your identity, to decide when it is necessary and when it is not necessary for your name and your personal information to be known to others, could well be the key to privacy, and . . . by extension, to intellectual freedom in our information future" (*Newsletter on Intellectual Freedom*, p. 169).

SUGGESTED READINGS

Agre, Philip, and Marc Rotenberg, eds. *Technology and privacy: The new landscape*. Cambridge, MA: MIT Press, 1998.

Newsletter on Intellectual Freedom, September 1995, p. 169.

Rotenberg, Marc. *The privacy law sourcebook 2000: United States law, international law and recent developments*. Washington, D.C.: Electronic Privacy Information Center, 2000.

Stepanek, Marcia. "Marc Rotenberg." *Business Week Online*, May 15, 2000, http://www.businessweek.com/

Web site for Electronic Privacy Information Center: http://epic.org

(Ahmed) Salman Rushdie

A Death Threat from the World of Islam

Born: June 19, 1947, Bombay, India
Education: M.A., King's College, Cambridge University, 1968
Current position: Writer

Salman Rushdie, an author of celebrated but complex novels, has suffered the ultimate in censorship, an international death sentence that offers a bounty in the millions of dollars to anyone who kills him. Rushdie was born in Bombay, India, in 1947. His father was a successful businessman who sent Rushdie to King's College, Cambridge, England, when he was ready for college. Rushdie graduated with honors in 1968 and began an acting career at the Fringe Theatre in London. He has been a successful author of novels and short stories since 1975. Rushdie has written five novels to date: *Grimus* (1975), *Midnight's Children* (1980), *Shame* (1983), *The Satanic Verses* (1988), and *The Moor's Last Sigh* (1997). His second book, *Midnight's Children*, is his most critically acclaimed work. The novel chronicles the history of modern India through the lives of 1001 children born during the first hour of India's independence from Great Britain on August 15, 1947. The novel has won numerous literary prizes, including the Booker McConnell Prize for fiction in 1981.

It is Rushdie's *Satanic Verses*, however, that resulted in an act of international censorship. The novel, which is a complex narrative that tells many stories within a story, angered Muslims all over the world with what they believed to be its blasphemy of and insult to Islam. The book has been banned in more than a dozen, mostly Muslim, countries. After its publication in 1988, riots broke out in Pakistan, India, and even South Africa. In 1989, the Ayatollah Ruhollah Khomeini, the leader of Iran, issued a *fatwa*, death sentence, against Rushdie and his publisher. Three people associated with the publication of *The Satanic Verses* have been attacked over the years, including Rushdie's Japanese translator, who was killed by Islamic

AP Photo/Bjarke Oersted. Courtesy of AP/Wide World Photos.

extremists. To protect his life and the lives of his family, Rushdie has been forced into hiding. He rarely makes public appearances, and those few that he makes are often made unannounced. His first public appearance after the death sentence was on December 12, 1991, when he spoke on the occasion of the 200th anniversary of the U.S. Bill of Rights to the surprise of journalism students at Columbia University.

Rushdie has argued that the death sentence is the product of "contemporary thought police" who have created an Islamic culture in which one "may not discuss Mohammed as if he were human with human virtues and weaknesses. One may not discuss the growth of Islam as a historical phenomena, as an ideology born out of its turn." Rushdie, who has often compared Jesus with Mohammed, has said that, unlike Jesus, Mohammed "is not granted divine status, but the text (of the Koran) is." Many literary critics of Rushdie's work believe that those Muslims who have condemned Rushdie have not read

Satanic Verses or have misunderstood the excerpts they have read. Most critics feel the misunderstanding arises in those sections of the book in which a religion that is similar to Islam is portrayed with a prophet named Mahoud (a derisive epithet for Mohammed). In these sections, a scribe named Salman changes the prophet's diction, which appears to call the Koran's validity into question. Rushdie is also accused of using irreverent names throughout the book. One critic feels that the outrage comes from the belief that the novel treats the Islamic Holy Word as myth, not truth, because it portrays Mohammed as a fallible human being rather than as a deity. Rushdie has pointed out that, in Islam, Mohammed is seen in a very human way.

In his surprise appearance at Columbia University in 1991, Rushdie said, in part, "Free speech is the whole thing; the whole ball game. Free speech is life itself" (*New York Times*, p. B8). Although he avowed his faith in Islam publicly in an essay entitled "Why I Have Embraced Islam" in 1991, perhaps in hopes of ending the fatwa, the death sentence remains in place. In fact, the threats were renewed when the paperback version of *The Satanic Verses* was announced. Several nations have attempted to persuade Iran to withdraw the death sentence. Some hope arose in 1998 when a moderate Iranian government announced that the state would not enforce the edict nor encourage anyone to carry out the death sentence. In 1999, however, the Ayatollah Hassan Sanei promised 2.8 million to anyone who killed Rushdie.

Rushdie continues to speak out against censorship. He is a member of International PEN, a writers' organization with a strong anticensorship stance, and continues to be a productive author. In 1995 he published both *East, West*, a collection of short stories that illustrate the contrasting social and emotional visions of Eastern and Western culture, and *The Moor's Last Sigh*. *The Moor's Last Sigh*, which has been described as a satirical look at India's politics, won the Booker Prize and became a bestseller as well. Because of its veiled references to India's first prime minister, Jawaharlal Nehru, including a pun on his first name, the novel has been censored in India, and the Indian government has placed an embargo on its importation into the country.

Salman Rushdie has been married three times. In 1976, he wed Clarissa Luard, a publicity manager and literary agent for the British publisher Paul Elek. Rushdie and Clarissa had a son, Zafar, born in 1979. The couple were divorced in 1987 but stayed close until Clarissa died of cancer in 1999. Shortly before the publication of *The*

Satanic Verses, Rushdie married Marianne Wiggins, an American writer. Their marriage underwent severe strain during the years of hiding caused by the fatwa, and they were divorced in 1993. He then married the British author and publisher Elizabeth West, and they had a son, Milan. In 2001, after announcing that he had fallen in love with the model and actress Padma Lakshmi, Rushdie moved to New York City.

SUGGESTED READINGS

Appignanesi, Lisa, and Sara Maitland, eds. *The Rushdie file*. Syracuse, NY: Syracuse University Press, 1990.
Blumenthal, Ralph. "Safeguarding Rushdie." *New York Times*, December 12, 1991, p. B8.
For Rushdie: Essays by Arab and Muslim writers in defense of free speech. Anovar Abdallah, ed. New York: G. Braziller, 1994.
Weatherby, William J. *Salman Rushdie: Sentenced to death*. New York: Carroll & Graf Publishers, 1990.
"Why I have Embraced Islam." in *Imaginary homelands: Essays and criticism, 1981–1991* by Salman Rushdie. London: Granta Books, 1991.

Frederic R. (Rick) Schatz

Teaching Others How to Protect Children and Families from Internet Pornography

Born: August 21, 1944
Education: B.S., University of Cincinnati, 1966; M.B.A., Harvard University, 1969
Current position: President and chief executive office, National Coalition for the Protection of Children and Families

"My chief motivation for serving in this way is my faith commitment to Jesus Christ, and despite the challenges of this work, it has been a great blessing," Frederic R. Schatz, or Rick, as he prefers to be called, told the authors during an interview on December 6, 2000. As president and chief executive officer (CEO) of the National Co-

alition for the Protection of Children and Families (NCPCF), Schatz works to stop the illegal traffic in pornography. The NCPCF was originally founded in 1983 by the Reverend Jerry Kirk as the National Coalition Against Pornography, an alliance of citizen action groups, foundations, and religious denominations. The NCPCF's web site states, "We are a national nonprofit organization focused on protecting children and families from the harms of pornography and its messages. All pornography carries the risk of harm. Hardcore pornography and child pornography have been shown to promote sexual violence, degradation, and abuse of children and adults. The National Coalition opposes censorship. We promote responsibility and enforcement of laws against pornography."

Schatz did not begin his career as an antipornography fighter. After graduating from the University of Cincinnati with a degree in chemical engineering, he went on to a successful career in business. In 1969, he received an M.B.A. from Harvard University and joined Xomox Corporation, an international manufacturer of industrial equipment. In 1984, after serving as vice president of the corporation, Schatz began his own company, Creative Waterworks, and successfully developed one of the most popular water parks in the Cincinnati, Ohio, area.

Schatz sold the company in 1990 to practice his religion and to promote "decency and family values." His association with the Reverend Jerry Kirk helped him to secure his present position as the president and CEO. "My background in the business world and the opportunity to help lead the National Coalition for the Protection of Children and Families helped prepare me to give something back to make our culture a better place for people to live, grow, and mature," Schatz told the authors during his interview. The coalition coordinates the activities of the Religious Alliance Against Pornography (RAAP) and the National Law Center for Children and Families. His work with the coalition and his support of numerous other antipornography organizations such as Enough Is Enough, the National Obscenity Law Center (NOLC), and Morality in Media have placed Schatz in the forefront of the fight against pornography. Schatz told the authors, "Because I have been blessed, I have felt it more than appropriate when I began ten years ago in an effort to help protect the lives of children, women, men, and families from the destructive influence of pornography and its messages."

The NCPCF has been active in two recent efforts to prevent access to pornography. The NCPCF became involved in Operation Blue Ridge Thunder in Bedford, Virginia, which began when a thirteen-year-old girl was solicited for sexual favors by a pedophile over the Internet. With the help of the NCPCF, Operation Blue Ridge Thunder worked to build a local coalition to stop pedophiles, child pornography, and Internet pornography. Schatz told the group's members that filters should be used on home, school, and library computers. In Memphis, Tennessee, Citizens for Community Values, a local organization, lobbied the Shelby County Commission for the creation of an Internet filtering policy that could be enforced at the Memphis public libraries. Much of the development and success of the Citizens for Community Values was due to the consulting advice provided by Schatz and the NCPCF.

The National Coalition also produces *Filtering Review*, an online magazine that provides product reviews of Internet filtering products. *Filtering Review* can be accessed at www.filteringreview.com/contact.asp. It includes links to other resources, such as the web sites for Enough Is Enough and other coalition partners.

Schatz is an elder and founding member of the Evangelical Community Church in Cincinnati, Ohio. He and his wife Sharon have been married for thirty-three years and have three sons and two grandchildren. Even though Schatz finds his task a daunting one because law enforcement does not always support the coalition, he plans to continue to lead the coalition in its fight to stop pornography.

SUGGESTED READINGS

Web site for the National Coalition for the Protection of Children and Families: http://www.nationalcoalition.org

Phyllis Schlafly

Eagle Forum

Born: August 15, 1924, St. Louis, Missouri
Education: B.A., Washington University in St. Louis, 1944; Master's in Government, Harvard University, 1945; J.D., Washington University Law School, 1978
Current position: President, Eagle Forum

Phyllis Schlafly has been a national leader of the conservative movement since the publication of her best-selling book in 1964, *A Choice Not An Echo*, promoting the candidacy of Barry Goldwater in the 1964 presidential election. She has been a leader of conservative causes that have attempted to counter the feminist movement and that promote conservative family values since 1972, when she founded and became president of the STOP-ERA organization (now called Eagle Forum). She is also the founder and president of the Eagle Forum Education & Legal Defense Fund, a think-tank that has its national headquarters at the Eagle Forum Education Center in St. Louis.

Phyllis Schlafly was born on August 15, 1924 to John Bruce Stewart and Odille Dodge Stewart, in St. Louis, Missouri. Schlafly attended a Catholic parochial school, where she graduated valedictorian in her class of 1941. After high school, she enrolled in Maryville College of the Sacred Heart, another Catholic school, but transferred to Washington University in St. Louis in her junior year. When she completed her bachelor's degree in 1944, she was awarded a $500

scholarship to do graduate work at the prestigious Radcliffe College, a women's college associated with Harvard University. Schlafly earned an M.A. in political science in 1945 and promptly found work as a campaign aide to Missouri congressman Claude Bakewell. For the latter part of the 1940s, she worked for the First National Bank of St. Louis as a librarian and researcher. It was here that she met her husband, John Fred Schlafly, a lawyer from a wealthy St. Louis family.

After they married in the fall of 1949, Schlafly quit her job to become active in volunteer work, especially in Republican Party politics. She ran for her first political office in 1952, winning the Republican primary for Missouri's Twenty-Fourth Congressional seat held by Melvin Price. Though she lost to Price in the general election, she remained active in the Republican Party, holding delegate positions at the 1956, 1964, and 1968 Republican conventions. Schlafly also attempted another run for Congress in 1960, as a write-in candidate.

Schlafly is a prolific writer, contributing syndicated columns to 100 newspapers, along with her own newsletter, *The Phyllis Schlafly Report*, published monthly since 1967. She has written or edited sixteen books on various topics, including *The Power of the Positive Woman* (1977) on family and feminism; *Strike from Space* (1966) and *Kissinger on the Couch* (1975) on nuclear strategy; *Child Abuse in the Classroom* (1984) on education; *Who Will Rock the Cradle?* (1989) on child care; and *First Reader* (1994), which is a complete system to enable every parent to teach a child to read. Schlafly has presented commentaries on both radio and television since the 1970s, currently producing a 3-minutes-a-day 5-days-a-week radio commentary on 460 stations and a radio talk show on education called "Phyllis Schlafly Live," which airs on 45 stations. Her commentaries also appear on the Eagle Forum's Web site: www.eagleforum.org. Schlafly is an attorney, admitted to the practice of law in Illinois, Missouri, the District of Columbia, and the U.S. Supreme Court, and has served on numerous commissions, as well as testifying before more than fifty congressional and state legislative committees on constitutional, national defense, foreign policy, education, taxes, encryption, and family issues.

Schlafly has received numerous awards for service in a variety of fields. In 2000, the *Ladies' Home Journal* named her one of the 100 most important women of the twentieth century. She has received many awards for volunteer service to the Republican Party, serving in active roles since 1952. She was named one of the Ten Most Admired Women in the world in the *Good Housekeeping* poll, 1977–1990. The *World Almanac* named her one of the twenty-five Most Influential Women in America, 1978–1985. The mother of six (three lawyers, one physician, one Ph.D. mathematician, and one business-woman), she was named the Illinois Mother of the Year in 1992.

While a student, Schlafly worked her way through college at a federal small arms factory that manufactured weapons for the war effort in World War II. She often worked on the night shift, 48 hours a week, while attending classes in the morning. Schlafly told the authors that this experience helped her develop her extensive knowledge of politics and government. "That's how, after I was married and spending my days nursing and feeding and doing laundry for babies, I kept current on national affairs and active with volunteer work in the community and especially in politics, which became my lifetime hobby."

Schlafly led what she has called "the pro-family" movement to oppose the passage of the Equal Rights Amendment. The amendment reads "Equality of rights under the law shall not be denied or abridged by the United States or by any State on account of sex." Schlafly argued that the "fundamental error of the Equal Rights Amendment, or ERA, is that it will mandate the gender-free, rigid, absolute equality of treatment of men and women under every federal and state law, bureaucratic regulation, and court decision, and in every aspect of our lives that is touched directly or indirectly by public funding" (Schlafly, 1977, p. 68). In her crusade, she assembled the movement called Stop ERA. Her objections to the ERA were based on her conviction that the amendment would undermine the family, draft women into military combat, and destroy the legal rights of wives.

After the Equal Rights Amendment failed to achieve ratification by the states, Schlafly and the Eagle Forum became very active in promoting other family values issues. Their Web site, which takes a strong family values stand, states, in part, "The Eagle Forum stands for the fundamental right of parents to guide the education of their own children" (http://www.eagleforum.org). The Eagle Forum philosophy backs parents of children in public schools who wish to protect their children from what they deem harmful materials and instruction, stating, in part, "parents have the right to expect that schools respect the religion and values of parents and children. Schools should not deprive children of their free-exercise-of-religion rights, impose on children courses in explicit sex or alternate lifestyles, profane or immoral fiction or videos" (http://www.eagleforum .org). Eagle Forum chapters exist all over the nation; they are organized to help educational institutions see the need to protect these parental rights and to promote the pro-family philosophy of the national organization. For instance, local chapters of the Eagle Forum have been active in objecting to school curriculums and books that they find harmful to children, including books that glamorize sex or contain anti-Christian themes or values.

Schlafly and her Eagle Forum promote many conservative causes and viewpoints. Educational issues have become one of the Forum's most significant areas of concern. For example, within the last two years, Schlafly and the Eagle Forum have objected to the use of

Outcomes-Based curriculums in the schools and whole language curriculums to teach reading. In past years, the Eagle Forum has launched other major initiatives important to traditional family values such as their opposition to sex education that does not emphasize abstinence. She has lectured or debated on more than 500 college and university campuses. She told the authors "Eagle Forum was built with volunteers in the cause of good government through political activism." Schlafly believes that the Eagle Forum has kept faith with their mission and with the people who share their principles and standards.

SUGGESTED READINGS

Felsenthal, Carol. *The sweetheart of the Silent Majority: The biography of Phyllis Schlafly*. New York: Doubleday, 1981.
Schlafly, Phyllis. *The power of the positive woman*. New Rochelle, NY: Arlington House, 1977.
Web site for Eagle Forum: http://www.eagleforum.org

C. James Schmidt

Library Advocate on the Commission on Online Child Protection

Born: June 27, 1939, Flint, Michigan.
Education: B.A., Catholic University, 1962; M.S.L.S., Columbia University, 1963; Graduate study, University of Texas, 1966–67; Ph.D., Florida State University, 1972
Current position: Professor of Library and Information Science, San Jose State University

One of the most active professional librarians in America today, James Schmidt is dedicated to protecting intellectual freedom. He has had a long and distinguished career since winning an LSCA scholarship from the Michigan State Library in 1962 to attend the graduate school of library science at Columbia University. Over the last thirty-eight years, Schmidt has established a solid reputation within his profession in both library administration and scholarship and teaching. His work has gained him many forms of recognition, and contributed to the positions he has held in the American Library Association (ALA).

Schmidt began his professional career as a public librarian in Flint, Michigan, working in the business and industry department. Because Flint is one of the leading automobile manufacturing centers, the assignment was one of the busiest for a new professional. His success at the Flint Public Library helped him to secure a position as head of reference for the General Motors Institute. From there, Schmidt went on to become an associate college librarian for Southwest Texas State University, in San Marcos, Texas. While living in Texas, he pursued graduate study in political science at the University of Texas in Austin. In 1967, he became head of the undergraduate and branch campus libraries at Ohio State University in Columbus, Ohio, and remained there until 1970. At that point, convinced that a doctoral degree was important for his career, he entered Florida State University in Tallahassee, to pursue a Ph.D. in library science.

Except for a brief period as a consultant, Schmidt has held high-level positions at major universities since completing his doctorate. Through much of the 1970s, he was director of the State University of New York at Albany (SUNY-Albany) libraries. In 1979, he became the university librarian at Brown University and three years later the vice president, chief operating officer and director of the Research Libraries Information Network, also known as RLIN. RLIN is one of two primary bibliographic information systems used by libraries throughout the United States and in other parts of the world to process materials for inclusion in library collections. Libraries also use RLIN to share material between library organizations through interlibrary loan. Throughout most of the 1980s, Schmidt furthered the development of RLIN as a national system and contributed to the changes RLIN had planned for its future in the bibliographic industry.

For the past nine years, Schmidt has been associated with San Jose State University in California. He began work there as the university librarian in 1992. In 1995, the university appointed him to the position of acting chief information officer. Since 1996, he has been a professor in the School of Library and Information Science.

Schmidt's defense of intellectual freedom and his commitment to combating censorship in libraries has brought him recognition as an articulate spokesperson for freedom of speech and freedom of the press. His greatest honor came in 1990 when he was awarded the 1991 Robert B. Downs Intellectual Freedom Award. The Downs award, which is given by the University of Illinois's Graduate School of Library and Information Science in honor of Robert B. Downs, dean of the graduate school and a champion of intellectual freedom, "acknowledges individuals or groups who have furthered the cause of intellectual freedom, particularly as it impacts libraries and information centers, and the dissemination of ideas" (http://alexia.lis. uiuc.edu/gslis/school/downs-awc). When Schmidt won the Downs award, he was president of the Freedom to Read Foundation, a coalition of organizations and individuals that promotes open access to resources, especially books, and opposes censorship. Schmidt has also been on the Intellectual Freedom Committee of the ALA and was the chairperson of the committee from 1985 to 1986 and from 1987 to 1989. It was during his tenure on the committee that the FBI's attempt to use library records as part of its surveillance of foreign nationals and other individuals came to light. Schmidt's leadership of the Intellectual Freedom Committee and, later, the Freedom to Read Foundation was instrumental in the development of the library profession's response to the FBI's intrusion into academia and confidential library records.

Schmidt has remained active in intellectual freedom circles. His reputation for astute and fair thinking on freedom of speech led to his appointment to the Commission on Online Child Protection, a commission studying the impact of the Internet on children. Both the commission and the Child Online Protection Act (COPA) were created in 1998, at least in part, in response to the U.S. Supreme Court's decision that the Communications Decency Act (CDA) was unconstitutional. The CDA made it a crime, with a prison sentence and/or fines to use what the law said was indecent or patently offensive speech on a computer network if that speech could be viewed by a minor. After the Court's ruling, the commission was asked to "study methods to help reduce access by minors to material that is harmful to minors on the Internet." When the commission filed its report in 2000, Schmidt wrote an opinion that was included in the report: "It has been said that the Internet is a 'worldwide conversation.' There is no limit to the number who may speak, the admission price for speakers is low, users can seek and 'hear' speech of their choosing. As is the case with the printed medium, where the cost of speaking—publishing—is higher, the Internet's worldwide conversation contains speech offensive to some." He went on to discuss the current legal limitations to the commission's work and then noted, "In the end, the protection of minors from Internet content that may be harmful to some will require active adult supervision. 'Too much to do, too little time' is the response from many parents, guardians, and caregivers. Hence a massive educational effort is needed, combined with the development of easily accessible tools, so parents and kids can participate in the worldwide conversation and realize the benefits while feeling safe" (Final Report, COPA, p. 82).

Schmidt has written several reports on intellectual freedom for the ALA, most notably for successive ALA yearbooks in the late 1980s and early 1990s. He continues to be a popular speaker for panels and seminars on intellectual freedom. He also has worked on issues concerning freedom of speech and the right to privacy on the Internet. He was on the steering committee for the 1993 Computers, Freedom, and Privacy Conference, the most active of those conferences promoting freedom of speech and the right to privacy on the Internet.

SUGGESTED READINGS

The Newsletter on Intellectual Freedom, a publication of the Office for Intellectual Freedom of the American Library Association.

U.S. Commission on Online Child Protection. *Final Report.* Washington, D.C.: US Government Printing Office, 2000.

Web site for Commission on Online Child Protection: http://www.copacommission.org

Jay Alan Sekulow

Protecting the Rights to Religious Expression

Born: June 10, 1956, Brooklyn, New York

Education: B.A., Mercer University, 1976; J.D., Mercer University, 1980

Current position: Chief Counsel, American Center for Law and Justice

AP Photo/Kamenko Pajic. Courtesy of AP/Wide World Photos.

Jay Sekulow has been an influential force in the protection of the rights of Christians, especially fundamentalist Christians. Jay Alan Sekulow was born on June 10, 1956, in Brooklyn, New York. Shortly thereafter, his parents moved to Long Island, where he was raised in the Jewish faith. When Sekulow was a teenager, his parents moved to Atlanta, Georgia. While attending a local community college there, Sekulow found he enjoyed learning and decided to enroll in what was then known as Atlanta Baptist College, now Mercer University.

While at Mercer Sekulow met Glenn Borders, who challenged his religious beliefs. The friendship led Sekulow to be introduced to Jews for Jesus, an organization founded in 1973 that uses evangelistic outreach to Jewish people to promote Jesus as the Messiah. People who belong to this organization consider themselves Jews but believe that the teachings of Jesus are the religious values to follow. Sekulow affiliated with the group and continued his academic career at Mercer

University. He enrolled in the law school at Mercer in 1977 and graduated in 1980 in the top 5 percent of his class. After law school he spent about eighteen months as a tax prosecutor for the IRS and then opened a law firm with his friend Stuart Roth. The firm flourished for the next several years. Sekulow also incorporated and managed a successful real-estate development firm. During this period, he remained committed to his faith and stayed in contact with his friends in Jews for Jesus. In time, he became a member of the organization's board of directors. His business continued to flourish, but Sekulow says, "There was something else I wanted to do. I thought more and more about using my legal skills to serve God. In 1986, I became the Jews for Jesus general legal counsel" (http://www.jewsforjesus.org/stories/jseku).

In 1990, Sekulow also became the chief counsel for the American Center for Law and Justice (ACLJ). The ACLJ is closely associated with Pat Robertson, who was instrumental in its creation. Robertson founded the ACLJ to counter some of the activism of the American Civil Liberties Union (ACLU), especially in the area of religious rights. The ACLJ is a public interest law firm that will enter into court cases to defend conservative Christian values, most notably anti-abortion groups when charged with offenses during protests or parents and groups wanting school prayer back in the schools.

Sekulow has argued a number of cases on religious rights before the U.S. Supreme Court, first as the general counsel for Jews for Jesus and then as chief counsel for ACLJ. Among his recent cases in which he was successful in the courts are *Board of Education of Westside Community Schools* v. *Mergens* (496 U.S. 226, 1990) where Sekulow argued that public secondary schools that receive federal funds be required to allow student religious groups to hold meetings before and after school; *Bray* v. *Alexandria's Women's Health Clinic* (506 U.S., 263, 1993) where he made the case that a law in Virginia that governed protests by hate groups such as the Ku Klux Klan, but applied to an anti-abortion rally, could not be used against pro-life protesters from Operation Rescue; and an *amicus curiae* (friend of the court) brief in *Boy Scouts of America* v. *Dale* (120 S. Ct. 246, 2000), in which he argued that the Boy Scouts of America had the right to refuse leadership positions to openly gay adults.

In 1999, Sekulow testified before the U.S. Congress then investigating the use of Internet filters in public libraries. In testimony before the Senate on Senate Bill 5.97, on March 4, 1999, Sekulow stated:

Public libraries were created to lend books, provide research tools, and make available educational opportunities to its citizens. The Supreme Court has described a library as "a place dedicated to quiet, to knowledge, and to beauty" (*Brown v. Louisiana*, 383 US 131. 1966). Libraries, therefore, have an affirmative duty to provide materials which will benefit the surrounding community and restrict illegal and harmful materials. Children's unrestricted access to the Internet fails to fulfill this duty.... The vast majority of pornography which saturates the web is neither educational nor beneficial, and in many jurisdictions, the exposure to minors to such material is illegal. Therefore, to avoid liability, libraries will have to adopt some form of Internet filtering process for minors. (http://www.aclj.org/issues/filtering.asp)

Sekulow is a frequent guest speaker on CBN's television show *The 700 Club*, a noted speaker at various evangelical Christian conventions, and a frequent substitute cohost on *Praise the Lord*, the primary television program for the Trinity Broadcast Network. He is also the host of syndicated *Case in Controversy*, a radio program that features legal issues important to Christians who do witnessing as part of their faith and the primary speaker for a similar show on the Trinity Broadcasting Network. The ACLJ web site features links to Sekulow's radio broadcasts and has a Speak-to-Jay link that submits questions on religious rights and similar legal matters to Sekulow for advice. Sekulow is married to Pam Sekulow, and they have two sons.

SUGGESTED READINGS

Sekulow, Jay. *And nothing but the truth*. Nashville, TN: T. Nelson, 1996.
———. *From intimidation to victory: Regaining the Christian right to speak*. Lake Mary, FL: Creation House, 1990.
Web site for the American Center for Law and Justice: http://www.aclj.org

Robert L. Simonds

The Dangers in Public School Education

Born: November 24, 1925, Los Angeles, California
Education: B.Th., M.A, Pacific Bible College, 1955
Current positions: President of the National Association of Chris-

tian Educators (NACE) and Citizens for Excellence in Education (CEE); Chairman of the Southern California National Association of Evangelicals (NAE), and a member of the National NAE Board of Directors

Christian educators have found an articulate advocate in Robert Simonds, a leader in promoting Christian values in the schools. His organization, Citizens for Excellence in Education (CEE), has been one of the most active groups challenging local schools to provide morally based instruction with materials that support Christian values. The CEE has played a significant role in assisting parents and citizens in organizing complaints against curriculums and resources considered contrary to these Christian values. Simonds also founded the National Association of Christian Educators (NACE). He has spoken at twenty-four national and state conventions of public school organizations in the recent past, seeking to reconcile Christian/public school differences in the education of twenty million Christian children in public schools.

Simonds did not start out to be a crusader; he wanted simply to make a difference in the lives of children through education. He began teaching in the public schools in 1960 as a high school teacher, and later served as a high school principal. Next, he became a professor of philosophy, architecture/engineering, and mathematics at Orange Coast College (Costa Mesa, California), as well as an adjunct professor in teacher education at the University of California at Los Angeles.

Under Simonds' leadership, the CEE in a strategy called RESCUE 2010 called for all Christian children to enroll in Christian schools or opt for home schooling. As of December 2000, over three million children had left the public schools in part because of this campaign. RESCUE 2010's most important aims are to halt the influence of secular humanism in the school curriculums and promote Christian teachings. The CEE has also organized a total of 1,710 CEE parents chapters in all fifty states to elect parents to school boards (http://www.nace.org). Local CEE chapters have been involved in challenging schools to provide better library materials and to remove books that are contrary to Christian values. The National CEE headquarters assists the local chapters in these efforts, especially with resources on organizing chapters and activities. Several CEE chapters have also been active in movements to promote the use of filters for the Internet in public libraries. After 13 years, CEE has elected 25,250 of the total 92,000 new local/state school board members.

Simonds has published three journals and newsletters and has written a number of books on reforming education, strengthening families, and electing school board members. Many of his most significant books are published by the CEE, including *A Guide to Public Schools for Christian Parents and Teachers and Especially for Pastors* (1993), written with Kathi Hudson, and *How to Elect Christians to Public Office* (1985). He travels and speaks to about eighty CEE banquets or conventions every year. His CEE groups include 350,000 parents. Alarmed by public school education's growing movement toward "secular humanism," which many conservatives consider anti-Christian, Simonds founded Citizens for Excellence in Education, a parents' advocacy group established "to assure academic excellence and character education to all American children in public schools" (interview with the authors). The CEE rapidly gained a reputation for tenacity within conservative circles and the Republican Party. As a result, Simonds has had a dramatic impact on national education policy in the United States. President Ronald Reagan, for example, appointed him to the Forum to Implement the National Commission on Excellence in Education Report: A Nation At Risk (1983).

Simonds states that two influences have inspired his efforts to make a lasting difference in people and especially children's lives: his faith in God and the Bible and his public school teaching experience.

Simonds' activities have drawn considerable criticism and even hatred. His life has been threatened thirty-four times, including an attack on his home when bricks were thrown through his windows. On a less perilous level, numerous articles have been written to impugn his character. Nonetheless, he remains dedicated to addressing the needs of American children in the public schools.

SUGGESTED READINGS

Web site for the CEE: http://www.nace-cee.org

Shari Steele

Advocate for Free Speech on the Electronic Frontier

Born: July 28, 1959, Killeen, Texas
Education: B.S., Widener University, 1980; M.S., West Chester University of Pennsylvania, 1984; J.D., Widener University School of Law, 1989; LL.M., Georgetown University Law Center, 1994.
Current position: Executive Director and president, Electronic Frontier Foundation

Shari Steele directs the organization that has been a pioneer in the protection of free speech on electronic networks. As the executive director and president of the Electronic Frontier Foundation (EFF), she has lent her legal skills to combating efforts to censor or limit access to electronic information. As a result, Steele is at the center of the debate on the censorship of information in the twenty-first century.

Shari Steele was born in Killeen, Texas, on July 28, 1959. Her family moved to the Philadelphia area shortly thereafter. After graduating from high school, Steele enrolled at Widener University in suburban Philadelphia and received a B.S. in 1980. She then went on to graduate school at West Chester University of Pennsylvania, where she earned a master's in instructional media. In the late 1980s, she enrolled in the Widener University School of Law, earning her J.D. in 1989. She began her legal career as a teaching fellow at the Georgetown University Law Center. While at Georgetown, she received an LL.M. degree in advocacy. Steele has said her inspiration for defending free speech arises from her admiration of Supreme Court Justice William Brennan, a strong advocate of civil liberties.

The EFF was founded in 1990 by Mitch Kapor, founder of Lotus Development Corporation, John Perry Barlow, lyricist for the Grateful Dead rock group, and John Gilmore, who was instrumental in the creation of the alt. newsgroups, an early form of Internet chat. Steele joined the EFF as a member of its legal team. By 1999, she was the director of legal services. She then took a brief sabbatical to cofound Bridges.org, a nonprofit corporation that works to ensure sound technology policy in developing nations. When she returned to the EFF in 2000, she was made executive director and president of the organization.

Steele has been in the forefront of some well-known cases involving the Internet, either as a member of a legal team in the case or as an author of an *amicus curiae* (friend of the court) brief. Among the cases she has worked on are *ACLU* v. *Reno*, which challenged the Child Online Protection Act (COPA) and *Bernstein* v. *Department of Justice*, which led to the decision that declared the export control laws on encryption unconstitutional. (COPA was a federal law that attempted to mandate Internet filtering systems be used in all institutions receiving federal money, where minors might access the Internet on computers, such as in schools and libraries.) Steele has also worked with the U.S. Sentencing Commission to develop sentencing guidelines for the Computer Fraud and Abuse Act and the No Electronic Theft Act, with the National Research Council on U.S. encryption policy, and with the National Telecommunications and Information Administration (NTIA) on hate crimes in telecommunications. She believes technological advances will present challenges to free speech and privacy in the future: "I see continued convergence between all multimedia into a single platform. I hope that technology will be used to enrich everyone's lives. I see expanded use of technology for delivering medical information, education, personal sharing, and selected entertainment. I hope that people will be working to win back the privacy protections that have started eroding away while technology was in its infancy (i.e., now)" (http://www. witi.com/center/witimuseum).

Steele has spoken about civil liberties law in newly emerging technologies in a number of venues. She has appeared on the *CBS News*, *Washington Journal*, on C-SPAN CNN, the BBC, and the *Today Show*. She has been featured on such national radio programs as *All Things Considered* on PBS and the National Public Radio's *Morning Edition*. She is also a frequent speaker on college campuses and at technology conferences. She was a keynote speaker at the Smithsonian Institution's lecture series on Internet law and a speaker before the American Bar Association's TechWorld Conference.

Steele lives in San Francisco, California, where the EFF is headquartered. When asked what she considers her greatest accomplishment, she has said, "Raising my two wonderful daughters (by the way, I'm not done yet)" (http:www.witi.com/center/witimuseum/ womeninscience). She is a powerful spokesperson for women in the world of technology. She has been actively involved with Women in Technology International, a professional association for women working in technology. Her advice to women who want to enter the demanding field of technology and advocacy is, "Don't take no for an answer. Just start doing the work. It's an extremely competitive field, but there is much more work than those currently engaged can handle. Find something that you feel passionate about and stick with it until you accomplish your goals" (http:www.witi.com/center/ witimuseum/womeninscience).

SUGGESTED READINGS

EFFector Online Newsletter, a publication of the Electronic Frontier Foundation.

Godwin, Mike. *Cyber rights: Defending free speech in the digital age.* New York: Times Books, 1998.

Nadine Strossen

Civil Libertarian Defending the Bill of Rights

Born: August 18, 1950, Jersey City, New Jersey
Education: B.A., Radcliffe College, 1972; J.D., Harvard University, 1975
Current position: National President, American Civil Liberties Union; professor, New York Law School

Nadine Strossen is a notable voice for the First Amendment. She is currently the national president of the American Civil Liberties Union (ACLU) and a prominent author and lecturer on free speech. The ACLU is the oldest and most well-known organization dedicated to defending the Bill of Rights.

Strossen was born in Jersey City, New Jersey, to Woodrow John Strossen and Sylvia (Simicich) Strossen on August 18, 1950. The family moved to Hopkins, Minnesota, eight years later when her father was transferred in his job. Strossen began to speak up for causes she believed in early in life. When she graduated from high school in 1968, she condemned the role of the United States in the Vietnam War during her speech to her graduating class. "I had a strong sense of individual rights and sticking one's neck out on behalf of unpopular causes, even at the risk of personal ostracism" (*New York Times*, p. 74).

She was not the first member of her family to take a stand for her beliefs. Her maternal grandfather was a pacifist during World War I. When taken to court, the court had ordered him to stand in front of the courthouse, where people had spat on him. Strossen's father, who grew up in Germany, had been imprisoned in the Buchenwald concentration camp for anti-Nazi activities.

Strossen attended Radcliffe College, which was later melded into Harvard University. She majored in history and literature, was inducted into Phi Beta Kappa, an honors society, and graduated in 1972 with honors. After graduation, she attended Harvard Law School and

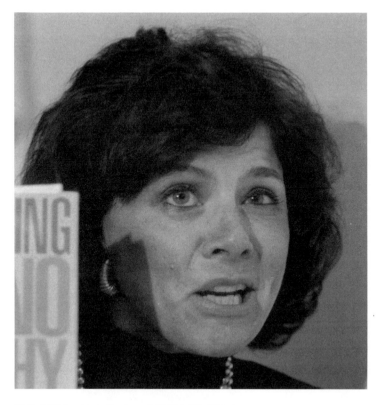

AP Photo/H. Rumph, Jr. Courtesy of AP/Wide World Photos.

became an editor of the *Harvard Law Review*. She received her degree *magna cum laude* in 1975. Strossen began her law career as a law clerk for the Minnesota Supreme Court and then took a position with a firm that specialized in commercial litigation. From 1984 through 1988, she held a faculty position at the New York University School of Law. As an associate professor, she taught courses in civil rights. She also became the supervising attorney for the civil rights clinic sponsored by the law school.

Strossen became a member of the ACLU in 1983 and was quickly named a member of the board of directors. In 1986, she became an ACLU national general counsel. In 1991, she became the first female president of the ACLU and the youngest person ever to hold that post. While the ACLU has been acused of being "too liberal" by some, Strossen told the *New York Times* on January 28, 1991, "I think this is the most important organization in the country, if not the world. To say what we do is controversial is to say the Bill of Rights is controversial. I want to emphasize the American in American Civil Liberties Union."

Strossen has written extensively on freedom of speech. Although her most noted book is *Defending Pornography: Free Speech, Sex, and the Fight for Women's Rights* (1995), Strossen rejects the apologist-for-pornographers label that antipornography feminists have applied to her. In her view, pornography is protected by the First Amendment, and she disagrees with those feminists, for example, Catherine MacKinnon and Andrea Dworkin, who espouse antipornography laws.

> While MacDworkinite laws would not criminalize pornography, they would subject it to such crippling penalties that it would probably be produced by underworld-type operators, not likely to abide by applicable laws and regulations. As Judge Posner U.S. Appeals Court judge for the Federal Seventh Circuit and critic of MacKinnon and Dworkin's writings, indicated, scarlet collar workers are already exploited because some sexual expression is now subject to legal sanctions; they would be even more exploited should more sexual expression be subject to legal sanctions. For the foregoing reasons, it is not surprising that virtually all of the organizations representing sex trade workers have opposed schemes to censor pornography. Sex workers, including pornography models and actresses, have repeatedly lobbied the National Organization for Women to refrain from supporting the antipornography movement.

Strossen is adamant, however, in her belief that any defense of pornography must exclude pornographic material that depicts children, animals, or nonconsensual activity by participating adults. She sees the importance of making a distinction between speech and action, something MacKinnon and Dworkin argue is irrelevant. Strossen has written, "Just as it is vitally important to enforce criminal and societal sanctions against real rape, it is also vitally important not to enforce sanctions against unreal rape—words or images describing or depicting nonconsensual sex" (Strossen, p. 170). In the book *Speaking of Race, Speaking of Sex: Hate Speech, Civil Rights, and Civil Liberties* (1985), a collection of essays edited by Henry Gates et al., Strossen argues that the defense of the First Amendment must not be sacrificed to preserve equality.

Recently, the ACLU and other organizations have struggled with the issues surrounding the censorship of electronic information. Under Strossen's leadership, the ACLU opposed the Communications Decency Act (CDA) of 1996, which made it a crime, with a prison

sentence and/or fines, to use what the law said was indecent or patently offensive speech on a computer network if that speech could
be viewed by a minor. The ACLU believed that the vague language
of the bill did not fit within any definition of illegal obscenity or
pornography. Strossen has noted that new forms of communication
technology often get blamed for societal worries and has pointed out
that the invention of the printing press created an immediate wave
of censorship. While Strossen has said she supports any technology
that helps parents choose what they want their children to see, she
opposes any type of technology that takes the freedom of choice
away from adults, as the V-chip is prone to do. (The V-chip is a
software program that allows parents or other adults to block out
programs. It uses the rating codes assigned to shows to block the
programs. Parents set the limits based on which codes they want
blocked.)

Strossen has won numerous awards in her career. In 1986, she became the first woman to receive the Jaycee International's Outstanding Young Person award. In 1991, the *National Law Journal* included
her in its list of the "100 most influential lawyers in America." She
was also honored by the Media Institute, which presented her with
its Freedom of Speech Award. She is married to Eli Michael Noam,
an economist and attorney who teaches business at Columbia University's Graduate School of Business.

SUGGESTED READINGS

Gates, Henry, Griffin, Anthony P., Lovely, Donald E., Post, Robert C.,
    *Speaking of Race, Speaking of Sex: Hate Speech, Civil Rights, and Civil
    Liberties.* New York: New York University Press, 1995.
New York Times, January 28, 1991, p 74.
Strossen, Nadine. *Defending pornography: Free speech, sex, and the fight for
    women's rights.* New York: Scribner, 1995.
Web site for the American Civil Liberties Union: http://www.aclu.org

Bruce Taylor

National Law Center

Born: November 13, 1950, Rutland, Vermont
Education: B.A., University of Vermont, 1971; J. D., Cleveland-
    Marshall College of Law, 1974

Current position: President and chief counsel, National Law
   Center for Children and Families

Bruce Taylor is one of the leading legal experts on pornography. He
has been president and chief counsel of the National Law Center for
Children and Families since 1995. Prior to joining the center, he was
senior trial attorney for the child exploitation and obscenity section
of the U.S. Department of Justice. As such, he prosecuted child pornography and hard-core pornography distribution. He has prosecuted
over 600 obscenity cases and 100 appeals, including the *Larry Flynt
v. Ohio* case in 1981 (Appeals Court for the Ohio district) while he
was a prosecutor and assistant director of law for the city of Cleve-
land. In this case, Larry Flynt, publisher of the men's magazine *Hustler*, was appealing his obscenity conviction for publishing and
distributing his magazine. Taylor has also been an assistant attorney
general for the state of Arizona.

As president and chief counsel for the center, Taylor supported
the Communications Decency Act (CDA), which was originally introduced by Senator James J. Exon of Nebraska in 1994. The act
made it a crime, with a prison sentence and/or fines, to use indecent
or patently offensive speech on a computer network if that speech
could be viewed by a minor. In a September 1996 online debate over
the act, Taylor explained that Congress was reacting to the online
proliferation of both hard-core pornography (which it deemed obscene even for adults) and soft-core pornography (which it deemed
indecent or harmful to minors, even if not obscene for adults), as well
as child pornography (which is a felony to make, distribute, or possess). He noted that these types of pornography are freely available
to all adults and minors on many parts of the Internet and pointed
out that, in all other areas of American life, adults are able to obtain
so-called adult material in ways that do not make it accessible to
minors. Taylor believed the CDA simply made it clear that federal
obscenity laws applied to the Internet and added provisions to protect children from indecent material. He argued that the CDA provided good-faith defenses for Internet access providers, computer
system operators, software and hardware suppliers, and phone carriers
that would protect them from liability as long as they made good-
faith efforts to protect children and comply with the CDA and would
also preserve existing privacy protection and copyright laws. Taylor

pointed out that indecent meant patently offensive sexual or excretory materials, not serious art or literature, and thus would not apply to Michelangelo's David, the Sistine Chapel, some books, or serious science materials for AIDS or safe-sex education. In Taylor's views, the computer, when it is hooked up to a telephone line, becomes the sender or receiver of indecent material and thus subject to legal regulation. Taylor represented congressional sponsors as the counsel of record in the amici curiae (friend of the court) briefs in support of the CDA before the U.S. District Court of the Eastern District of Pennsylvania in *ACLU* v. *Reno* and *ALA* v. *Department of Justice* (1995), before the U.S. District Court for the Southern District of New York in *Shea* v. *Reno* (1995), and before the Supreme Court in *Reno* v. *ACLU* (1996). In 1998, he appeared in support of the Child Online Protection Act of 1998 (COPA) before the U.S. District Court for the Eastern District of Pennsylvania and the U.S. Court for Appeals for the Third Circuit in *ACLU* v. *Reno*. He has testified as an expert law enforcement witness before various congressional committees and subcommittees at national and state levels. He has also appeared on national and local television and radio shows and lectured in forty-eight states, Canada, Puerto Rico, the Bahamas, and the Philippines.

It is Taylor's belief that the National Law Center for Children and Families should provide legal advice and assistance to prosecutors, law enforcement officers, public officials, legislators, community and civic leaders, and concerned citizens on the issues of obscenity, sexual exploitation of children, Internet pornography, regulation of sexually oriented businesses, and First Amendment jurisprudence.

SUGGESTED READINGS

Web site for the National Law Center for Children and Families: http://www.nationallawcenter.org

C. Delores Tucker

Fighting the Influences of Obscene and Violent Music

Born: October 4, 1927, Philadelphia, Pennsylvania
Education: Attended Temple University, Pennsylvania State

AP Photo/str. Courtesy of AP/Wide World Photos.

University, the University of Pennsylvania, and the North
Philadelphia School of Realty
Current position: Founder and chairperson, National Political
Congress of Black Women

Since 1993, C. Delores Tucker has waged an uphill battle to shut
down purveyors of musical lyrics that are violent and demeaning to
African Americans, especially African American women. "These ma-
licious lyrics grossly malign Black women, degrade the unthinking
young Black artist who create it, pander pornography to our innocent
young children, hold Black people (especially young Black males)
universally up to ridicule and contempt, and corrupt its vast audience
of listeners, white and Black throughout the world" (http://www.
npcbw.org/press/newo6server.htm). Tucker is not alone in her efforts, which began when several well-known entertainers and musicians, including Dionne Warwick, contacted her through Dorothy
Height, president of the National Council of Negro Women. Since
beginning her crusade in 1993, Tucker has picketed record stores,

invaded corporate boardrooms, and appeared on many talk shows. She also has been vilified by elements in the music industry.

Tucker did not begin her career as a crusader against violence and obscenity in music. Born to the Reverend Whitfield and Captilda Nottage in 1927, she was inspired by her parents' Christianity and deep commitment to the work ethic:

> My parents were strict fundamental, Puritan Christians. We couldn't smoke, play cards, drink, dance, or listen to popular music. No male company until I was twenty-one. My father was a minister, from a family of ministers. He never took a salary, always believing God would provide, even though he had 11 children. But my mother realized she had to feed us, so she opened up an employment agency, then a grocery store, then she rented houses. We weren't taught to value material things, but we were taught that we were spiritual aristocracy, that we were special, were children of the King, and were taught to place all our values in relationships—to heal the sick, to love everybody, to feed the poor, not to care about anything worldly. (*Biography News*, p. 73)

As an African American growing up in the 1930s and 1940s, Tucker experienced racial discrimination. She was the only African American in her junior high school, and because her family lived on a farm, her schoolmates called her "Black Beauty." She felt she was under constant scrutiny. When she graduated from Girl's High School in Philadelphia in 1946, her father took her on a trip to the Bahamas. On board the ship, she was told she could not sleep in the compartments assigned to whites. She refused to accept segregated accommodations and slept on an open-air deck instead. As a result, she was ill by the time she returned home. Although she had wanted to become a doctor, she required a year of convalescence to overcome her illness, which ended her chance to go to college and study medicine. Over the years, however, she has attended Temple University, the University of Pennsylvania, and Pennsylvania State University and often acted as a surrogate parent for students.

In time, Tucker married William J. Tucker, a Philadelphia real estate executive, and managed a lucrative real estate brokerage. As a result of her prominence in the Philadelphia real estate market, she was named to the Philadelphia zoning board. She was the first African American woman to be on the board.

Tucker has always been active in the civil rights movement. A long-time member and officer of the National Association for the Advancement of Colored People (NAACP), she was an ardent follower of Reverend Martin Luther King, Jr., and participated in the Selma to Montgomery March in 1965, a seminal event in the civil rights movement. She is also the president of the Philadelphia chapter of the Martin Luther King, Jr., Association. She has also been a supporter of Reverend Jesse Jackson, his Rainbow Coalition, and PUSH, People United to Save Humanity. In 1984, she was a leading spokesperson for his presidential election in 1984 and a leader in his Pennsylvania campaign organization.

Tucker first became active in politics in 1950 when she worked for the campaign of Joseph Clark, who was running for mayor of Philadelphia. Since 1972, *Ebony* magazine has named her as one of the 100 most influential Black Americans. She is an articulate and powerful speaker and often tells groups of African American women, "Many of you are in the position to bring influence to bear if you have the courage of Esther, who could say, 'I'll go unto the King, which is not according to the law, and if I perish, I perish'" (*Ebony*, p. 60).

In 1971, Governor Milton Shapp appointed her to the post of Secretary of the Commonwealth of Pennsylvania. She was the first African American to hold that position and the highest ranking African American woman in state government at the time. Her role was to regulate business and industry, and she pursued her duties with zeal and competence. In 1975 and 1976, *Ladies Home Journal* nominated her for its "Woman of the Year" award. In 1987, she made an unsuccessful run for lieutenant governor in Pennsylvania but finished third out of a field of fourteen candidates in the Democratic primary. In the late 1990s, Tucker set out to encourage other African American women to become politically active. After founding the National Political Congress of Black Women, she was named by *People* magazine as one of twenty-five of the world's most intriguing people.

Tucker began to go after companies that produce gangsta rap and rock and roll music with excessive violence and obscenity in 1993. In 1997, she testified before the Senate Governmental Affairs Subcommittee on Oversight and Management of the District of Columbia during its hearings on the social impact of music violence. During her testimony, she urged the subcommittee to find a way to stop the proliferation of what many see as pornographic music that degrades and demeans women and said "the poison exists not just in the inner cities but is spreading to the more affluent suburbs as well" (*Philadelphia New Observer*, p. 10).

SUGGESTED READINGS

Biography News, July–August 1979, p. 73.

Ebony, July 1972, p. 60.

Newton, David E. *Violence and the media: A reference handbook*. Santa Barbara, CA: ABC-CLIO, 1996.

Philadelphia New Observer, November 19, 1997, p. 10.

Straub, Deborah Gillan, and Ray Broadus Browne. *Contemporary heroes and heroines*. Detroit: Gale Research, 1998.

Web site for the National Political Congress of Black Women: http://www.npcbw.org

John Wayne Whitehead

Leading Spokesperson for Conservative Christian Causes

Born: July 14, 1946, Pulaski, Tennessee
Education: B.A., University of Arkansas, 1969; J.D., University of Arkansas, 1974
Current position: President, The Rutherford Institute

The Rutherford Institute, one of the most active and effective organizations supporting conservative Christian causes, was founded in 1982 by John Whitehead, along with Frank Schaefer. Whitehead was born in Pulaski, Tennessee, a small city in southern Tennessee. After graduating from high school, he attended the University of Arkansas and earned a B.A. in 1969. He went on to study law at the university and completed his Juris Doctor in 1974. After a brief period working in private practice, Whitehead, who is committed to his faith, turned his attention to protect-religious-freedom:

> When founding the Rutherford Institute, my goal was to create an organization that would defend the people who were persecuted or

AP Photo/William Philpott. Courtesy of AP/Wide World Photos.

oppressed without charging for such services. The Rutherford Institute exists to ensure that people are treated fairly in the courts and are free to express themselves without fear. (http://www.rutherford.org/about/jww.asp)

In 1995 alone, the institute provided legal aid to almost 750 people. In one recent case, the Rutherford Institute defended a member of the Sons of Confederate Veterans (SCV) who wanted to buy a Virginia vanity license plate that included a graphic of the Confederate battle flag. In a decision by the U.S. District Court for Virginia, Jackson Kiser, the federal judge, ruled that the specialty plate statute had been made expressly to exclude the SCV's official logo and that this was discrimination favoring one viewpoint over another. After the ruling, Whitehead noted, "This is a victory for the free speech rights of all Virginia organizations. By this ruling, the court has said 'hands off' to government officials who would censor the free speech rights of private organizations in the name of misguided political correctness" (http://www.sierratimes.com/archives/sarticles/2001/Jan).

Whitehead has written numerous books and articles on a variety of subjects, primarily religious freedom, abortion, home schooling, the right to picket, and the rights of parents. He has written a number of law review articles for such university law school reviews as the *Emory Law Journal, Pepperdine Law Review*, and *The Washington and Lee Law Review*. Whitehead has also been an active spokesperson for Christian causes and freedom of religious expression in the media. In the late 1990s, *60 Minutes*, the CBS news program, included a profile of him. He has been a featured guest on numerous shows, including *Larry King Live, Crossfire, Nightline, This Week with Sam and Cokie, Burden of Proof, Hardball with Chris Matthews*, and *Late Edition with Wolf Blitzer*.

In the late 1990s, Whitehead became nationally known as the attorney for Paula Jones, in her sexual harassment lawsuit against President Clinton. After many legal maneuvers by both sides, Jones, following her attorneys' advice, dropped the lawsuit and accepted a cash settlement of $850,000 in November 1999.

Whitehead has written eleven books. His most well known is *The Second American Revolution* (1982), which examines the way in which misinterpretation of the Constitution has affected United States law. His first book, *The Separation Illusion* (1977), also discusses his views on how the Constitution has been misinterpreted. Because the Rutherford Institute has been active in the anti-abortion movement, Whitehead wrote *The Right to Picket and the Freedom of Public Discourse* in 1984 as a means of explaining to anti-abortion protesters what their rights are and where the limits are set for public demonstrations. Recently, Whitehead and the institute have turned their attention to the home school movement. Whitehead has written a legal guide for parents and institutions entitled *Home Education and Constitutional Liberties* (1986). Whitehead has also written two books on church-state relations, *Schools on Fire* (1980) and *The New Tyranny* (1989). Both books argue that religious input and expressions of religion have been unconstitutionally excluded from public education and that the "wall of separation" concept that is often used as an argument to eliminate religion from public schools was never meant to exclude religious expression.

Whitehead is married to Carolyn Nichols Whitehead and has four children. He is a veteran of the U.S. Army and a member of the American Bar Association as well as the Arkansas and Virginia bar associations. He and his wife live in Manassas, Virginia. The Rutherford Institute has its headquarters in Charlottesville, Virginia. It was named after Samuel Rutherford, a seventeenth-century theologian who challenged the concept of the divine right of kings in his book *Lex Rex* (*The Law and the King*) (1644).

SUGGESTED READINGS

Web site for *The Rutherford Institute*: http://www.rutherford.org

Whitehead, John W. *The separation illusion: A lawyer examines the First Amendment*. Milford, MI: Mott Media, 1977.

Whitehead, John W., and Wayne Stayskal. *The second American revolution*. Wheaton, IL: Crossway Books, 1982.

Donald E. Wildmon

Crusader for Family Values in Television Programming

Born: January 18, 1938, Dumas, Mississippi

Education: B.A., Millsaps College, 1960; M. Div., Emory University, 1965

Current position: Founder and executive director, American Family Association

---

For the past twenty-five years, Donald Wildmon has crusaded for a reduction in violence and obscenity in television programming. Wildmon was born in the small, northeastern Mississippi town of Dumas on January 18, 1938, to Ellis Wildmon, an investigator for the Mississippi Department of Health, and Johnnie (Tigrett) Wildmon, a schoolteacher. He was raised in Ripley, Mississippi, thirty-five miles from Tupelo, the birthplace of Elvis Presley. He was a member of the high-school football and track teams, editor of the school newspaper's sports section, and active in the Boy Scouts. Wildmon has described his childhood as "wholesome fun, clean fun, fun, fun" (*People*, p. 24).

After graduating from Millsaps College in 1960, Wildmon chose a career as a minister. He attended Emory University, in Atlanta, Georgia, and earned his divinity degree in 1965. In 1968, after spending

AP Photo/fls. Courtesy of AP/Wide World Photos.

two years in the military, he accepted a call as pastor for the Lee
Acres United Methodist Church in Tupelo. During his tenure at the
church, he wrote a number of inspirational works, including *Thoughts
Worth Thinking* (1968), *Practical Help for Daily Living* (1972), and *Stand
Up to Life* (1975).

In 1976, Wildmon took on a new call at another Methodist church
in Southaven, Mississippi. His crusade against what he calls violence
and obscenity in television programming began during the Christmas
season of that year. After sitting down one evening with his children
to watch television and finding several programs with adultery, profanity, and violence, including a scene in which a hammer was used
to torture someone, he made up his mind to do something to bring
alternative programs to TV. He began his advocacy at the local level.
His first act was to ask his congregation to participate in a turn-the-
TV-off week.

Four months later, Wildmon left his pastorate to devote all his time to his campaign and to founding the National Federation for Decency (NFD), which later became the American Family Association (AFA). The NFD began by attempting to gather information that could be used to persuade the networks to create better programming. However, Nielson ratings are the most significant source of data for network executives in determining whether to keep or remove program, and these ratings remained high for programs the NFD felt were indecent. Thus the NFD's initial efforts had little impact on programming. Wildmon came to believe that the public was being manipulated by those in Hollywood whose lifestyles were different from those of the average American. Reassessing his strategies, he decided to concentrate on advertisers.

Since beginning his crusade, Wildmon has had numerous successes in influencing, directly and indirectly, the content of television programming and commercials. His first, and most heralded, success came in 1981. In that year, Wildmon's NFD joined forces with Jerry Falwell's Moral Majority and Phyllis Schlafly's Eagle Forum, among others, to form a coalition called the Coalition for Better Television (CBTV). The new coalition threatened a boycott of those companies that sponsored shows the coalition deemed too violent or obscene. This effort began with a survey by members of the coalition to gather information on current programming at the time. Before the boycott began, however, the chairman of the board of Procter & Gamble, the largest sponsor of television programs at the time, announced to television executives, "We think the coalition is expressing some very important and broadly held views about gratuitous sex, violence, and profanity. I can assure you that we are listening very carefully to what they say, and I urge you to do the same" (*Inside Prime Time*). Wildmon considered this a victory, and the boycott was called off.

These and subsequent efforts have led to criticisms of Wildmon and the AFA by members of the television industry. He told the authors that James Duffy, former president of ABC Television has claimed that Wildmon leads "a band of moral zealots . . . busy inventing a national problem." In the same interview with the authors, he said that Gene Mater, from CBS Television, remarked: "We look upon Wildmon's efforts as the greatest frontal assault on intellectual freedom this country has ever faced." Wildmon has responded to these criticisms on a number of occasions. He told *Time* magazine in 1989 that he's not trying to deny people their rights. He just doesn't want anyone to infringe upon his rights. The Coalition for Better Television was disbanded in 1982. Wildmon has expressed satisfaction with the success that he was able to achieve through the coalition.

By 1987, the NFD had changed its name to the AFA. The association has been active in a number of nationally focused movements. In the mid-1980s, it was influential in the decision by the Southland Corporation, parent company of the 7–11 convenience store chain, to drop *Playboy* from its sales inventory. The association was also influential in a decision by K-Mart, owner of Waldenbooks, to drop pornographic titles from that bookstore chain and has lobbied the Holiday Inn Corporation to stop offering adult films in its hotel rooms.

In 1989, the association threatened to boycott PepsiCo because of the company's advertising campaign, which featured Madonna singing her hit song "Like a Prayer." Wildmon and the association considered the video version of the song to be sacrilegious because of its visuals which included burning crosses and Madonna kissing a saint. The ad was run only once in the United States before PepsiCo pulled it off the airwaves. The association has also criticized funding by the National Endowment for the Arts (NEA). In Wildmon's view, "the NEA has been insulated from mainstream American values for so long that it has become captive to a morally decadent minority which ridicules and mocks decent, moral taxpayers while demanding taxpayer subsidies" (*Wall Street Journal*, p. 1).

Wildmon continues to work from his Tupelo, Mississippi, headquarters. He has written over twenty-two books and is a frequent commentator or guest on such shows as the *McNeil-Lehrer Report*, *Nightline*, the *700 Club*, and *Meet the Press*. Married to Lynda Lou Bennett since 1961, Wildmon has four children and six grandchildren. He sees the need to continue his crusade for sometime. As he noted in an interview in the March 1988 issue of *Conservative Digest*, "It has taken fifty years or longer to reduce our culture to its present sorry state. We are just beginning to swing the pendulum back to the other way, and it will not be accomplished in my lifetime" (p. 75).

SUGGESTED READINGS

Conservative Digest, March 1988, p. 75.
Inside Prime Time, 1983.
People magazine, July 6, 1981, p. 24.
Wall Street Journal April 17, 1989, p. 1.

Web site for the American Family Association: http://www.afa.net
Wildmon, Donald E., and Randall Nulton. *Don Wildmon: The man the networks love to hate*. Wilmore, KY: Bristol Books, 1990.

Frank Zappa

Champion of Unconventional Music

Born: December 21, 1940, Baltimore, Maryland
Died: December 4, 1993, Los Angeles, California
Education: Attended Antelope Valley Junior College and Chaffee Junior College
Former position: Rock and roll musician

Frank Zappa was a musician, composer, lyricist, guitarist, and bandleader. For three decades, he was known for his innovative and iconoclastic contributions to progressive rock. Despite the unconventional musical structures and controversial lyrics of his songs and the contempt they expressed for political, social, and musical establishments, he had a devoted cult following for several decades.

Zappa was born in Baltimore, Maryland, in 1940, but his family moved to California in the early 1950s. His father was a metallurgist and meteorologist who researched poisonous gases for the military. His mother was a librarian. Zappa once said that his musical tastes and life changed in 1954 when he read a *Look* magazine article discussing the ability of the Sam Goody record chain to sell such music as *The Complete Works of Edgar Varese*. Zappa found a copy of the album and became inspired by Varese's avant-garde dissonance, although he still enjoyed Howlin' Wolf and the Orioles.

As a sophomore in high school, Zappa began composing classical music. He disliked the rock and roll of the 1950s, which he called "fake black music," and preferred the black do-wop groups of this era and such rhythm and blues performers as Howlin' Wolf, Muddy Waters, Lightning Slim, and Sonny Boy Williamson. He also wrote the soundtrack for *Run Home Slow*, a film written by his high-school

English teacher, and "The World's Greatest Sinner," which required a fifty-two piece orchestra.

Zappa always enjoyed having an audience. In his late teens, he formed a rhythm and blues group called Black-Outs, and he performed with a number of small bands in the Los Angeles area when he began writing rock-and-roll music in his early twenties. In 1963, he set up a small recording studio so that he could produce his unconventional music. In 1964, he played guitar with the Soul Giants, which later became the Mothers of Invention. In most of the work he did with this group, he collaborated with Don Van Vliet, another self-proclaimed music "freak." Using vocal and visual effects as well as electric or amplified guitars, bass, percussion, keyboard, and wind instruments and synthesizers, Zappa constantly changed the music produced by the Mothers of Invention. Although the group did not get a great deal of play on the radio, it had an enthusiastic following. The first double album of the group, *Freak Out*, produced in 1966 by MGM Records, included "Return of the Son of the Monster Magnet," in honor of Edgar Varese, an American composer of primarily classical music who pioneered the use of electric instruments in the early 1950s.

Between 1970 and 1981, Zappa wrote and performed such songs as "Road Ladies" and "Don't Eat the Yellow Snow," his first hit single, which was cut by a disc jockey from its original ten minutes to three minutes. His other hit was the 1979 "Dancin' Fool," which satirized disco. In 1981, Zappa founded Barking Pumpkin Records. His first release under this label was *Tinseltown Rebellion*. It was under the Barking Pumpkin label that he recorded the now famous single, "Valley Girls," in 1982, which satirized California's shopping mall culture. His label also provided a place for such artists as Alice Cooper, Captain Beefheart, GTOs, Tim Buckley, the Persuasions, and Lord Buckley.

In 1985, Zappa, who had written "Joe's Garage," which dealt with what would happen if music were illegal, testified before a Senate hearing investigating the negative influences of rock music. He accused the committee of fostering censorship and branded the Parents Music Resource Center (PMRC), which had urged the labeling of popular music as "a group of bored Washington housewives" who wanted to "housebreak all composers and performers because of the lyrics of a few" (*New Yorker*, p. 33). Zappa later memorialized his Senate committee encounter in *Frank Zappa Meets the Mothers of Prevention*. The album included the twelve-minute song "Porn Wars," which used sound bites from the hearing. Zappa devoted much of his energy to crusading against the censorship of recordings from 1985 on. He testified before several state legislatures and wrote many articles against the concept of voluntary labeling and censorship in general. Zappa's views on censorship, particularly the censorship of music, are detailed in his memoir *The Real Frank Zappa Book* (1993).

Zappa viewed politics as "not a matter of conservative vs. liberal" but "fascism vs. freedom" and saw himself as a traditional conservative. Although he was a registered Democrat, he said he could be a Republican "if you were to subtract . . . the evil influence of the religious Right" from the Republican Party. Zappa thought of himself as a devout capitalist and "composer-businessman" (*Newsmakers*, p. 629). Zappa was unconventional, but his intelligence, wit, and humor made him a legend. His strong feelings about protecting creativity and independence made him an outspoken advocate for protecting the right of free expression in the music industry. He died of prostate cancer in December 1993 at the age of fifty-two. After his death, his family designated the American Library Association's Office for Intellectual Freedom and the Freedom to Read Foundation for memorial donations. The Freedom to Read Foundation then established the Frank Zappa Memorial Fund for such contributions. In 1995, the American Library Association presented its intellectual freedom award to Zappa posthumously.

SUGGESTED READINGS

Colbeck, Julian. *Zappa: A Biography*. London: Virgin Books, 1987.
Current Biography Yearbook. Judith Graham, ed. New York: H. W. Wilson, 1994.
Newsmakers, 1994, p. 629.
New Yorker, January 25, 1999, p. 33.
Zappa, Frank. *Them or us*. New York: Barking Pumpkin Press, 1984.
———. *The real Frank Zappa book*. New York: Poseidon Press, 1993.

The First Amendment to the United States Constitution

Congress shall make no law respecting an establishment of religion, or pro-hibiting the free exercise thereof; or abridging the freedom of speech, or of the press; or the right of the people peaceably to assemble, and to petition the Government for a redress of grievances.

Historical Documents Related to the First Amendment

ENGLISH ANTECEDENTS:

Magna Carta, 1215

Bernard Schwartz, a constitutional scholar, has said, "In the Magna Carta is to be found the germ of the root principle that there are fundamental rights above the State, which the State—otherwise sovereign power that it is—may not infringe." Signed by King John on June 15, 1215, at Runnymeade in England, the Magna Carta, or Great Charter, was the first document to challenge the divine right of kings and thus declare that people had rights that could not be violated by government. This concept is the essence of the Bill of Rights, especially the First Amendment. The Magna Carta, which came about as a result a series of abuses of power by King John, is a feudal grant that enumerates the basic liberties of the nobility of the day. Among the most important of these liberties is the right to a trial by jury.

Petition of Right, 1628

The Petition of Right of 1628 is the second great charter of English liberty. The Petition of Right was enacted as a statute at the time when Charles I was asserting the divine right of kings. The Petition of Right, introduced in the House of Commons in 1628 by the English jurist, Sir Edward Coke, declared fundamental rights of Englishmen such as no taxation without an act of parliament, no quartering of soldiers in civilian homes, and no imprisonment without a formal legal cause. This petition, which helped to establish basic liberties for all Englishmen, greatly influenced the Constitution and the Bill of Rights.

Agreement of the People, 1649

After the execution of Charles I and the ascent of the commonwealth government under Oliver Cromwell, the Agreement of the People was created as a form of a republican constitution. When Parliament took the reins of power from the king, some feared that it would abuse its power. The Agreement of the People set out to create the boundaries of Parliament's power. Among other things, the agreement set forth six fundamental "points in Reserve": a provision for freedom of religion, restrictions to military conscription, amnesty for those involved in the wars surrounding the removal of Charles I, sanctity of the public debt, a prohibition against *ex post facto* laws, and equality before the law. Many constitutional scholars consider this document to be a landmark in the history of constitutional theory.

The English Bill of Rights, 1689

The Bill of Rights, enacted in 1689, is considered the third great charter of English liberty and the direct ancestor of the American Bill of Rights. The Bill of Rights came about as a result of the Glorious Revolution of 1688, when Parliament invited William of Orange and his wife Mary to overthrow James II. To create a government capable of carrying on affairs of state, a new parliament was formed and a bill was introduced to enact a declaration of rights that addressed the abuses of power by the Stuart kings, especially Charles II and James II, and included prohibitions against raising or keeping an army without the consent of Parliament, a rudimentary declaration on the right of the people to bear arms, a prohibition against quartering troops, the right to trial by jury, and prohibitions against such legal abuses as excessive bail or fines and cruel and unusual punishment.

COLONIAL CHARTERS

First Charter of Virginia, 1606

Some American colonies were established when the King granted a charter for the colonies. These royal colonial charters also impact American constitutional history and are the oldest documents affecting American constitutional law. The Virginia charter was the first of the colonial charters and established the precedent that the colonists were entitled to the rights of Englishmen. Bernard Schwartz has noted that the Virginia Charter did not enumerate those rights but merely established the connection of American colonists to the rights of Englishmen. Because of this connection, the charter played a pivotal role in the American Revolution and the Constitution. The roots of Patrick Henry's famous speech before the Virginia House of Burgesses in 1765—"Give me liberty or give me death!"—lie in the Virginia Charter.

Fundamental Orders of Connecticut, 1639

While on the surface the Fundamental Orders of Connecticut, drawn up in 1639, do not appear to have contributed to the Bill of Rights, constitutional scholars agree that the orders constituted what James Bryce has characterized as "the oldest truly political Constitution in America." The Fundamental Orders of Connecticut were created by the people of the colony and thus established the precedent in America that constitutional government is government of the people, by the people, and for the people. Constitutional scholars see this as an important step in limiting government powers over personal liberties.

Other Colonial Charters

Most other colonial charters contained statements or provisions that established the rights of the people of those colonies. While each is similar to the Virginia charter, their cumulative effect was the extension of the concept of individual liberties to all colonists. The most important of these charters are

Maryland Act for the Liberties of the People, 1639

Massachusetts Body of Liberties, 1641

Maryland Act Concerning Religion, 1649

Charter of Rhode Island and Providence Plantations, 1663

Fundamental Constitutions of Carolina, 1669

Concessions and Agreements of West New Jersey, 1677

Pennsylvania Frame of Government, 1682

New York Charter of Liberties and Privileges, 1683

Pennsylvania Charter of Privileges, 1701

DOCUMENTS OF THE AMERICAN REVOLUTION

Declaration of Rights and Grievances, 1765

The rallying cry of the American Revolution was "No taxation without representation." In the eyes of the colonists, the most onerous act passed by the English Parliament was the Stamp Act, which taxed the importation and sale of tea among other things. Opposition to the act was fierce. Perhaps nothing more symbolizes this opposition than Patrick Henry's famous "Give me liberty or give me death" speech in 1765. It was Henry's eloquence on law, especially on the legal precedents set down by Sir Edward Coke, the English jurist who framed the Petition of Right of 1628, that sparked the call for a congress of all the colonies to protest the act. The Stamp Act Congress, as it came to be called, wrote the Declaration of Rights and Grievances of 1765. The declaration was a statement of a fundamental concept: Taxes may be levied only by representatives of those who are being taxed. The declaration made it clear to the king and Parliament the colonists intended to be afforded their full rights as Englishmen.

The Rights of the Colonists and A List of Infringements and Violations of Rights, 1772

On the eve of the revolution, much of the ferment against the king centered in Massachusetts and was led by Sam Adams and the Sons of Liberty. In 1772, Thomas Hutchinson, the newly appointed governor of Massachusetts, declared that his salary and that of all the judges would be paid by the crown, not the colonists. Adams and his fellow revolutionaries believed this meant that the Massachusetts government would not be answerable to the colonists. At a town meeting in Boston, the governor was questioned about the matter, but he brushed the colonists off without answering their concerns. Adams called for a committee of correspondence, which drafted two documents, The Rights of the Colonists and A List of Infringements and Violations of Rights. While these documents, much like the Declaration of Rights and Grievances, declared that the colonists had the rights of Englishmen and that those rights had been violated, they included liberties not mentioned previously, especially the right against unreasonable searches and seizures.

Declaration and Resolves of the First Continental Congress, 1774

As tensions between the colonists and George III and Parliament grew, revolution became more imminent. The Coercive Acts, also known as The Intolerable Acts, were the final straw for the colonists. The Coercive Acts were designed to control the Massachusetts colony after the Boston Tea Party, where American patriots threw a tea shipment into the harbor to protest taxes. These acts included rules prohibiting town meetings without the approval of the King, among others. An intercolonial congress was called to address the complaints of the colonists. This became the First Continental Congress. In 1774, this congress drafted the Declaration and Resolves, which has sometimes been called a Bill of Rights as well because a page entitled Bill of Rights added by the printer reflected the sentiment of many colonists, most notably Sam Adams. The Declaration and Resolves closely mirrors the current Bill of Rights. Its provisions include a right to petition the government for a redress of grievances and many of the rights of arrest and trial now in the Bill of Rights.

Virginia Declaration of Rights, 1776

The Virginia Declaration of Rights is considered to be the first true Bill of Rights in the United States because it was the first guarantee of the rights of people written in a constitution that was then adopted by the people through an elected governmental body or convention. This document was created in the last of five Virginia conventions that were held after Lord Dunmore, the last colonial governor of Virginia, disbanded Virginia's House of Burgesses. On May 15, 1776, the convention formed a committee, which included George Mason and James Madison, to draw up a declaration of rights. It was Mason who virtually wrote the Virginia Declaration of Rights. The declaration omitted any reference to English law and colonial charters and, instead, asserted that the law of nature is the source of individual rights. Madison drafted much of the Constitution's Bill of Rights after the revolution.

The Declaration of Independence, 1776

The Declaration of Independence is crucial to U.S. history and to the Constitution because it declared that the people had right to abolish a government that disregarded their rights and establish a new government. It was not intended to be a declaration of rights. Instead, it was drawn up to justify the actions against the colonists of George III and Parliament. In enumerating the rights that had been violated by the king, however, it included a list of basic rights. These served as a foundation to the Bill of Rights.

Thomas Paine on a Bill of Rights, 1777

In a letter written in response to criticism of the 1776 constitution of Pennsylvania, Thomas Paine wrote a powerful justification for a bill of rights. In his letter, Paine asserted that a bill of rights needed to be a plain and positive declaration of the rights themselves, not a statement on the great principles of natural liberty. Paine also rejected the notion that a bill of rights is unalterable and argued that laws should be declared unconstitutional if they are not consistent with a bill of rights.

Awards

INTELLECTUAL FREEDOM AWARD WINNERS RELATED TO LIBRARY SERVICES

SIRS Intellectual Freedom Award

Founded in 1981 in conjunction with the North Carolina Library Association, the SIRS Intellectual Freedom Award is given to individuals or groups who have met or have resisted attempts at censorship and have otherwise furthered the cause of intellectual and academic freedom (http://www.sirs.com/corporate/freedom.html).

1982 Frances Dean, Montgomery County Public Schools, Rockville, Maryland

1983 Pat Scales, Greenville Middle School, Greenville, South Carolina

1984 Vicki H. Hardesty, Findlay High School, Greenville, South Carolina

1986 Carolyn Kellerman, Santa Fe High School, Santa Fe, New Mexico

1987 Gayle Kersey, East Arcadia School, Ridgewood, North Carolina

1988 Nancy Moreno, Kocurek Elementary School, Austin, Texas

1989 William A. Murray, Jr., Aurora Public Schools, Aurora, Colorado

1990 Linda L. Waddle, Cedar Falls High School, Cedar Falls, Iowa

1991 Neva Thompson, Humboldt Unified District, Dewey, Arizona

1993 Jean Kern, Linden West Elementary School, Gladstone, Missouri

1994 Ruth E. Dishnow, Texas Woman's University, Denton, Texas

1996 Ann K. Symons, Juneau Douglas High School, Juneau, Arkansas

1997 Ginny Moore Kruse and Cooperative Children's Book Center, Madison, Wisconsin

Eli M. Oboler Award

Established in 1985 by the Intellectual Freedom Roundtable of the American Library Association, the Oboler Award, named and dedicated to Eli M. Oboler, a librarian and champion of intellectual freedom, is given to the best published work in the area of intellectual freedom during a two-year period (http://www.ala.org/alaorg/oboler_a.html).

1985 *Emergence of a Free Press* by Lawrence W. Levy

1988 *Choosing Equality: The Case for Democratic Schooling* by Colin Greer, Norman Fruchter, Kenneth Haskins, Marilyn Gittel, and Ann Bastian

1990 Missouri Association of School Librarians, Spring, 1988, edition of *Media Horizons*, edited by Aileen Helmick and Floyd Pentlin.

1992 *Libraries, Erotica, and Pornography* by Martha Cornog

1994 *What Johnny Shouldn't Read: Textbook Censorship in America* by Joan Delfattore

1996 *Beyond the Burning Cross* by Edward Cleary

1998 *Free Speech in Its Forgotten Years* by David M. Rabban

2000 *The Transparent Society: Will Technology Force Us to Choose Between Privacy and Freedom* by David Brin

John Phillip Immroth Memorial Award

Named for and dedicated to John Phillip Immroth, a librarian and intellectual freedom advocate, this award is sponsored by the Intellectual Freedom Roundtable of the American Library Association. The Immroth Award honors intellectual freedom fighters within and outside the library profession who have demonstrated remarkable personal courage in resisting censorship, either from a lifetime of advocacy or through a difficult censorship battle (http://www.ala.org/alaorg/oif/immroth.html).

1976 I. F. Stone

1977 Irene Turin

1978 Sonja Coleman

1979 Alex P. Allain

1980 Elizabeth A. Phillips

1982 Steven Pico

1983 Nat Hentoff

1984 Gene Lanier

1985 William D. North

1986 Thomas J. Mills

1987 Charles Levendosky

1988 Elliot and Eleanor Goldstein

1989 Cooperative Children's Book Center

1990 Pamela G. Bonnell

1991 Christopher Merritt

1992 Dorothea A. Hunter

1993 William A. Moffett

1994 John Swan

1995 Fort Vancouver Regional Library Board of Trustees

1996 Plaintiffs in *Annie On My Mind* case

1997 Dr. Ronald F. Sigler

1998 Paula Baker, Marjorie Meany, Elizabeth Gibson, William Meub, Barry Ferraro, and Paul Bortz of the Rutland [VT] Free Library

1999 Mainstream Loudon

2000 Gordon Conable

2001 Linda Hughes

Robert B. Downs Intellectual Freedom Award

Named for Robert B. Downs, dean of the Graduate School of Library Science at the University of Illinois and a champion of intellectual freedom, this award is given annually to acknowledge individuals or groups who have furthered the cause of intellectual freedom, particularly as it impacts libraries and information centers and the dissemination of ideas (http://alexia.lis. uiuc.edu/gslis/school/downs-award.html).

1973 Alex P. Allain, president, Freedom to Read Foundation

1974 Everett Moore, author, *Issues of Freedom in American Libraries*

1975 No award

1976 Eli Oboler, director, Idaho State University Library, Pocatello, Idaho

1977 Irene Turin, librarian, Island Trees High School, Levittown, New York

1978 Judith F. Krug, director, Office for Intellectual Freedom, American Library Association

1979 Ralph McCoy, dean emeritus of library affairs, Southern Illinois University, Carbondale, Illinois

1980 Jeanne Layton, director, Davis County Library, Farmington, Utah

1981 Dr. E. B. Stanley and the seven other members of the Washington County [Virginia] Library Board of Trustees

1982 No award

1983 No award

1984 Marie Bruce, Huntington Memorial Library, Oneonta, New York

1985 Donald Miedema, superintendent of Springfield, Illinois, public schools

1986 Dorothy Broderick, author, educator, Virginia Beach, Virginia

1987 Gene Lanier, professor, East Carolina State University, Greenville, North Carolina

1988 Paula Kaufman, dean of library services, University of Tennessee, Chattanooga, Tennessee

1989 Cooperative Children's Book Center, University of Wisconsin, Madison, Wisconsin

1990 C. James Schmidt, president, Freedom to Read Foundation

1991 Dennis Barrie and the Cincinnati Contemporary Arts Center, Cincinnati, Ohio

1992 Mary Jo Godwin, former editor, *Wilson Library Bulletin*

1993 Nat Hentoff, author and journalist

1994 Maggie Breen, collection coordinator, Jefferson County Public Library, Lakewood, Colorado

1995 Eleanor and Elliott Goldstein, founders, Social Issues Resources Series, Inc. (SIRS)

1996 Sanford Berman, head cataloger, Technical Services Division, Hennepin County Public Library, Minnesota

1997 Bruce J. Ennis, attorney

1998 Mainstream Loudon, Loudon Country, Virginia

1999 Ann Symons, librarian, Douglas High School, Juneau, Alaska

2000 Nancy Garden, author, and Bennett Haselton, Peacefire.org

Freedom to Read Foundation Roll of Honor

Established in 1987, this award recognizes and honors those individuals who have contributed substantially to the Freedom to Read Foundation through their adherence to its principles and/or substantial monetary support (http://www.ftrf.org/rollofhonoraward.html).

1988 Everett T. Moore and Sydney Sheldon

1989 Jeanne Layton and Alex P. Allain

1990 Russell Shank and William D. North

1991 Judy Blume and Carrie C. Robinson

1992 R. Kathleen Molz and Elliot and Eleanor Goldstein

1993 Jerry Thrasher and Lillian Bradshaw

1994 Frank Zappa and the Juneau, Alaska, school districts, including the superintendent, the board of education, and the school librarian

1995 Judith F. Krug and J. Dennis Day

1996 Gordon M. Conable

1997 Bruce J. Ennis

1998 Dorothy M. Broderick

1999 Charles Levendosky

2000 Emily Wheelock Reed

The Intellectual Freedom Roundtable/SIRS State and Regional Intellectual Freedom Achievement Award

This award is given to the most innovative and effective intellectual freedom project covering a state or region (http://www.ala.org/alaorg/oif/ifrt_spa.html).

1984 South Carolina Library Association, Intellectual Freedom Committee

1985 North Carolina Library Association, Intellectual Freedom Committee

1986 Indiana Library Association, Intellectual Freedom Committee

1987 Wisconsin Library Association, Intellectual Freedom Committee

1988 New York Library Association, Intellectual Freedom Committee

1989 Alabama Library Association, Intellectual Freedom Committee

1990 No award

1991 Oregon Intellectual Freedom Clearinghouse

1992 Oklahoma Library Association, Intellectual Freedom Committee

1993 Oregon Library Association, Intellectual Freedom Committee

1994 Freedom to Read Foundation

1995 Northern Virginia Citizens Against Censorship

1996 Long Island Coalition Against Censorship

1997 Georgia First Amendment Foundation

1998 Illinois Library Association, Intellectual Freedom Forum

1999 Oregon Coalition for Free Expression

2000 Ohio Library Council

2001 West Virginia Library Association Intellectual Freedom Committee

OTHER IMPORTANT INTELLECTUAL FREEDOM AWARDS

The Jefferson Muzzles

Sponsored by the Thomas Jefferson Center for the Protection of Free Expression, the Jefferson Muzzles have been awarded to individuals and groups since 1992. According to the center's web site, the award has been designed "to call attention to those who in the past year forgot or disregarded Mr. Jefferson's admonition that freedom of speech 'cannot be limited without being lost.' " The Jefferson Muzzle is awarded on Thomas Jefferson's birthday to highlight abridgements of free speech and freedom of the press and to build an appreciation for the tenets of the First Amendment. Web address: http://www.tjcenter.org/muzzles.html.

PEN/"Newman's Own" First Amendment Award

Sponsored by PEN American Center and substantially supported by Paul Newman and his food corporation, this award is "presented to a U.S. resident each Spring who has fought courageously, despite adversity, to safeguard the First Amendment right to freedom of expression as it applies to the written word." Web address: http://www.pen.org/freedom/nomination.html.

Hugh M. Hefner First Amendment Award

Established in 1979 by the Playboy Foundation, the Hugh M. Hefner First Amendment Award is designed "to honor individuals who have made significant contributions in the vital effort to protect and enhance the First Amendment rights for Americans." Nominees for the award come from a variety of professional fields, including print and broadcast journalism, the arts and entertainment, education, publishing, and law and government. Web address: http://www.playboyenterprises.com/foundation/amendment_awards.html.

The William J. Brennan, Jr., Award

The William J. Brennan, Jr., Award is also sponsored by the Thomas Jefferson Center for the Protection of Free Expression and is designed to honor the legacy of William J. Brennan, Jr., one of the Supreme Court's most ardent defenders of the First Amendment. The award is presented to "an individual or group whose commitment to free expression is consistent with Justice Brennan's abiding devotion. Such commitment might be shown to be a single act or through a lifetime of activity to enhance the liberties of free speech and press." Web address: http://www.tjcenter.org/brennan.html.

The National Council of Teachers of English NCTE/SLATE National Intellectual Freedom Award

The purpose of the National Council of Teachers of English award is "to honor individuals, groups, or institutions that merit recognition for advancing the cause of intellectual freedom." The award uses specific criteria, including evidence of the courage in advancing the cause of intellectual freedom and activity related to particular recent events. It is not limited to educators. Nominees are judged on the impact of their activities at the national level. Web address: http://www.ncte.org/censorship/slate_award.html.

The National Council of Teachers of English NCTE/SLATE State, Regional, and Provincial Affiliate Awards

The National Council of Teachers of English also sponsors an award at the state, regional, and provincial level. The purpose of this award is the same as the NCTE National Intellectual Freedom Award, but the nominees are judged on their contributions at the state, regional, or provincial level. Web address: http://www.ncte.org/censorship/slate_award.html.

Glossary of Terms on Censorship

ACLU et al. **v.** *Reno* (521 US 884, 1997): Also known as *Reno* v. *ACLU et al.* in the U.S. Appeals Court, this is the U.S. Supreme Court case that struck down the Communications Decency Act of 1996 as unconstitutional. The case was heard simultaneously with a similar case, *ALA* v. *Reno*, filed by the American Library Association. The U.S. Supreme Court ruled that the provisions of the Communications Decency Act of 1996 were vague and constitutionally overbroad and therefore unconstitutional.

ALA **v.** *Reno* (521 US 884, 1997): The U.S. Supreme Court case, heard with the case *ACLU et al.* v. *Reno*, that struck down the Communications Decency Act of 1996 as unconstitutional. This case was filed on the behalf of the American Library Association and other organizations but was decided by the Supreme Court in its ruling in the case *ACLU et al.* v. *Reno*.

Bias: Personal, especially unreasonable or distorted, judgment; prejudice.

Blacklisting: The act of excluding persons from their work or social engagements because their views or beliefs are considered unacceptable. The most well-known episode of blacklisting occurred during the early 1950s against writers and actors in Hollywood who were suspected of ties to Communist organizations.

Book burning: A severe act of censorship. Book burning is an attempt to eradicate entirely any ideas contained within the books. The most famous incident of book burning in modern times was that mounted by the German Nazi Party in the 1930s to eliminate political viewpoints opposed to Nazism.

Bowdlerize: The act of expurgating or removing words or parts of a work because of objectionable language or ideas. The term is derived from the name of an English family. In the eighteenth and nineteenth centuries, Thomas Bowdler and other family members rewrote the works of William Shakespeare and Edward Gibbon to remove offensive language and sections they considered immoral.

Censor: One who supervises conduct and morals and examines materials for objectionable content.

Censorship: Removal, suppression, or restricted circulation of literary, artistic, or educational materials on the grounds that these are morally or otherwise objectionable.

Challenges: Attacks made on books or materials in a public school curriculum or public library because of objections to the content or nature of the material.

Child Online Protection Act (COPA): Also known as CDA II, this legislation was introduced into the U.S. Congress on April 30, 1998, as a response to the Supreme Court ruling that declared the Communications Decency Act unconstitutional in 1997. This law required anyone engaged in the business of selling or transferring materials through the World Wide Web to restrict access to any material deemed harmful to minors. The law did not define what was to be deemed harmful to minors. It also formed the Child Online Protection Act Commission to study strategies that could be recommended to the federal government for protecting minors from access to materials over the Internet that might be harmful. This law was challenged by the ACLU and other organizations in 2001. The Supreme Court agreed to hear the case, *John Ashcroft, Attorney General* v. *ACLU, et al.*, in the Fall of 2001 but had not announced a decision as of March 2002.

Chilling effect: An argument that censorship of a creative work will cause creators of similar works to limit what they produce in the future for fear that it may be censored. This has the effect of eliminating works.

Communications Decency Act (CDA): Also known as the Exon Amendment because it was introduced by Senator James Exon of Nebraska as an amendment to the Telecommunications Reform Act of 1996. This legislation became known as the Communications Decency Act after it was signed into law by President Bill Clinton on February 8, 1996. The law made it illegal for anyone to engage in speech that is indecent or patently offensive on computer networks if the speech could be viewed by a minor. It did not define "indecent" or "patently offensive" speech. Punishment for violation of the law included up to two years in prison and/or a $250,000 fine. This law was struck down as unconstitutional by the U.S. Supreme Court on June 26, 1997, as language that was too broad to be constitutional. This ruling was made through two Supreme

Court cases heard by the Court simultaneously, *ACLU et al.* v. *Reno* and *ALA* v. *Reno*.

Contemporary community standards: A central part of the test for obscenity. According to Supreme Court decisions on obscenity (*Roth* v. *United States* [1957], *Miller v. California* [1973]), a work must be judged by current understandings of what is acceptable to the average person within a community. Under the Roth test, the community was considered to be a national standard. With the advent of the Miller test, the community became more local in nature and is defined to be the state or a region within the state.

Cryptography: the enciphering and deciphering of messages in a secret code or writing. Cryptography is often used to create secure electronic communications.

Defamation: A form of unprotected speech, defamation is the printed or written or spoken word that tends to injure a person's reputation, causing him or her to be subjected to public hatred or ridicule or financial loss. It can also call into question a person's character, integrity, or morality.

Encryption: The encoding of material so that it cannot be detected by unwanted parties.

Exon Amendment: See Communications Decency Act

Family values: A phrase often used to define beliefs and goals identified with traditional forms of families, that is, man and wife in a monogamous marriage, usually with children and religiously active in a church or synagogue. Some groups also promote biblical, especially Christian, teachings as part of the definition of family values, and those groups often oppose abortion on demand, pornography, and homosexual lifestyles.

Filtering programs: Software blocking programs that allow individuals to select and screen out any content they wish to avoid while navigating the Internet.

First Amendment: The first of twenty-six changes or additions to the U.S. Constitution. Added in 1791, it guarantees all citizens four basic freedoms: freedom of religion, freedom of speech, freedom of the press, and the right to assemble peaceably.

Hate speech: Speech designed to inflict harm on a person or group, usually because of gender, sexual orientation, or ethnic or racial background.

Labeling: The assignment of a code, name, or symbol to categorize or otherwise indicate the level or type of objections to a work. The movie rating code is a form of labeling that indicates the relative level of violence and/or sexual themes in a film. Books, recordings, and television programs are sometimes labeled to indicate content. Some labels are designed to indicate the presence of something controversial and the nature of that controversy.

Libel: A form of unprotected speech, libel is a written statement that attacks the reputation of a person. The statement does not have to be false to injure someone but needs to be shown to have a deliberate harmful effect that caused pain and suffering to at least one person. There is a difference between criticism and libel. Criticism is an expression of opinion based on facts that provide grounds for a difference of opinion and that do not attack a person's private or personal affairs. Libel attacks the personal qualities of the character of an individual.

Obscenity: Any written or visual work that offends moral standards or incites to lust or depravity. A legal definition has been considered difficult to formulate and apply to all possible works. Legally constituted obscenity must be defined by an appropriate judicial body using acceptable case law and tests for obscenity.

Patent offensiveness: A term used in the *Miller* v. *California* obscenity decision. Under the Miller test, the concept usually applies to hardcore pornography. The Supreme Court used the Miller case to provide some examples of what was to be considered patently offensive but left any actual definition up the individual states.

Political correctness: A term that evolved in the early 1980s to stand for language and behavior that was tolerant and accepting of diversity and multiculturalism and intolerant of those unwilling to go along with this movement.

Pornography: Material that depicts sexual behavior and is designed to cause sexual arousal. Pornography is generally categorized in the media as either "hard core" or "soft core." Hard core pornography depicts penetration during a sex act. Soft core pornography usually depicts forms of nudity and sexual themes but without showing penetration in a sexual act. Some publications with only nudity are referred to as soft core pornography by some groups but not others.

Prior restraint: The removal or attempt to remove an exercise of free speech or press before it has been made or distributed without a proper judicial determination to establish that exercise as unprotected speech or press. This concept was first developed in *Near* v. *Minnesota* (1931). It prohibits authorities from stopping speeches, published works, or other types of expression from being made or delivered until the courts can decide whether the expression is illegal. Once a type of speech or material has been judged as unprotected, prior restraint can occur.

Production codes (also known as movie rating codes): Standards applied to the film industry in order to maintain a particular level of morality in a film. The industry calls this a system of "production codes," driving the type of production. The result of the production code system is the movie ratings the public sees when going to the movies.

Profanity: Vulgar, irreverent language, such as swear words.

Secular humanism: A term used to describe the belief that ultimate values reside solely in the human individual and not with a Supreme Being or the teachings of religious tenets and beliefs, especially the Bible.

V-Chip: Technology currently in use in television, and proposed for the Internet, that allows individuals to block channels with content they consider inappropriate.

Voluntary ratings system: A proposed method of blocking inappropriate or pornographic material online that would require all creators of Web sites to rate their site according to a set scale, much the way movies are now rated as G, PG, PG-13, NC-17, R, and X.

Bibliography of Additional Readings

Axelrod, Lauryn. *TV-proof your kids: A parent's guide to safe and healthy viewing.* New York: Carol Publishing Group, 1997.

Beahm, George, ed. *War of words: The censorship debate.* Kansas City, MO: Andrews and McMeel, 1993.

Bedford, Carmel. *Fiction, fact, and the fatwa: The Rushdie defence campaign.* London: Article 19, 2000.

Black, Gregory D. *Hollywood censored: Morality codes, Catholics, and the movies.* Cambridge: Cambridge University Press, 1994.

Bollinger, Lee C. *The tolerant society: Freedom of speech and extremist speech in America.* New York: Oxford University Press, 1986.

Bolton, Richard. *Culture wars: Documents from the recent controversies in the arts.* New York: New Press, 1992.

Bosmajian, Haig. *The freedom to read: Books, films, and plays.* New York: Neal-Schuman, 1987.

———. *Censorship, libraries, and the law.* New York: Neal-Schuman, 1983.

Burress, Lee. *The battle of the books: Literary censorship in the public schools, 1950–1985.* Metuchen, NJ: Scarecrow Press, 1989.

Burstyn, Varda. *Women against censorship.* Vancouver, B.C.: Douglas & McIntyre, 1985.

Burt, Richard, ed. *The Administration of aesthetics: Censorship, political criticism, and the public sphere.* Minneapolis: University of Minnesota Press, 1994.

Byerly, Greg, and Rick Rubin. *Pornography: The conflict over sexually explicit materials in the United States: An annotated bibliography.* New York: Garland Publishing, 1980.

Carmilly-Weinberger, Moshe. *Fear of art: Censorship and freedom of expression in art.* New York: R.R. Bowker & Co., 1986.

Cline, Victor B., comp. *Where do you draw the line? An exploration into media violence, pornography, and censorship.* Provo: Brigham Young University Press, 1974.

Clor, Harry M. *Obscenity and public morality: Censorship in a liberal society.* Chicago: University of Chicago Press, 1969. Reprinted 1985.

Cooper, Jonathan, ed. *Liberating cyberspace: Civil liberties, human rights, and the Internet.* Chicago: Pluto Press, 1998.

Cornog, Martha, *Libraries, erotica and pornography.* New York: Oryx Press, 1991.

Day, Gary, and Clive Bloom, eds. *Perspectives on pornography: Sexuality in film and literature.* New York: St. Martin's Press, 1988.

DeGrazia, Edward, and Riger K. Newman. *Banned films: Movies, censors, and the First Amendment.* New York: R. R. Bowker & Co., 1982.

Downs, Donald Alexander. *The new politics of pornography.* Chicago: University of Chicago Press, 1989.

Downs, Robert B., and Ralph E. McCoy, eds. *The first freedom today: Critical issues relating to censorship and to intellectual freedom.* Chicago: American Library Association, 1984.

Dubin, Steven. C. *Arresting images: Impolitic art and uncivil actions.* New York: Routledge, 1994.

Dworkin, Andrea. *Letters from a war zone: Writings.* New York: Dutton, 1989.
———. *Pornography: Men possessing women.* New York: G.P. Putnam's Sons, 1981.

Foerstel, Herbert. *Banned in the media: A reference guide to censorship in the press, motion pictures, broadcasting, and the Internet.* Westport, CT: Greenwood Press, 1998.

Friedman, Samuel Joshua. *Children and the world wide web: Tool or trap?* Lanham, MD: University Press of America, 2000.

Friendly, Fred. *Minnesota rag: The dramatic story of the landmark Supreme Court case that gave new meaning to freedom of the press.* New York: Random House, 1981.

Gardiner, Harold C., S.J. *The Catholic viewpoint on censorship.* Revised edition Garden City, NJ: Doubleday & Co., 1961.

Gardner, Gerald C. *The censorship papers: Movie censorship letters from the Hays office.* New York: Dodd, Mead, and Co., 1987.

Garry, Patrick. *An American paradox: Censorship in a nation of free speech.* Westport, CT: Greenwood Press, 1993.

Gelman, Robert B., Stanton McCandish, and Esther Dyson. *Protecting yourself online: The definitive resource on safety, freedom, and privacy in cyberspace.* New York: Harper Collins, 1998.

Goodman, Michael B. *Contemporary literary censorship: The case history of Burroughs'* Naked Lunch. Metuchen, NJ: Scarecrow Press, 1981.

Green, Jonathan. *The encyclopedia of censorship.* New York: Facts on File, 1990.

Griffin, Susan. *Pornography and silence: Culture's revenge against nature.* New York: Harper & Row, 1981.

Gubar, Susan, and Joan Hoff, eds. *For adult users only: The dilemma of violent pornography*. Bloomington, IN: Indiana University Press, 1989.

Haight, Anne Lyon. *Banned books, 387 B.C. to 1978 A.D.* 4th ed. Updated and enlarged by Chandler B. Grannis. New York: R. R. Bowker & Co., 1978.

Harer, John B. *Intellectual freedom: A reference handbook*. Santa Barbara, CA: ABC-Clio, 1992.

Harer, John B., and Steven R. Harris. *Censorship of expression in the 1980s: A statistical survey*. Westport, CT: Greenwood Press, 1994.

Hawkins, Gordon, and Franklin G. Zimring. *Pornography in a free society*. New York: Cambridge University Press, 1988.

Heins, Marjorie. *Not in front of the children: "Indecency," censorship, and the innocence of youth*. New York: Hill and Wang, 2001.

———. *Sex, sin, and blasphemy: A guide to America's censorship wars*. New York: New Press, 1993.

Hentoff, Nat. *The day they came to arrest the book*. New York: Delacorte Press, 1982.

———. *The first freedom: The tumultuous history of free speech in America*. New York: Delacorte Press, 1980.

———. *Free speech for me but not for thee: How the American left and right relentlessly censor each other*. New York: HarperCollins, 1993.

Hoffman, Frank. *Intellectual freedom and censorship: An annotated bibliography*. Metuchen, NJ: Scarecrow Press, 1989.

Holbrook, David, ed. *The case against pornography*. LaSalle, IL: Open Court, 1973.

Hughes, Donna Rice, and Pamela T. Campbell. *Kids online: Protecting your children in cyberspace*. Chicago: Fleming H. Revell Company, 1998.

Hurwitz, Leon. *Historical dictionary of censorship in the United States*. Westport, CT: Greenwood Press, 1985.

Ingelhart, Louis Edward. *Press law and press freedom for high school publications*. Westport, CT: Greenwood Press, 1986.

Jansen, Sue Curry. *Censorship: The knot that binds power and knowledge*. New York: Oxford University Press, 1988.

Jenkinson, Edward B. *The schoolbook protest movement*. Bloomington, IN: Phi Delta Educational Foundation, 1986.

Jensen, Carl. *Stories that changed America: Muckrakers of the 20th century*. New York: Seven Stories Press, 2000.

Johnson, Claudia. *Stifled laughter: One woman's story about fighting censorship*. Golden, CO: Fulcrum Publishers, 1994.

Jones, Frances M. *Defusing censorship: The librarian's guide to handling censorship conflicts*. Phoenix, AZ: Oryx Press, 1983.

Karolides, Nicholas, Jr., and Lee Burress. *Celebrating censored books*. Racine, WI: Wisconsin Council of Teachers of English, 1985.

Kendrick, Walter. *The secret museum: Pornography in modern culture.* New York: Viking, 1987.

Keough, Peter. *Flesh and blood: The national society of film critics on sex, violence, and censorship.* San Francisco: Mercury House, 1995.

Kristof, Nicholas D. *Freedom of the high school press.* Lanham, MD: University Press of America, 1983.

Lederor, Laura, ed. *Take back the night: Women on pornography.* New York: William Morrow Company, 1980.

Levine, Madeline. *See no evil: A guide to protecting our children from media violence.* San Francisco: Jossey-Bass Publishers, 1996.

Levy, Leonard W. *Emergence of a free press.* New York: Oxford University Press, 1985.

Lewis, Jon. *Hollywood v. hard core: How the struggle over censorship saved the modern film industry.* New York: New York University, 2000.

Lyons, Charles. *The new censors: Movies and the culture wars.* Philadelphia: Temple University Press, 1997.

Mack, Dana. *The assault on parenthood: How our culture undermines the family.* New York: Simon and Schuster, 1997.

Marsh, Dave. *50 ways to fight censorship and important facts to know about censors.* New York: Thunder's Mouth Press, 1991.

Miller, Frank. *Censored Hollywood: Sex, sin, and violence on screen.* Atlanta: Turner Publishers, 1994.

Miller, Steven E. *Civilizing cyberspace: Policy, power, and the information superhighway.* Reading, MA: Addison Wesley, 1995.

Monks, Merri M., and Donna Reidy Pistolis, eds. *Hit list: Frequently challenged books for young adults.* Chicago: American Library Association, 1996.

Moretti, Daniel S. *Obscenity and pornography: The law under the First Amendment.* London: Oceana, 1984.

Neuharth, Al. *How you can get the most out of life at any age . . . free spirit: . . . and how it might make you a millionaire.* Arlington, VA: Newseum Books, 2000.

Nobile, Philip, and Eric Nadler. *United States of America vs. sex: How the Meese Commission lied about pornography.* New York: Minotaur Press, 1986.

Noble, William. *Bookbanning in America.* Middlebury, VT: Paul S. Eriksson, 1990.

Nuzum, Eric D. *Parental advisory: Music censorship in America.* New York: Perennial, 2001.

Oboler, Eli M. *Defending intellectual freedom: The library and the censor.* Westport, CT: Greenwood Press, 1980.

———. *The fear of the word: Censorship and sex.* Metuchen, NJ: Scarecrow Press, 1974.

Osanka, Franklin Mark, and Sara Lee Johann. *Sourcebook on pornography.* Lexington, MA: D.C. Heath, 1989.

Petrie, Ruth, ed. *Film and censorship: The index reader.* London: Cassell Academic, 1997.

Reichman, Henry. *Censorship and selection: Issues and answers for schools.* Chicago: American Library Association/American Association of School Administrators, 1988.

Robbins, Louise S. *The dismissal of Miss Ruth Brown: Civil rights, censorship, and the American library.* Norman, OK: University of Oklahoma Press, 2000.

Saunders, Kevin W. *Violence as obscenity: Limiting the media's First Amendment protections.* Durham, N.C.: Duke University Press, 1996.

Sellen, Betty-Carol, and Patricia Young. *Feminists, pornography and the law: An annotated bibliography of conflict, 1970–1986.* Hamden, CT: Library Professional Publications, 1987.

Smolla, Rodney A. *Jerry Falwell v. Larry Flynt: The First Amendment on trial.* New York: St. Martin's Press, 1988.

Spizor, Matthew L. *Seven dirty words and six other stories: Controlling the content of print and broadcast.* New Haven, CT: Yale University Press, 1986.

Stay, Byron L., ed. *Censorship: Opposing viewpoints.* San Diego: Greenhaven Press, 1997.

Theiner, George, ed. *They shoot writers, don't they?* Winchester, MA: Faber & Faber, 1984.

Thomas, Cal. *Book burning.* Wheaton, IL: Good News Publications, 1983.

Vitz, Paul C. *Censorship: Evidence of bias in our children's textbooks.* Ann Arbor, MI: Servant, 1986.

Walker, Alice. *Banned.* San Francisco: Aunt Lute Books, 1996.

Wallace, Jonathan, and Mark Mangan. *Sex, laws, and cyberspace: Freedom and censorship on the frontiers of the online revolution.* New York: M and T Books, 1996.

Walsh, Frank. *Sin and censorship: The Catholic Church and the motion picture industry.* New Haven, CT: Yale University Press, 1996.

White, Harry. *Anatomy of censorship: Why censors have it wrong.* Lanham, MD: University Press of America, 1997.

Wilson, Elizabeth. *Women who censor.* London: Writers and Scholars International, 2000.

Woods, L. B. *A decade of censorship in America: The threat to classrooms and libaries, 1966–1975.* Metuchen, NJ: Scarecrow Press, 1979.

Zurcher, Louis A., Jr., and R. George Kirkpatrick. *Citizens for decency: Anti-pornography crusades as status defense.* Austin: University of Texas Press, 1976.

Resources

ORGANIZATIONS

Accuracy in Media (AIM)
4455 Connecticut Ave., NW, Suite 330
Washington, DC 20008
(202) 364–4401
Web site: *http://www.aim.org*

American Center for Law and Justice (ACLJ)
P. O. Box 64429
Virginia Beach, VA 23467
(757) 226–2489
Web site: *http://www.aclj.org*

American Civil Liberties Union (ACLU)
132 West 43rd St.
New York, NY 10036–6599
(212) 549–2500
Web site: *http://www.aclu.org*

American Family Association, Inc. (AFA)
P. O. Drawer 2440
Tupelo, MS 38803
(601) 844–5036
Web site: *http://www.afa.net*

American Library Association (ALA)
Office for Intellectual Freedom
50 East Huron St.
Chicago, IL 60611–2795
(800) 545–2433
Web site: *http://www.ala.org/alaorg/oif*

Author's Guild
31 East 28th St.
10th Floor
New York, N.Y. 10016
(212) 563–5904
Web site: *http://www.authorsguild.org*

Christian Broadcasting Network
977 Centerville Turnpike
Virginia Beach, VA 23463
(757) 226–7000
Web site: *http://www.cbn.org/*

Christian Coalition
499 So. Capitol St. SW
Suite 615
Washington, DC 20003
(202) 479–6900
Web site: *http://www.cc.org/*

Citizens for Community Values (CCV)
11175 Reading Road, Suite 103
Cincinnati, OH 45241
(513) 733–5775
Web site: *http://www.ccv.org*

Citizens for Excellence in Education (CEE)
National Association of Christian Educators (NACE)
P. O. Box 3200
Costa Mesa, CA 92628
(949) 251–9333
Web site: *http://www.nace-cee.org*

Computer Professionals for Social Responsibility (CPSR)
P. O. Box 717
Palo Alto, CA 94302
(650) 322–4748
Web site: *http://www.cpsr.org*

Disability Rights Education and Defense Fund
2212 Sixth St.
Berkeley, CA 94710
(510) 644–2555
Web site: *http://www.dredf.org/*

Eagle Forum
Operations Center
P. O. Box 618
Alton, IL 62002

(618) 462–5415
Web site: *http://www.eagleforum.org*

Electronic Frontier Foundation (EFF)
1550 Bryant St., Suite 725
San Francisco, CA 94130–4832
(415) 436–9333
Web site: *http://www.eff.org*

Electronic Privacy Information Center (EPIC)
666 Pennsylvania Ave. SE, Suite 301
Washington, DC 20003
(202) 544–9240
Web site: *http://www.epic.org*

Enough Is Enough
P.O. Box 888
Fairfax, VA 22030
(703) 278–8343
Web site: *www.enough.org*

Fairness and Accuracy in Reporting (FAIR)
130 West 25th St.
New York, NY 10001
(212) 633–6700
Web site: *http://www.fair.org*

Family Friendly Libraries (FFL)
7597 Whisperwood Ct.
Springfield, VA 22153
(703) 440–3654
Web site: *http://www.fflibraries.org*

Family Research Council (FRC)
801 G Street NW
Washington, DC 20001
(202) 393–2100
Web site: *http://www.frc.org*

Feminists for Free Expression (FFE)
2525 Times Square Station
New York, NY 10108–2525
(212) 702–6292
Web site: *http://www.well.com/user/freedom/*

Filtering Facts
210 S. State Street #7
Lake Oswego, OR 97034
(503) 635–7048
Web site: *http://www.filteringfacts.org*

First Amendment Center (associated with Freedom Forum)
Vanderbilt University
1207 18th Ave., South
Nashville, TN 37212
(615) 321–9588
Web site: *http://www.freedomforum.org*

Focus on the Family
P.O. Box 35500
Colorado Springs, CO 80995
(719) 531–5181
Web site: *http://www.family.org*

Freedom Council (defunct).
See Christian Broadcasting Network

Freedom Forum (associated with The First Amendment Center)
1101 Wilson Blvd.
Arlington, VA 22209
(703) 528–0800
Web site: *http://www.freedomforum.org*

Human Rights Watch
350 Fifth Ave., 34th Flr
New York, NY 10118–3299
(212) 290–4700
Web site: *http://www.hrw.org/*

Journalism Education Assoc.
Kansas State University
103 Kedzic Hall
Manhattan, KS 66506–1505
(785) 532–5532
Web site: *http://www.jea.org/*

Morality in Media (associated with the National Obscenity Law Center)
475 Riverside Dr., Suite 239
New York, NY 10015
(212) 870–3222
Web site: *http://www.netcom.com/~mimnyc*

National Association for the Advancement of Colored People (NAACP)
4805 Mt. Hope Dr.
Baltimore, MD 21215
(877) 622–2798
Web site: *http://www.naacp.org/*

National Coalition Against Censorship (NCAC)
275 7th Ave.
New York, NY 10001
(212) 807–6222
Web site: *http://www.ncac.org*

The National Coalition to Protect Children and Families (NCPCF)
800 Compton Rd., Suite 9224
Cincinnati, OH 45231
(513) 521–6227
Web site: *http://www2.nationalcoalition.org/ncpcf*

National Law Center for Children and Families (NLC)
4103 Chain Bridge Rd, Suite 410
Fairfax, VA 22030–4105
(703) 691–4626
Web site: *http://www.nationallawcenter.org*

National Legal Foundation
P.O. Box 64427
Virginia Beach, VA 23467
(757) 463–6133
Web site: *http://www.nlf.net/*

The National Obscenity Law Center (NOLC) (associated with Morality in
   Media)
475 Riverside Dr., Suite 239
New York, NY 10115
(212) 870–3232
Web site: *http://www.netcom.com/~nolc*

National Perspectives Institute (defunct). See Christian Broadcasting Network

Parents, Families and Friends of Lesbians and Gays (PFLAG)
1726 M St. NW, Suite 400
Washington, DC 20036
(202) 467–8180
Web site: *http://www.pflag.org/*

PEN American Center
568 Broadway
New York, NY 10012–3225
(212) 334–1660
Web site: *http://www.pen.org*

People for the American Way
2000 M Street NW, Suite 400
Washington, DC 20036
(202) 467–4999
Web site: *http://www.pfaw.org*

Rock Out Censorship
P.O. Box 147
Jewett, OH 43986
(740) 946–2011
Web site: *http://www.theroc.org*

The Rutherford Institute
P.O. Box 7482
Charlottesville, VA 22906
(804) 978–3888
Web site: *http://www.rutherford.org*

Society of Professional Journalists
3909 N. Meridian St.
Indianapolis, IN 46208
(317) 927–8000
Web site: *http://www.spj.org/*

Southern Christian Leadership Council (SCLL)
334 Auburn Ave, NE
Atlanta, GA 30312
404–522–1420
Web site: *http://www.scll.org*

Student Press Law Center (SPLC)
1101 Wilson Blvd, Suite 1910
Arlington, VA 22209–2248
(703) 807–1904
Web site: *http://www.splc.org*

RELEVANT WEB SITES

Banned Books Online:
http://digital.library.upenn.edu/books/banned-books.html

Bonfire of Liberties: Censorship of the Humanities:
http://www.humanities-interactive.org/bonfireindex.html

The Censorship Pages:
http://www.booksatoz.com/censorship

Electronic Frontier Foundation's Blue Ribbon Campaign:
http://www.eff.org/blueribbon

Free Expression Network (FEN):
http://www.freeexpression.org

Green Ribbon Campaign for Responsibility in Free Speech:
http://www.zondervan.com/green.htm

Internet Free Expression Alliance:
http://www.ifea.net

Peacefire.org:
http://www.peacefire.org

Index

Note: Page numbers in **bold** denote main entries in the work.

About the Authors

JOHN B. HARER is an Associate Professor of Library Science at Texas A&M University. He is the author of *Censorship of Expression in the 1980's* and *Intellectual Freedom: A Reference Handbook.*

JEANNE HARRELL is an Associate Professor of Library Science at Texas A&M University.